E-Mail For Dummies, 2nd Edition

Your Own Customized Cheat Sheet!

Build your own customized cheat sheet! Just fill in the details from the appropriate chapters in the book to describe your personal mail setup:

My e-mail address: _____@_____ (Chapter 3)

My mail system: _____ (Chapters 5–13)

The rest of these items can be cribbed from the chapter that describes your mail program. Note the pages where they're described so that you can check for details.

To start my mail program: _____ (page ___)

To retrieve incoming messages: _____ (page ___)

To create a new message: _____ (page ___)

To send outgoing messages: _____ (page ___)

To reply to a message: _____ (page ___)

To forward a message: _____ (page ___)

To file away a message: _____ (page ___)

To delete a message: _____ (page ___)

To open the address book: _____ (page ___)

Internet E-Mail Address Formats

To Send To	With This Address	Type This
AOL	SteveCase	stevecase@aol.com
BITNET	user@node	user@node.bitnet or user%node.bitnet@cunyvm.cuny.edu
CompuServe	77777,7777	77777.7777@compuserve.com
Delphi	jsmith	jsmith@delphi.com
EasyLink	1234567	1234567@eln.attmail.com
FIDONET	MarySmith 1:2/3.4	mary.smith@p4.f3.n2.z1.fidonet.org
GEnie	J.SMITH7	J.SMITH7@genie.geis.com
MCI Mail	555-2468	5552468@mcimail.com
MSN	BillGates	billgates@msn.com
Prodigy	ABCD123A	abcd123a@prodigy.com

...For Dummies: #1 Computer Book Series for Beginners

E-Mail For Dummies, 2nd Edition

Cheat Sheet

Host Name Zones

Internet host zone names are represented by a three-letter abbreviation or four-letter word. (For two-letter country codes, see Appendix A.)

Zone	Host
arts	organization emphasizing cultural and entertainment activities
com	company or individual
edu	educational institution
firm	business
gov	government
info	organization providing information services
int	international organization
mil	military
net	network organization
nom	individual or personal names
org	non-profit or other non-commercial organization
rec	organization emphasizing recreational activities
store	business offering goods to purchase
web	organization emphasizing activities related to the Web

Favorite Nicknames (Aliases)

Fill in the names you pick when you make a nickname:

_____

_____

_____

_____

_____

_____

_____

_____

_____

E-Mail Addresses You'd Hate to Lose

_____

_____

_____

_____

_____

_____

_____

_____

_____

_____

_____

_____

...For Dummies: #1 Computer Book Series for Beginners

COMPUTER BOOK SERIES FROM IDG

References for the Rest of Us!®

Are you intimidated and confused by computers? Do you find that traditional manuals are overloaded with technical details you'll never use? Do your friends and family always call you to fix simple problems on their PCs? Then the *...For Dummies*® computer book series from IDG Books Worldwide is for you.

...For Dummies books are written for those frustrated computer users who know they aren't really dumb but find that PC hardware, software, and indeed the unique vocabulary of computing make them feel helpless. *...For Dummies* books use a lighthearted approach, a down-to-earth style, and even cartoons and humorous icons to diffuse computer novices' fears and build their confidence. Lighthearted but not lightweight, these books are a perfect survival guide for anyone forced to use a computer.

> *"I like my copy so much I told friends; now they bought copies."*
>
> **Irene C., Orwell, Ohio**

> *"Quick, concise, nontechnical, and humorous."*
>
> **Jay A., Elburn, Illinois**

> *"Thanks, I needed this book. Now I can sleep at night."*
>
> **Robin F., British Columbia, Canada**

Already, millions of satisfied readers agree. They have made *...For Dummies* books the #1 introductory level computer book series and have written asking for more. So, if you're looking for the most fun and easy way to learn about computers, look to *...For Dummies* books to give you a helping hand.

E-MAIL FOR DUMMIES®
2ND EDITION

**by John R. Levine, Carol Baroudi,
Margy Levine Young, and Arnold Reinhold**

IDG Books Worldwide, Inc.
An International Data Group Company

Foster City, CA ♦ Chicago, IL ♦ Indianapolis, IN ♦ New York, NY

E-Mail For Dummies®, 2nd Edition

Published by
IDG Books Worldwide, Inc.
An International Data Group Company
919 E. Hillsdale Blvd.
Suite 400
Foster City, CA 94404
www.idgbooks.com (IDG Books Worldwide Web site)
www.dummies.com (Dummies Press Web site)

Library of Congress Catalog Card No.: 97-72416

ISBN: 0-7645-0131-3

Printed in the United States of America

10 9 8 7 6 5 4 3 2

2O/SZ/QU/ZY/IN

Distributed in the United States by IDG Books Worldwide, Inc.

Distributed by Macmillan Canada for Canada; by Transworld Publishers Limited in the United Kingdom; by IDG Norge Books for Norway; by IDG Sweden Books for Sweden; by Woodslane Pty. Ltd. for Australia; by Woodslane Enterprises Ltd. for New Zealand; by Longman Singapore Publishers Ltd. for Singapore, Malaysia, Thailand, and Indonesia; by Simron Pty. Ltd. for South Africa; by Toppan Company Ltd. for Japan; by Distribuidora Cuspide for Argentina; by Livraria Cultura for Brazil; by Ediciencia S.A. for Ecuador; by Addison-Wesley Publishing Company for Korea; by Ediciones ZETA S.C.R. Ltda. for Peru; by WS Computer Publishing Corporation, Inc., for the Philippines; by Unalis Corporation for Taiwan; by Contemporanea de Ediciones for Venezuela; by Computer Book & Magazine Store for Puerto Rico; by Express Computer Distributors for the Caribbean and West Indies. Authorized Sales Agent: Anthony Rudkin Associates for the Middle East and North Africa.

For general information on IDG Books Worldwide's books in the U.S., please call our Consumer Customer Service department at 800-762-2974. For reseller information, including discounts and premium sales, please call our Reseller Customer Service department at 800-434-3422.

For information on where to purchase IDG Books Worldwide's books outside the U.S., please contact our International Sales department at 650-655-3200 or fax 650-655-3295.

For information on foreign language translations, please contact our Foreign & Subsidiary Rights department at 650-655-3021 or fax 650-655-3281.

For sales inquiries and special prices for bulk quantities, please contact our Sales department at 650-655-3200 or write to the address above.

For information on using IDG Books Worldwide's books in the classroom or for ordering examination copies, please contact our Educational Sales department at 800-434-2086 or fax 817-251-8174.

For press review copies, author interviews, or other publicity information, please contact our Public Relations department at 650-655-3000 or fax 650-655-3299.

For authorization to photocopy items for corporate, personal, or educational use, please contact Copyright Clearance Center, 222 Rosewood Drive, Danvers, MA 01923, or fax 978-750-4470.

is a trademark under exclusive license to IDG Books Worldwide, Inc., from International Data Group, Inc.

About the Authors

John R. Levine was a member of a computer club in high school — before high school students, or even high schools, had computers. He met Theodor H. Nelson, the author of *Computer Lib/Dream Machines* and the inventor of hypertext, who reminded us that computers should not be taken seriously and that everyone can and should understand and use computers.

John wrote his first program in 1967 on an IBM 1130 (a computer roughly as powerful as your typical modern digital wristwatch, only more difficult to use). He became an official system administrator of a networked computer at Yale in 1975. He began working part-time, for a computer company, of course, in 1977 and has been in and out of the computer and network biz ever since. He got his company on to Usenet early enough that it appears in a 1982 *Byte* magazine article in a map of Usenet, which then was so small the map fit on half a page.

He used to spend most of his time writing software, but now he mostly writes books (including *The Internet For Dummies*, *UNIX For Dummies* and *Internet Secrets,* published by IDG Books Worldwide, Inc.) because it's more fun and he can do so at home in the tiny village of Trumansburg, New York. He also speaks on the Internet and related topics and and co-hosts a weekly radio call-in show on the Internet. (Catch it at `http://iecc.com/radio/`.) He holds a B.A. and a Ph.D. in computer science from Yale University, but please don't hold that against him. Gluttons for punishment can find out more at `http://iecc.com/johnl`.

Carol Baroudi first started playing with computers in 1971 at Colgate University where two things were new: the PDP-10 and women. She was lucky to have unlimited access to the state-of-the-art PDP-10 where she learned to program, operate the machine, and talk to Eliza. She taught Algol and helped to design the curricula for Computer Science and Women's Studies. She majored in Spanish and studied French, which, thanks to the Internet, she can now use every day.

For six years, she developed software and managed software devopment. For a while, she had a small business doing high-tech recruiting (she was a headhunter). For the last several years, she's been writing books for ordinary people who want to use computers and speaking to academic, business, and general audiences around the world about the Internet, the impacts of technology on society, and other related topics.

She's the mother of a fantastic six year old. She loves acting and singing and will fly to France on any excuse. She believes that we are living in a very interesting time when technology is changing our lives faster than we can imagine. She hopes that as we learn to use the new technologies, we don't loose sight of our humanity and feels that that computers can be useful and fun but are no substitute for real life.

Margy Levine Young has used small computers since the 1970s. She graduated from UNIX on a PDP/11 to Apple DOS on an Apple II to MS-DOS and UNIX on a variety of machines. She has done all kinds of jobs that involve explaining to people that computers aren't as mysterious as they might think, including managing the use of PCs at Columbia Pictures, teaching scientists and engineers what computers are good for, and writing and co-writing computer manuals and books, including *Understanding Javelin PLUS* (Sybex, 1987), *The Complete Guide to PC-File* (Center Books, better known as Margy and her Dad, 1991), *UNIX For Dummies, MORE Internet For Dummies, WordPerfect For Windows For Dummies,* and *Internet FAQs: Answers to the Most Frequently Asked Questions, Dummies 101: The Internet For Windows 95,* and *Dummies 101: Netscape Navigator.* Margy has a degree in computer science from Yale University and lives with her husband, two children, and chickens near Middlebury, Vermont.

Arnold Reinhold has been programming computers since they had filaments. His first introduction to the hype/so what?/wow! cycle that governs computer industry evolution was the invention of the transistor. He has gotten to do cool stuff in spacecraft guidance, air traffic control, computer-aided design, robotics, and machine vision. Arnold has been on and off the Internet for over twelve years. Recent writing includes "Commonsense and Cryptography" in *Internet Secrets* and *The Internet For Dummies Quick Reference,* 3rd Edition, both from IDG Books Worldwide, Inc. Arnold studied mathematics at CCNY and MIT, and management at Harvard. You can check out his home page at `http://world.std.com/~reinhold/`.

Dedication

John dedicates his parts of the book to Tonia and Sarah Willow, who surprises us every day.

Carol dedicates her parts of the book, the invisible parts, to her friends that remind her that only the impossible is worth doing.

Authors' Acknowledgments

We particularly thank Mary Bednarek and Diane Steele at IDG Books, whose support and trust encouraged us to do what we all knew perfectly well was impossible.

John thanks Tonia Saxon, for taking such good care of both him and Ms. Pook during the often exciting process of writing this book.

Carol thanks Joshua for *really* explaining things, Steve Dyer for keeping her connected, and Arnold and John for being such great friends.

Margy would like to acknowledge Barbara Begonis and the folks at Lexington Playcare, without whom she would have been typing with one hand while holding two kids. She would also like to thank Meg and Zac, the two kids in question, for being such extraordinary people.

Arnold thanks Barbara Lapinskas for her help and many useful suggestions, Joshua Reinhold for his tour of the Eiffel Tower, and Max and Grete Reinhold of blessed memory.

Thanks to Tim Gallan for rallying to the cause and producing this book despite all odds.

The entire contents of this book were submitted by the authors to the publisher over the Internet. Edited chapters were returned for review in the same way. We thank Finger Lakes Technology Group (Trumansburg, N.Y.), CENTNet (Cambridge, Massachusetts), the World (Brookline, Massachusetts), and Lightlink (Ithaca, New York), our Internet providers.

ABOUT IDG BOOKS WORLDWIDE

Welcome to the world of IDG Books Worldwide.

IDG Books Worldwide, Inc., is a subsidiary of International Data Group, the world's largest publisher of computer-related information and the leading global provider of information services on information technology. IDG was founded more than 25 years ago and now employs more than 8,500 people worldwide. IDG publishes more than 275 computer publications in over 75 countries (see listing below). More than 60 million people read one or more IDG publications each month.

Launched in 1990, IDG Books Worldwide is today the #1 publisher of best-selling computer books in the United States. We are proud to have received eight awards from the Computer Press Association in recognition of editorial excellence and three from *Computer Currents'* First Annual Readers' Choice Awards. Our best-selling *...For Dummies*® series has more than 30 million copies in print with translations in 30 languages. IDG Books Worldwide, through a joint venture with IDG's Hi-Tech Beijing, became the first U.S. publisher to publish a computer book in the People's Republic of China. In record time, IDG Books Worldwide has become the first choice for millions of readers around the world who want to learn how to better manage their businesses.

Our mission is simple: Every one of our books is designed to bring extra value and skill-building instructions to the reader. Our books are written by experts who understand and care about our readers. The knowledge base of our editorial staff comes from years of experience in publishing, education, and journalism — experience we use to produce books for the '90s. In short, we care about books, so we attract the best people. We devote special attention to details such as audience, interior design, use of icons, and illustrations. And because we use an efficient process of authoring, editing, and desktop publishing our books electronically, we can spend more time ensuring superior content and spend less time on the technicalities of making books.

You can count on our commitment to deliver high-quality books at competitive prices on topics you want to read about. At IDG Books Worldwide, we continue in the IDG tradition of delivering quality for more than 25 years. You'll find no better book on a subject than one from IDG Books Worldwide.

John Kilcullen
CEO
IDG Books Worldwide, Inc.

Steven Berkowitz
President and Publisher
IDG Books Worldwide, Inc.

Eighth Annual
Computer Press
Awards ≥1992

WINNER
Ninth Annual
Computer Press
Awards ≥1993

WINNER
Tenth Annual
Computer Press
Awards ≥1994

Eleventh Annual
Computer Press
Awards ≥1995

Publisher's Acknowledgments

We're proud of this book; please register your comments through our IDG Books Worldwide Online Registration Form located at: http://my2cents.dummies.com.

Some of the people who helped bring this book to market include the following:

Acquisitions, Development, and Editorial

Project Editor: Tim Gallan

Acquisitions Editor: Michael Kelly

Media Development Manager: Joyce Pepple

Associate Permissions Editor:
Heather Heath Dismore

Copy Editor: Felicity O'Meara

Technical Editors: Jim McCarter, Kevin Spencer

Editorial Manager: Leah P. Cameron

Editorial Assistant: Michael D. Sullivan

Production

Associate Project Coordinator:
E. Shawn Aylsworth

Layout and Graphics: Angela F. Hunckler, Drew R. Moore, Mark C. Owens, Brent Savage

Proofreaders: Mildred Rosenzweig, Betty Kish, Christine D. Berman, Joel K. Draper, Nancy Price, Robert Springer, Karen York

Indexer: Sherry Massey

General and Administrative

IDG Books Worldwide, Inc.: John Kilcullen, CEO; Steven Berkowitz, President and Publisher

IDG Books Technology Publishing: Brenda McLaughlin, Senior Vice President and Group Publisher

Dummies Technology Press and Dummies Editorial: Diane Graves Steele, Vice President and Associate Publisher; Mary Bednarek, Director of Acquisitions and Product Development; Kristin A. Cocks, Editorial Director

Dummies Trade Press: Kathleen A. Welton, Vice President and Publisher; Kevin Thornton, Acquisitions Manager

IDG Books Production for Dummies Press: Beth Jenkins Roberts, Production Director; Cindy L. Phipps, Manager of Project Coordination, Production Proofreading, and Indexing; Kathie S. Schutte, Supervisor of Page Layout; Shelley Lea, Supervisor of Graphics and Design; Debbie J. Gates, Production Systems Specialist; Robert Springer, Supervisor of Proofreading; Debbie Stailey, Special Projects Coordinator; Tony Augsburger, Supervisor of Reprints and Bluelines; Leslie Popplewell, Media Archive Coordinator

Dummies Packaging and Book Design: Patti Crane, Packaging Specialist; Kavish + Kavish, Cover Design

◆

The publisher would like to give special thanks to Patrick J. McGovern, without whom this book would not have been possible.

◆

Contents at a Glance

Cartoons at a Glance

By Rich Tennant

page 97

page 279

page 79

page 57

page 321

page 7

page 309

page 171

Fax: 978-546-7747 • E-mail: the5wave@tiac.net

Table of Contents

Introduction

. . . .

*W*e happen to think that electronic mail, henceforth *e-mail*, is one of the greatest inventions since the telephone. And it appears that the rest of the world agrees with us. With estimates of more than sixty million users, e-mail is here to stay.

It's hard to go anywhere today without someone asking if you have e-mail — your Aunt Alice and Uncle Erling, your cousin Bertha, your nephew Timmy, even Gramma and Gramps. Employers are telling you to send your resume in via e-mail. TV shows suggest you write to them at their e-mail address. Yes, e-mail is everywhere.

We happen to think this is good news (not just because we like writing books). We realize however, that this great e-mail avalanche is causing problems for some people, and that's why we're here to help. We here at Dummies Central have been using e-mail for decades. Some of us have even been writing about e-mail for decades. And here is our professional opinion:

- ✔ Everyone can learn e-mail.
- ✔ Everyone can learn something *new* about e-mail.

And hence, this book.

Who Are You?

In writing the book, we assumed that

- ✔ You have or would like to have e-mail.
- ✔ You want to use it to communicate effectively with others.
- ✔ You are not interested in becoming an expert on building worldwide e-mail systems; you just want to learn how to use them.

Our first goal is to help you get familiar with the basic concepts of e-mail and to get you using some e-mail system. (We give you lots of choices, and even put some on the handy CD-ROM in the back of the book.)

Our second goal is to show you lots of wonderful things you can do with e-mail beyond the basics — like joining mailing lists about topics that interest you, sending pictures to friends and relatives, making your e-mail snoop-proof and even chatting online.

About This Book

We understand that e-mail is pretty utilitarian stuff and won't be offended if you don't read every page of this book. Part I gives you a general understanding of e-mail and why you might want it, and tells you what you need to get started.

In Parts II, III, and IV we cover many different e-mail programs. Obviously, you won't be interested in all of them. Here's how to tell them apart.

If you are already using Netscape or Internet Explorer to access the World Wide Web, we show you how to set them up to do e-mail as well. If you use America Online or CompuServe, we take you through the steps of using e-mail on those systems. For people who have straight UNIX shell accounts, we describe Pine. For the rest of the world who's probably using a PPP or SLIP account, we provide a variety of e-mail programs from which to choose. We even include a few on the CD at the back of the book. Don't worry though, if you can't read a CD, as we tell you other ways to get the software we include there. Here are the other e-mail programs we describe:

- ✔ Eudora Light from QUALCOMM
- ✔ Outlook 97 and Exchange by Microsoft
- ✔ Pegasus Mail
- ✔ Juno

In Part V, we covers some advanced topics, including mailing lists (there are oodles of great ones), ways to find someone's e-mail address, attaching different kinds of things to your e-mail (like word-processing documents, pictures, sound, and movies), keeping your e-mail private, and online chat.

Part VI talks about using e-mail at work and in the rest of our lives. We cover such important things as using e-mail effectively in the office and using e-mail effectively in a romance. We provide mailing lists of special interest to kids and their parents.

We provide our pithy advice about e-mail and more fascinating mailing lists in Part VII. In Part VIII, Appendix A lists countries and their country codes so that you can decipher where your new friends are writing to you from. The glossary in Appendix B provides a handy list of geeky e-mail terms. Appendix C tells you about the nifty CD stuck in the back of the book.

How to Use This Book

To begin, please read the first four chapters. You can skip Chapter 2 if you already have e-mail service. These chapters give you an overview of e-mail and some important tips and terminology. Besides, we think that they're interesting.

From there, pick one e-mail program to get started with. If you have America Online or CompuServe, start with their mail systems. If you have a PPP or SLIP account and can read a CD or know how to download software from the Net, start with Eudora. If you don't know how to download software, but you have Netscape or Internet Explorer, start with the program you have. If you know you have a UNIX shell account, go straight to the chapter on Pine. If you already have some e-mail program, but it's not one of the ones we talk about or if this whole paragraph is making you crazy, just turn to the Eudora chapter and start there. E-mail programs all do pretty much the same things; some do them more easily than others, but if you read about enough of them, you'll know what to expect even from the most obscure e-mailer someone has inflicted on you.

Once you're up and running, take a peek at Parts VI and VII, just to know what's there. After that, use this book as a reference. Look up your topic or command in the Table of Contents or the Index, either of which should refer you to the part of the book in which we describe what to do and perhaps define a few terms (if absolutely necessary).

In order to emphasize e-mail addresses and other important things that you may need to type in, we present that information in the book like this:

```
cryptic command or address
```

If you want to type in this information (say it's an address to a mailing list you'd like to join), just type it as it appears. Use the same capitalization we do — some systems care very deeply about CAPITAL and small letters.

How This Book Is Organized

This book has eight parts. The parts stand on their own, so you can begin reading wherever you like, but you should at least skim Part I first to get acquainted with some unavoidable Internet jargon and learn how to get your computer on the Net.

Here are the parts of the book and what they contain:

Part I: What Is E-Mail All About?

We give you an introduction to e-mail and tell you why we think it's important, give you strategies for getting you set up with e-mail, and introduce you to the basic concepts. We talk some about the nuances of e-mail use.

Part II: Using Your Browser for E-Mail

Many people already using the World Wide Web can use e-mail from their Web browser. We tell you how to use Netscape and Internet Explorer to do e-mail.

Part III: Using Online Services for E-Mail

America Online and CompuServe users have e-mail built into their services. We tell you how to use them.

Part IV: Using Real E-Mail Programs

The world is full of e-mail programs. We picked out what we think are the best and most popular options for e-mail and help you pick the one that's right for you.

Part V: Advanced E-Mail Topics

Once you have the e-mail basics under your belt, you can delve into more advanced e-mail topics. We include sending attachments and talk about the various kinds of things you can attach. We tell you all about mailing lists and how to participate in them. We teach you about the mysterious world of cryptography and how to keep nosy people from reading your e-mail. We've added a chapter on online chat for those of you who want instant gratification.

Part VI: What to Do with E-Mail

We tell you all kinds of ways to use e-mail both privately and professionally.

Part VII: The Part of Tens

This part is a compendium of sound advice on e-mail (which, we suppose, suggests that the rest of the book is full of bad advice). We also provide more mailing lists to get you started.

Part VIII: Appendixes

Appendix A contains some useful information pertaining to Internet e-mail addresses. In Appendix B, you will find a nifty e-mail glossary. Appendix C tells you about your new CD ROM.

We also include a comprehensive index at the back of the book.

Icons Used in This Book

Lets you know that some particularly nerdy, technoid information is coming up so that you can skip it if you want.

Indicates that a nifty little shortcut or time-saver is explained.

Arrrghhhh! Don't let this happen to you!

We really want this to stick in your mind, as in "It's cold out. Wear a sweater."

Feedback, Please

We love to hear from our readers. If you want to contact us, please feel free to do so in care of

> IDG Books Worldwide
> 7260 Shadeland Station, Suite 100
> Indianapolis, IN 46256

Better yet, send us e-mail at email2@dummies.net. (We answer our e-mail a lot more quickly than we answer our paper mail, which isn't saying much. E-mail is like that.) You can also visit our new World Wide Web home page at http://net.dummies.net, where you'll find the latest updated information on this and other *...For Dummies* books that we've written. These electronic addresses just contact the authors of this book; to contact the publisher or authors of other *...For Dummies* books, send e-mail to info@idgbooks.com or write to the postal address we just provided.

Part I

What Is E-Mail All About?

In this part . . .

Everybody's talking about e-mail these days, but if you've never seen it, it may seem pretty scary. We start with the very basics and gently guide you through the important concepts. We help you understand how e-mail can enhance our businesses and enrich our lives.

Chapter 1

A Gentle Introduction to Electronic Mail

*E*lectronic mail, or *e-mail,* is a way for people to send and receive messages using computers. It has become a primary communication tool for both business and pleasure. Tens of millions of people are using e-mail now, and thousands more are signing up every day. It is very likely that someone you care about is reachable by e-mail. Many of us feel that e-mail is the greatest invention in the history of humanity since the VCR.

The basic idea of e-mail is simple enough:

✔ You type your message on a computer keyboard.

✔ You type in someone's e-mail address — it's sort of like a phone number but usually has letters in it.

✔ You press a button.

✔ Almost instantly your message appears on that person's computer screen, anywhere in the world.

In many cases, e-mail really is about that easy. Best of all, e-mail is usually free, even for messages sent halfway round the world.

Here is what a typical e-mail message looks like:

```
From cb@dummies.net  Fri Jan  3 01:08:51 1997
Mime-Version: 1.0
Content-Type: text/plain; charset="us-ascii"
Date: Thu, 2 Jan 1997 20:08:51 -0500
To: Margaret Levine Young <mly@dummies.net>agr@dummies.net
(Arnold G Reinhold), Mary Bednarek <mbee@dummies.net>,
Waterside Productions <agent@dummies.net>
From: cb@dummies.net (Carol Baroudi)
Subject: Paris contact info

I arrive Saturday, January 4th, and return Tuesday,
January 14th.
I am staying at the Hotel d'Albe, phone 011 33 1 46
34 09 70
Carol Baroudi (cb@dummies.net)
Coauthor, The Internet For Dummies, Internet Secrets
```

What's So Great about E-Mail?

Why all the fuss? Couldn't you make a phone call instead, or send a fax, or just put a stamp on a letter and drop it in the mailbox? Well, in many ways, e-mail combines the best characteristics of all the methods of communicating that preceded it and adds important new benefits of its own. To understand what e-mail is like, let's compare it with other communication methods.

The letter

Postal mail is slow. Overnight delivery is the best you can expect, and you can't rely on that unless you pay a lot of money. Overseas surface mail can take weeks or even months to reach its destination. E-mail, by contrast, often arrives within seconds. Because it is so slow compared to e-mail, postal mail is often called *snail mail* in the electronic world.

Letters are written on paper. You can read them again if you want, photocopy them and pass them on to someone else, and file them for later reference. But you'd better have stationery, envelopes, and stamps on hand to send a letter, and it is awkward to correct a mistake in a handwritten note. You can edit e-mail with a flick of your mouse, and you never have to weigh your e-mail message to figure out the right postage. Just as easily, you can forward a message to a zillion of your closest personal friends and file it on your disk.

You need to know where people live in order to address letters to them. The post office has a tradition of delivering mail that is poorly addressed, but when you move, after a few months' forwarding grace period, you are expected to inform correspondents of your new address. Unless you change e-mail service providers, you can usually keep your e-mail address when you move.

On the other hand, a personal letter is still perhaps the warmest way to communicate. The sender's aura is somehow affixed to the piece of paper. E-mail, by contrast, can feel quite cold. Experienced users work to keep their messages from sounding too harsh. We tell you how in Chapter 4.

The telephone

Phoning is the most immediate form of electronic communication. Most of us use it many times per day. We often get as much information from pauses and tone of voice as we do from the words. Getting emotions across in e-mail is a lot harder. Some people have taken to using cute abbreviations in e-mail to make their feelings a little clearer. We tell you all about those in Chapter 2.

A big problem with the telephone is that the other person has to be there to answer your call. Answering machines and voice mail have helped a little, but it's tough to get a long message just right. Also, it is very hard to save a voice message in any useful way. By contrast, a typical computer hard disk can store thousands of e-mail messages, all neatly indexed by subject, correspondent, and date.

The need for the other person to be there to recieve a phone call is a particular problem for calls to different time zones. France is 9 hours ahead of California, and Japan is 11 hours ahead of New York, for example. E-mail makes communicating across the planet a breeze.

The phone is also very intrusive. Most of us have a Pavlovian need to answer a ringing phone no matter what. Frequent calls make it very hard to put quality time into one's work or life. But *you* decide when to read your e-mail.

Because the phone is so intrusive, many busy people have their calls screened. The "Whom shall I say is calling?" followed by a pause, followed by "I'm sorry, but Mr. Gates is out of the office right now" routine can get pretty tiring. Most people still read their own e-mail or at least scan the subject lines that start off most e-mail messages.

The phone system is persnickety about phone numbers. If you goof on a single digit, you get a wrong number or a nasal recording saying, "The number you have reached is not in service." E-mail also bounces if you get a single letter or number wrong in the address, and the messages are just as unfriendly.

Within North America, phoning is fairly inexpensive, although you can get socked with all kinds of charges when you're away from home. Calling overseas is another matter. People with overseas relationships can run up hundreds of dollars every month in phone bills. E-mail messages are usually free.

The fax

The facsimile machine, or fax, is another recent addition to the general public's communications vocabulary. Because most fax transmissions take place over ordinary phone lines, it shares some of the characteristics of the phone call, including phone numbers and calling rates.

There are two big ways in which a fax is less like a phone call and more like e-mail: A fax is a written form of communication, and the recipient usually doesn't have to be there to receive it. These features made fax the medium of choice for international commerce for many years, though e-mail is rapidly supplanting it.

Now that you can buy fax machines at a reasonable price that use plain paper instead of that yucky thermal stuff, the biggest problem with fax is that the messages cannot be easily and accurately read by computers, which makes it hard to automate the handling of fax messages. If someone faxes you text to include in a document, you typically have to retype and proofread the text. With e-mail, you can paste in the text electronically with complete accuracy.

Another advantage of fax is its ability to easily transmit graphics and messages in any language including the logographic characters used in China, Japan, and Korea. The latest e-mail systems can do this too.

E-Mail Is the Best of All Worlds, Sort Of

E-mail combines most of the best — and a few of the worst — characteristics of the more well-known methods of communicating described above.

- ✔ It's written. You get to review and edit your message before you send it, and the other person can reread it, forward it to someone else, and file it away.
- ✔ The other person doesn't have to be there. E-mail is great for international conversations.

- ✔ E-mail addresses are as persnickety as phone numbers — you have to get every letter in the address right — but they can also follow you around when you move. And many e-mail providers let you pick up your messages even when you are out of town. (We've picked up our e-mail in Australia, Canada, France, Argentina, Hong Kong, and Japan, as well as all corners of the United States.) We'll talk a lot more about e-mail addresses in Chapter 3.

- ✔ E-mail is fast — at least usually. It is not uncommon for messages to be delivered halfway around the world in seconds.

- ✔ E-mail is cheap. After you've paid for the computer, modem, phone line, and access account and any hourly charges, each e-mail message is usually free. It doesn't matter how long the message is or how far away the recipient lives.

- ✔ E-mail is nonintrusive. You can set aside a fixed time each day to read and respond to your e-mail, or you can read it whenever you have time.

- ✔ People who would never take your call are often reachable via e-mail. Senior managers can get feedback from every level of their organization without being swamped. The head of a large semiconductor plant sent all 1,400 of his employees an e-mail message asking, "What are we doing that is keeping you from doing your job to the best of your ability?" and expects to read all the responses.

E-mail's unique advantages

You can do several things with e-mail that are difficult or impossible with any other form of communication. These e-mail advantages include the following:

- ✔ It's easy to send your message to more than one person. You just type in several e-mail addresses. You can also keep mailing lists on your computer, which allows for quick distribution to many people, thousands even.

- ✔ Most e-mail systems have a reply button that lets you include, or *quote*, all or part of the original message when you are writing a reply. This one small feature can save you an enormous amount of time. Here is an example:

```
Subject: Re: ST:A Final Unity for Mac?
    >Would you please tell me if you have plans to put
      out a version
    >of "Star Trek: A Final Unity" for the Mac, and if
      so, when?
    It's out now!
Spectrum HoloByte Tech Support
```

✔ You can attach drawings, sounds, video clips, and other computer files to your e-mail.

✔ You can easily save thousands of e-mail messages and search saved message files electronically.

✔ You can paste all or part of an e-mail into other computer documents.

✔ You can use e-mail to access vast pools of information stored on the Internet.

E-mail's disadvantages

Okay, so e-mail isn't perfect. Here are some of the pitfalls:

✔ While the post office goes everywhere and phones are nearly universal in developed countries, a lot of people don't have e-mail yet.

✔ Your messages are not received until the recipients check their e-mail. While most active users check their mail daily, people who don't get mail often can't be counted on to check their mail regularly.

✔ E-mail isn't always reliable. Messages between different e-mail systems can be held up for days by computer glitches.

✔ Some e-mail service providers lack the equipment to handle peak demands. You may have trouble accessing your e-mail at certain times of the day. Consider this when choosing your service provider.

✔ Because it can pass through many multiuser computers on its way, your e-mail messages can be intercepted by others. But programs are available that protect your messages with secret codes. See Chapter 17, which covers e-mail security.

✔ Because it is a new medium, there are fewer legal privacy protections for e-mail messages. In particular, your employer may have the right to read — without your consent or knowledge — any e-mail messages you send or receive at work.

✔ Because your message is copied from computer to computer, it is hard to destroy e-mail messages. As they were leaving office, members of the Bush administration were embarrassed when copies of e-mail messages they thought they had erased showed up on archived computer backup tapes.

✔ You can be flooded with incoming mail. Some users get hundreds of messages each day. It can take some time to go through them all.

✔ Some people are using e-mail to send unsolicited advertising — called *junk e-mail*, or *spam*. We'll tell you how to deal with spam in Chapter 4.

These disadvantages notwithstanding, e-mail will become a part of most of our lives in the course of the next few years. We hope the rest of this book will help you make e-mail a valuable and pleasant way to communicate.

Chapter 2
Getting Started

In This Chapter
▶ What you need to get connected
▶ What your e-mail software can do
▶ What e-mail providers can offer

*G*etting hooked up to e-mail can be much more difficult than using it. The process can be hard on new users. We try to help.

You may already have e-mail — most college students do, and many employees of large corporations get their accounts the first day on the job. If so, you can skip this chapter, although parts may come in handy later as a reference. If you are part of an organization that has e-mail, but you don't yet have an account, talk to your supervisor or look for someone with the name "System Administrator" on her door. Tell her *E-Mail For Dummies* sent you and bring cookies.

If you are an individual or part of a small organization and want to communicate using e-mail, grab your favorite beverage and settle in someplace comfortable while we lead you through the process.

To use e-mail, you need access to the following:

✔ A computer

✔ A connection to the network. Often this means a modem and phone line

✔ Some software that lets your computer talk to other computers

✔ Some software that lets you send and receive e-mail

✔ A copy of this book

I have e-mail at work.
Does this mean I'm on the Internet?

Maybe yes, maybe no. Many companies hook their computers together with other computers at the same company to form a *network* of computers. Some then connect that network to the Internet, the worldwide association of computer networks all linked together. If so, you can use your computer at work to send e-mail to anyone anywhere on the Internet — for business purposes only, of course.

Other companies are not connected to the Internet, either because they don't want to be or because they haven't gotten around to it yet. If your company is one of those non-Internet types, you can exchange e-mail with coworkers but not with outsiders. This fact does not mean you should put this book back on the bookstore shelf and browse elsewhere. We have a lot to tell you about making more effective use of the e-mail you already have and we prepare you for the day you get Internet access at work (it's coming soon, trust us). You may even want to get your own e-mail account at home. It will give you a real leg up on your coworkers. We tell you how in this chapter.

Different kinds of internal e-mail software exist. Some companies run e-mail programs on their mainframes — large, very expensive computers that live in rooms with glass walls

and false floors and special air conditioning. Other companies wire together all their personal computers into a local area network, or *LAN*. Novell, AppleTalk, Lotus Notes, and cc:Mail are names you might see if your company is hooked up this way. Some organizations have even set up their own internal version of the Internet. These systems are called *intranets*, and use some of the same software, such as Eudora, that we describe in this book.

The best way to find out if your organization's e-mail system is on the Internet is to ask a coworker. You might also try sending an e-mail message addressed to `email2@ dummies.net` This is the address of the Dummies Central e-mail robot. We'll send a reply if we get your message, and you'll know you are on the Internet. If you don't get a reply, or if you get a reply saying your message cannot be delivered, it's a bad sign, but it doesn't mean for sure that you are not connected. You may have to do something special to get mail out to the Internet. Again, ask.

If you get fired just for trying, send a message to `sympathy@dummies.net`. If that message is returned to you as undeliverable, it means that you are actually a decent person with a great future and should accept this minor career setback as a learning experience.

You don't need exclusive control of any of the preceding items, though e-mail is more convenient and private if you have it. You can share. One thing you do need for your very own is an e-mail account. This gives you an *e-mail address* — the letters and numbers that people type into *their* e-mail system when they want to send mail to you — and a place where mail for you is kept until you get around to reading it. Your account is set up on a computer called a *mail server*. This computer is usually *not* the one on your desk. It may be in your building or at a *service provider* — a company that connects you to the Internet so you can send and receive e-mail.

There are now several way to connect your computer to the network. Some users, typically at universities and large corporations, are lucky enough to have a *direct connection* for e-mail. These people do not need a modem or phone line, but they may need a network interface card. In almost every organization that provides direct connections there is someone, usually the System Administrator, who can help you get started.

Many cable companies are now offering Internet access. While cable service is expensive if e-mail is all you need, it does provide fast access to other Internet tools like the World Wide Web. Cable companies often set up and configure your e-mail account for you, including installing a network card in your computer. Contact them for information about availability and price.

The rest of us connect to the network over an ordinary telephone line using a device called a *modem*. Many computers now come with a modem built in. If yours did not, you'll have to get one. We tell you what to get later in this chapter.

Finding a Computer for E-Mail

If you don't already have access to a computer, you need to borrow or buy one. Almost any computer will do for e-mail; however, technology is changing very rapidly, so here are a few things we think you should know:

If you want complete Internet access (not just e-mail, but access to the World Wide Web, for example), be aware that new machines are significantly different from old machines. If you're going to buy a computer, buy a new one with Internet software and modem already installed. If you're thinking about buying a used computer, make sure you're not spending a lot of money, and make sure the person who's selling it to you will come and install it and get you up and running. Otherwise, we fear you're wasting your time and your money.

If you borrow a computer, be sure to borrow its owner until you're up and running.

It Takes Two to E-Mail

Let's face it, sending e-mail to yourself is of limited value. You probably want e-mail to communicate with someone other than yourself. That someone (or those someones) are at the other end of some sort of computer network. In order to talk to them, you too must have to be connected to a network, most likely the Internet. If you're not already connected at school or at work, you have only a couple of options. If you don't like them, wait a year — they're bound to be different. For the time-being, the two common ways to connect to the Internet (that great network of networks) are

- Cable access
- Using a modem (a device that lets your computer talk over your phone line)

If your work or school has a network and you're not connected to it, it's worth finding out if you can connect to it, because chances are it'll save you some money. However, you may lose some autonomy when you find yourself restricted to the rules your organization has created regarding network access.

Cable TV without the TV

Right now, in the spring of 1997, the easiest way to get connected to the Internet is through access provided by cable TV companies that come and install the necessary hardware and software for you. Cable access is not yet universally available and is more costly than some stripped-down, e-mail-only services, but it's significantly faster and easier to get started. You don't need a TV, by the way.

Managing with a modem

Don't feel bad if cable access isn't available to you; none of us authors have it yet. All of us except John continue our daily e-mail connections via modem.

A modem is a device that connects your computer to the phone line. Back when the telephone was invented, no one ever dreamed of computers, much less computers that could talk to each other. Your modem converts the data that you want to send into soundlike signals that can go down an old-fashioned telephone line.

Because your modem is the key link between your computer and your e-mail provider, you want to get the fastest one on the market. The good news is that you can afford it.

If you are buying a new modem, try to get a 33,600-bps modem. These units cost less than $200. If you are tight for cash, get a 28,800-bps modem. It runs a bit slower but is still adequate for e-mail use. 14,400-bps modems are very cheap and provide adequate service for e-mail.

See *Modems For Dummies,* 3rd Edition (IDG Books Worldwide, Inc.), for more detailed information on modem selection.

Mommy, what's a protocol?

When your phone rings, you pick it up and say something short like "Hello," "Bonjour," or "White House, how can I direct your call?"

If the other person recognizes your voice or the name of your organization, he or she then says who he or she is, or makes a request, and the conversation proceeds.

If the other person doesn't recognize who picked up, you might hear something like, "Is this 202-456-1616?" or "I was trying to reach Dummies Central . . . "

And so on.

When your conversation is nearly over you might say

"It's been nice chatting, but I have to get back to work."

"We should do lunch."

"Give me a call."

"Bye."

Computers have similar rules for starting and ending phone calls and dealing with any problems that may arise. Protocols are just sets of rules that computers use to establish a conversation. Computers use different sets of rules, or protocols, for different purposes, just as people have different rules for calls to business acquaintances, friends, and lovers. And, like people, computers rarely do lunch.

What every modem user should know

- ✔ If someone picks up an extension phone while you are logged in, your connection usually breaks and you have to call back.

- ✔ If you have call waiting, put *70 in front of the number of your e-mail service provider in your communications software to turn off call waiting while your modem is on the line. Otherwise, those incoming calls may break your e-mail connection. (This hint applies in the U.S. and Canada only.)

- ✔ If your modem isn't working, check that all the cables are plugged in nice and tight at the computer, the modem, and the phone jack; that the power supply is plugged into the wall; and that the modem's on-off switch, usually hidden in the back, is on (usually up).

- ✔ If you use voice mail, the special *beep-beep-beep* dial tone that you get whenever you have new messages can confuse your modem. Pick up those voice messages before logging in to get your e-mail.

- ✔ If your modem dies, buy a new one unless the old one is still under warranty. Modems are usually not worth repairing.

Telephone tips for modem users

Your ordinary phone line is all you need to connect to your e-mail. But it must have a modular phone jack, the same kind of jack that telephones use, for your modem to plug into. If you don't have one, Radio Shack stores carry a wide line of adapters and wiring stuff.

Here are some other tips:

- ✔ If your phone company gives you a choice of local service options, pick one that lets you call your e-mail provider without per-minute charges.

- ✔ Business service costs a lot more than residential service.

- ✔ If you end up tying up the phone a lot, you may want to get a second line.

- ✔ If you do get a second line, don't add extensions to it and don't get call waiting. Just use it for your computer.

- ✔ Compare the cost of a second phone line, plus what your service provider is charging you, with the cost of Internet access from the local cable TV company, if that option is available in your area.

Selecting an E-Mail Provider

We could have titled this section "Selecting an Internet Service Provider" because, with one major exception, most e-mail service is provided by Internet service providers. A major exception is the e-mail–only service provided by Juno. If you know that all you want (for now) is e-mail, you can skip the rest of this chapter and turn straight to Chapter 11. We should warn you that e-mail itself is evolving into a multimedia organism; limiting yourself to e-mail is not a good long-term strategy.

Once you have a computer and a modem, you're ready to find a service provider. A provider is a business that offers electronic communications services, usually for a fee. You have to call the provider up to ask for an account, either by voice or using your computer and modem. Many give you free disks with everything you need to get started. When you connect for the first time, you will be asked for your name and address and for a credit card number, and you'll be billed monthly for the services you use. Some providers ask you to pay in advance or offer a discount if you do. Providers get a lot of deadbeats.

When you send mail, your provider forwards it to its destination. Mail addressed to you is held by the provider until you call up and log in to check your mail. You don't have to worry about missing mail when your computer isn't connected.

Types of service providers are described in the following sections as *value-added online services* and *local service providers*. Competition between the different types of service providers is intense, and the boundaries between them are blurring.

Value-added online services

This type of provider tries to offer much more than basic e-mail access in order to get you to use its services. Needless to say, these providers often charge more as a result.

The most popular value-added providers at the time of this writing are America Online, CompuServe, and Microsoft Network.

Reasons for picking a value-added online service include

- ✔ User-friendly software that provides all the tools you need in a single package
- ✔ Additional services that are only available to customers of that provider. For example, online chatting, which we tell you about in Chapter 20
- ✔ Capability of logging in from any major city just by making a local phone call

If you call one of the major value-added provider's phone number listed in Table 2-1, below, the provider will send you a starter kit with the software you need and usually some promotional offer.

Table 2-1	Major Value-Added Online Service Providers
Service	*Phone Numbers*
America Online (AOL)	800-827-6364; 703-448-8700
CompuServe	800-848-8990; 614-718-2800
The Microsoft Network (MSN)	800-386-5550

Local Internet e-mail providers

Local service providers come in two flavors:

- ✔ PPP/SLIP dial-up
- ✔ Terminal or shell dial-up

PPP or SLIP service connects you directly to the Internet, and you can use (and will need) a powerful Internet e-mail program like Eudora or Netscape. PPP stands for *point-to-point protocol* (see the sidebar "Mommy, what's a protocol?" earlier in this chapter), and SLIP stands for *serial line Internet protocol*. These protocols do pretty much the same thing. Ask your service provider which one they support. If you have a choice, PPP is slightly more reliable and a lot easier to set up. For more information on SLIP and PPP, see *The Internet For Dummies,* 4th Edition (IDG Books Worldwide, Inc.).

Terminal or shell dial-up service connects you to a computer, usually one using the UNIX operating system. You can send and receive your e-mail using a UNIX e-mail program, such as Pine. See Chapter 12 to learn how these UNIX e-mail programs work. This kind of service is great if you have an older computer that cannot run the latest graphical interface software.

Why go with the little guys?

Reasons to go local include the following:

- ✔ Lower cost. Many local providers offer a flat monthly rate, though the hourly rate may make more sense if you only plan to use e-mail. Either way they are often cheaper than the value-added providers.

- ✔ Choice of access tools. Many programs are available for reading e-mail, such as Eudora and Netscape, and with a PPP or SLIP account, you can use any program you want. Competition among e-mail programs is fierce, and new features are being added all the time. If you go with a value-added service provider, you are generally locked into the e-mail program they provide.

- ✔ Ability to use the latest Internet services as soon as they hit the Net. The value-added providers usually take half a year to a year to add a new capability — if they ever do.

- ✔ Less censorship. CompuServe once cut *all* its customers' access to some allegedly racy Internet newsgroups due to pressure from a German state government. Local providers tend to be more nimble.

- ✔ Friendly, local, personal service. If they don't act like they want your business, find a different provider who does.

Here are the best ways we know to find a local service provider close to home:

- ✔ Check the business pages of your local newspaper for advertisements from local access providers.

- ✔ Ask your public library's research librarian or online services staff.

- ✔ Look in your local Yellow Pages under "Internet Services."

- ✔ Ask friends and acquaintances who already have e-mail what service they're using and how they like it.

Consider the following things when picking a local service provider:

- ✔ Flat fee versus hourly charge. Monthly Internet access is available for $20/month or less in all major U.S. cities and a surprising number of rural areas. (One of your authors is typing this while connected to his local provider in Trumansburg, New York, population 1611, and another is in Cornwall, Vermont, population 1101.) Some providers charge less for e-mail–only use. A flat monthly fee is a great buy if you're using other Internet services besides e-mail. An hourly rate might be a lot cheaper if you are only using e-mail.

✔ Local phone access. In most areas in the United States, phone calls are free or at least not charged by the minute if they don't go too far. If at all possible, select a service provider that has an access phone number within your local (free or untimed) calling area.

✔ System availability during peak periods. Some providers cut costs by not having enough equipment to provide good service during peak periods. The result is busy signals when you try to dial in and painfully slow response when you do get through, especially on weekday evenings.

✔ Modem speeds. If you go out and buy a fast modem, make sure your provider has modems just as fast, and computers big enough to keep up.

✔ Ability to call in from remote locations. Some providers, like The World in Brookline, Massachusetts, have arrangements with large data networks to enable their customers to dial in from the road by making a local call. Some, like ClarkNet in Washington, D.C., have an 800 number for use on the road. They usually charge extra for this service.

✔ Support for neophytes. If the provider's technical support staff has no patience for questions from a beginner, look elsewhere.

✔ If you are a Macintosh user, make sure that your provider offers whole-hearted support for Macintosh e-mail applications.

Don't feel unreasonable if you want to try several services before picking the one you like best. But remember, once you start giving out your e-mail address, you may find it harder to switch services.

Understanding Your E-Mail Program

An e-mail program is software that runs on your computer and lets you read and compose your e-mail. If you are using a value-added service provider, your e-mail program is included in the program disk you use to start your service. We talk about using value-added online services for e-mail in Part III.

If you are using a local Internet service provider, you generally need to choose an Internet e-mail program. The most popular programs are described in Part II and Part IV. These parts also tell you how to get copies of these programs.

If you are using a shell account, you might want to use the UNIX e-mail program Pine, which is described in Chapter 12.

Finally, if you are using e-mail at work, you'll likely be told which e-mail program to use. We tell you about the most common types in Chapter 13.

Common features of e-mail programs include the following:

- ✔ Selecting and reading e-mail. Most e-mail programs present a list of incoming messages from which you can select.

- ✔ Composing, addressing, and sending outgoing messages. E-mail programs usually provide you with a built-in word processing program that lets you type in your message and make edits until you are satisfied with what you wrote. Some even have spell checkers.

- ✔ Replying to a message that someone has sent you. You can usually include all or part of the message that was sent.

- ✔ Forwarding a message you receive to someone else with your comments.

- ✔ Redirecting or bouncing a message to someone else without any edits or changes.

- ✔ Saving and organizing your messages. Many programs let you set up a number of folders on your computer and make it easy to put each message in the right folder.

- ✔ Filtering and threading incoming messages. Some e-mail programs have features that let you tell the program to put different types of mail into a separate list so you can easily read them in order of the priority you choose. Mail from your boss can be read first (or last!), for example.

- ✔ Saving and organizing e-mail addresses.

- ✔ Creating a short block of text that is automatically added to the end of messages you send. These files are called *signature files*.

- ✔ Creating personal nicknames, or aliases, that you can use to address mail without typing the entire address.

- ✔ Creating personal electronic mailing lists that let you send messages to a number of people at once.

- ✔ Importing a computer file into an e-mail message so that its text is part of the message.

- ✔ Attaching files to an e-mail message. These files might be anything from a word processing document, to a picture, to a video clip.

Whew!

We've given you an awful lot of information in this chapter. Don't panic if you haven't absorbed it all — in later chapters we get down to the nitty-gritty, step-by-step operations, and you can always come back here when you have a general question.

Chapter 3

Basic E-Mail Concepts

• •

In This Chapter

▶ Learning about e-mail addresses

▶ Sending and receiving mail

▶ Replying to and forwarding messages

▶ Saving messages

• •

You probably can't wait to start using e-mail. In this chapter we tell you the essential things you need to know in order to get going. We cover some of the finer points of e-mail in Chapter 4. Chapter 15 has some techy stuff that you certainly don't need to know about to get started, but you will be very glad to have if you ever *do* need it.

The basic concepts we talk about here apply whether you are on an isolated e-mail system and can only talk to people in your own company, or your e-mail system is connected to the Internet and you can talk to any other Internet-connected e-mail user in the world. We start at the top with e-mail addresses.

The Skinny on E-Mail Addresses

Understanding addresses may be the hardest part of learning e-mail — and definitely the most important. To send an e-mail message to someone or something (some e-mail goes to robots), you have to have his, her, or its address. An e-mail address is a lot like a phone number. Phone number styles vary somewhat around the world — some countries have 6-, 7-, or even 8-digit local numbers, for example — and you'll find that e-mail address styles vary a lot, too.

Here is the good news! If your computer has a cut-and-paste feature — as all Mac OS and Windows computers do — you can usually copy e-mail addresses and paste them where they are needed. Just be sure to copy the correct address, the whole address, and nothing but the address, so help you. If you just started using a computer for the first time and you don't know what we mean by "copy and paste," don't worry — typing the address works just fine. In your spare time, pick up *Macs For Dummies* or *Windows For Dummies* and read at your leisure — you might find the background helpful even if it's not absolutely necessary for your task at hand.

Local e-mail addresses

Local e-mail addresses, or *mailbox names*, are usually just a bunch of letters and numbers like margy, john1, Carol_Baroudi, or AGR12745. Often your local e-mail address is the same as the name you use when you log in to your computer — your *login name*. Many services let you pick any e-mail name you want, just so long as it isn't taken already. Often this means you end up with a name like joshua819 on a big, popular service like America Online.

Traditionally, CompuServe, for reasons having to do with long-forgotten computer operating systems, has used a pair of numbers separated by a comma for its e-mail addresses (for example, 102554,3060). Nowadays CompuServe also gives you the alternative of using a name instead of a number if you insist, although you still get a number as your default address.

That pesky comma is a source of considerable confusion because Internet mail programs use a comma to separate the different addresses when you want to send e-mail to multiple recipients. We tell you how this conflict is handled later. (Okay, if you can't stand the suspense: You replace the comma with a period when you want to send mail to a CompuServe member via the Internet. But please don't tell the other readers yet.)

Capitalization normally does not matter in e-mail addresses. Or, as computer types say it, e-mail addresses are not *case sensitive*. This means e-mail addressed to margy, Margy, and MARGY all end up at the same place. On the other hand, margy, margaret, and margy1 are all different, of course. (In fact, a few ancient systems still care about capitalization, but unless you're really unlucky, you'll never run into one.)

The general rule is that you can use the local e-mail name by itself whenever you are sending mail to someone who uses the same e-mail provider that you use. For example, if you use America Online, you can send mail to other America Online users without tacking "@aol.com" onto the user name. If you are sending a message to someone on a different e-mail service, you usually have to use a full Internet e-mail address.

Internet e-mail addresses

So what's an Internet address? Roughly speaking, an Internet e-mail address consists of the following parts:

- ✔ A mailbox name (like we told you about above)
- ✔ @ (the *at* sign)
- ✔ A domain name (the name of the computer the message is going to, sort of)

For example, here is a typical address: elvis@iecc.com.

Here, elvis is the mailbox name and iecc.com is the domain name. We tell you more about domain names in Chapter 4.

Internet e-mail addresses are more complicated than local e-mail addresses for several reasons:

- ✔ Internet e-mail connects over 40 million people today, and that number will grow to billions in the next century. We can't all have a simple e-mail address like Bob.
- ✔ The Internet has to accommodate addresses from many different e-mail systems. All of these were developed separately, and the developers had different ideas of what an e-mail address should look like.
- ✔ The computer programmers who invented the Internet never expected it to go on as long as it has without being redesigned. Had they known, they might have made it a bit more user-friendly. (Then again, they might have done worse — see Chapter 4.)

Actually, the @ sign, pronounced "at," was first selected as the way to separate a user's name from a machine's name in 1972 by Ray Tomlinson, a programmer at BBN, a company that did a lot of the early Internet development. He thought it was the obvious choice because when you read an address out loud, carol@iecc.com becomes "Carol at yech.com" — the @ sign tells where the user is at, so to speak.

Some e-mail services make you put an access code in front of the address, to tell your mail system that this message is destined for the Internet. It's kind of like dialing 9 to get an outside line. For example,

Internet:elvis@iecc.com

SMTP:elvis@iecc.com

SMTP in this example stands for simple mail transfer protocol, the optimistically named set of rules that say how Internet e-mail is transferred from one computer to another. For the most part, you never have to pay attention to these rules; your e-mail program takes care of them.

One rule that you do have to pay attention to says that Internet addresses can contain the following: letters, numbers, and some punctuation characters such as periods, hyphens, and underscores.

Internet addresses should *not* contain the following: commas, spaces, or parentheses.

The most common situation in which these restrictions cause problems is that of CompuServe addresses, which consist of two numbers separated by a comma. When converting a CompuServe address to an Internet address, you have to change the comma to a period. For example, `71053,2615` becomes `71053.2615@compuserve.com`.

Another common problem is spaces in AOL mailbox names. For example, John Doe's mailbox name might be `John Doe`. America Online in fact lets you leave out the space, so you would send mail to `JohnDoe@aol.com`.

While America Online may be forgiving about missing spaces, there are some other mail systems that are not so forgiving. If, for some reason, you must send Internet mail to an address that does include commas, spaces, or parentheses, enclose the address in double quotes, like this: `"John Doe"@fooble.com`.

Where am I on the Internet?

The most important address you need to know is your own. You should keep a copy in your wallet until you have it memorized. That way you will be prepared when someone asks, "What's your e-mail address?"

If you are accessing the Internet through a service provider, your address is most likely

```
yourloginname@yourproviderdomainname
```

The domain name is usually your provider's domain name. In the case where your company or school is your provider, it's your company's or school's domain name. If your login name is `elvis` and your provider's computer is `shamu.strat.ntw.org`, your mail address may be

```
elvis@shamu.strat.ntw.org
elvis@strat.ntw.org
elvis@ntw.org
```

or even

```
elvis-presley@ntw.org.
```

If you're not sure what your e-mail address is, send an e-mail message to Dummies Central — our e-mail address is `email2@dummies.net`.

Our mail robot will send back a note containing the address from which your message was sent, which is your e-mail address. While you're at it, add a sentence or two telling us whether you like this book because we authors do read all the mail, too.

Once you know your own e-mail address, the next thing you need is the address of the person you want to send that hot e-mail message to. We tell you how to find out someone else's e-mail address in Chapter 14. (Spoiler: The best way is to call that person on the phone and ask.)

We hope this is enough about addresses to get you started. We return to this fun topic in Chapter 4, where we tell you how to decode those intriguing domain names and deal with something called X.400 addresses, which you encounter only if you have done something really bad in a previous life.

What's the difference between an e-mail address and a URL?

URLs, or *uniform resource locators,* have become ubiquitous in a few short years. They show up on everything from movie credits to billboards. A URL tells a program called a browser (Netscape Navigator or Microsoft Internet Explorer, for example) where to find information on the Internet's World Wide Web. URLs are not e-mail addresses, so don't try to send mail to them. We tell you more about them in Chapter 15.

E-mail addresses have an @ sign, like `email2@dummies.net`. URLs have slashes and colons, like `http://net.dummies.net`.

Using Your E-Mail Program

To use e-mail, you need an e-mail program. E-mail programs typically let you do the following:

- Read your incoming e-mail messages.
- Send new messages.
- Reply to messages you receive.
- Forward messages to other people.
- Save messages for later.
- Read saved messages.

Sometimes you have a choice of which e-mail program to use. Other times you don't. If you're using AOL, for example, you use AOL's mailer. In this book, we cover the following e-mail programs:

- Eudora (Mac OS and Windows) (Chapters 9 and 10)
- Internet Explorer's Internet Mail (Mac OS and Windows) (Chapter 6)
- Netscape Navigator's Messenger (Mac OS and Windows) (Chapter 5)
- America Online's mail program (Mac OS and Windows) (Chapter 7)
- CompuServe's mail program (Mac OS and Windows) (Chapter 8)
- Juno (Windows only) (Chapter 11)
- Pine (UNIX) (Chapter 12)
- Microsoft's Outlook 97, Exchange and Microsoft Mail (Windows) (Chapter 13)
- Pegasus (Mac OS, Windows, and DOS) (Chapter 13)

Although many other e-mail programs are in use, the basic principles are pretty much the same. In this chapter, we paint a broad picture of what a generic e-mail program is supposed to do. When you are actually ready to send mail, turn to the chapter that deals with your very own e-mail program for the picky details.

Where is my mail, anyway?

When your mail arrives, unless you are one of the lucky few whose computers have a permanent Internet connection, the mail doesn't get delivered to your computer. Your messages are delivered instead to a *mail server,* a computer that is sort of like your local post office. In order for you to actually get your mail, your mail program has to contact your mail server and ask for your messages. To send mail, your mail program has to take it to the post office; that is, transmit it to the server.

If you're using a commercial online service or a UNIX shell account, the mail server is in the same group of computers you connect to when you're dialed in. So when you run your provider's mail program, the mail is right there for you to read, and the program can drop outgoing mail directly in the virtual mail chute.

If you're using a PPP/SLIP account, when your mail program picks up the mail, it sucks your messages from your provider to your computer at top speed. After you have your mail on your local computer, you can disconnect — a good idea if your provider charges by the hour. Then you can read and respond to your mail while the meter isn't ticking — that is, while you're offline. After you've composed and are ready to send your responses or new messages, you can reconnect and transmit your outgoing mail to the mail server, again at top network speed.

A five-step program for sending e-mail

You complete these five steps to send an e-mail message:

1. **Tell the mailer that you want to send a new message.**

2. **Address the message.**

3. **Fill in the subject line.**

4. **Compose the message.**

5. **Tell your computer to send the message on its way.**

Most mailers have a command called something like New Message that lets you create new e-mail. Usually a window or screen appears with *fields* (spaces for you to enter something) for the address, the subject, and the actual text of the message, often called the *message body*.

Where to, buddy?

Normally you address the new message by typing or pasting the recipient's e-mail address into a To field. Simple enough. Most mailers also let you keep an address book on your computer. If your mailer does, you can just select the recipient's name from a list, assuming you've entered the address into the address book beforehand.

You can send your message to more than one recipient. Most mailers let you enter several addresses into the To field. Most mailers (but not CompuServe's) ask you to separate the different addresses with commas.

Now move on to the next field. On most mailers you move from field to field by pressing the Tab key or by clicking with the mouse inside the field you want.

So what's carbon paper anyway? (ccs and bccs)

You will also notice fields labeled *cc* and maybe even *bcc*. The abbreviation *cc* stands for "carbon copy." Way back when, typists made multiple copies of a letter by inserting a sandwich of stationery separated by sheets of carbon paper. Use the cc field for the addresses of people who aren't the primary recipients of your message but who need to be kept informed. Everyone who gets the message sees the cc field and knows who else has received the message.

Some mailers have a *bcc* field. This abbreviation stands for "blind carbon copy." A person whose address is entered into the bcc field gets a copy of the message, but because the other recipients don't see what's been entered into the bcc field, they have no clue that this person got a copy. Use this feature judiciously. If people think their communications with you are private and confidential, only to find you've been copying their mail to someone else, you'd best have your ducks all lined up.

What's the message all about?

Another universal feature of mailers is the Subject field. It's a place for you to enter a short description of what the message is about. The recipient sees the subject and your name in an incoming-messages list when he or she picks up mail (many e-mail users find a hundred or more messages on their computer every morning). Your recipient can choose what order to read the messages in, so state your subject as clearly as possible. Here are some examples of subject lines:

Poor: "Need information"

Fair: "Real estate question"

Better: "About the Binkley sale"

Best: "What's the closing date for Binkley?"

Most e-mail programs let you have a blank subject, but we wish they would at least warn you when you forget the subject line. Always include a subject.

I have something to say

You are now ready to type what you want to say into the message body field.

When you are done, we recommend that you read over your message carefully. Most mailers have built-in editing features such as cut and paste that let you correct what you have written. Many mailers even have a built-in spelling checker.

If your mailer doesn't have a spelling checker, you can always copy the message, paste it into your word processor, and check the spelling there.

See Chapter 4 for some ideas on writing more effective e-mail.

You can also include text in your message that's in a file on your hard disk. To do so, look for a message import command in your e-mail program or open the file with your favorite word processor, select and copy the text you want included, and then paste that text into the message's body field.

Many mailers let you *attach* files to your message. These files can be word processing documents, graphics, sounds, or even video clips. You need to make sure that your recipient has the necessary programs to read the files you send. See Chapter 15 to learn about some of the more popular formats for e-mail attachments.

Ship it

After you're really, really sure your message says what you want it to say, it's time to send it on its way. Most e-mail programs have a send button or command. If you are online to your provider, just click this button or enter the command and your message is on its way.

Most mail system have *no* provision for recalling a message once you have sent it. In fact, e-mail messages are often delivered in less than a minute.

If you are working offline, you can put the message aside for transmission the next time you connect with your service provider. If your mailer is equipped to do this, you see a command like "Drop mail in out box" or "Send later." Not only does this way of working save on connect-time charges, but it also gives you a chance to reconsider.

Receiving mail

You follow four steps to read your mail:

1. **Get the mail from your service provider.**
2. **Review your list of messages.**
3. **Select, open, and read messages.**
4. **Dispose of messages.**

Beam them up, Scotty

You usually have to connect to your e-mail service provider or connect to your mail server to get your e-mail. Once you do this, you may have to enter a command like "Check mail." You then get to wait a moment while your messages are brought over the network to your computer. (If you are using a UNIX shell provider, you don't have to go through the "check mail" step.)

Your e-mail program presents you with a list of incoming e-mail messages. This list typically contains a line for each message containing the date, sender, and subject of that message. The list usually includes old messages that you have not dealt with and has new messages at the end. Different e-mail programs use different codes and icons to indicate the status of each message on the list: new, old-but-unopened, read.

You can now select a message to read, usually by double-clicking the message line using the mouse, or by using the arrow and Tab keys to move to the message line you want and then pressing Enter.

You can read the message on-screen, print it out, or close it and read it later. You can also send a reply message and send the message on to someone else. We talk about those options later in this chapter.

File this message, please

Finally, you can dispose of your message, either throwing it out or saving it for later reference. Different mailers have different names for the place in the computer where messages are saved. Most call them *mailboxes*. You can create as many of these mailboxes as you want and give them whatever names you want. Many mailers let you organize your mailboxes into *folders* — kind of like files within files in traditional filing systems.

Most mailers let you open any of these mailboxes and see a list of the messages that are in it. You can then select a message and open it, read it again, copy stuff out of it, send a belated reply, or whatever.

Mailers also usually let you save individual messages as separate text files that you can then open with a word processor, spreadsheet program, or some other type of software.

If you choose to save a message, you can use two general organizational approaches: filing by sender and filing by topic. Whether you use one or the other or both is mostly a matter of taste. Some mail programs (such as Pine) help you file stuff by the sender's name, so if your friend Fred has the address `fred@something.or.other`, when you press S to save a message from him, Pine asks whether you want to put it in a folder called fred.

For filing by topic, you come up with the folder names. The most difficult part is coming up with memorable names. If you're not careful, you end up with three folders, for example, Accounts, Bills, and Finances, with different names, each with a third of the messages about a particular topic. Sometimes you should just use the first name you come up with. That way you are more likely to pick the same name again to save future messages with similar topics.

When in doubt, throw it out

The hard disk manufacturers' association doesn't want us to tell you this but, umm, you really don't have to save all your incoming messages. In fact, saving them all is usually a really bad idea. This issue may not be high on your list of concerns if all the e-mail you've gotten so far is the welcome letter from the president of your service provider and the response from the Dummies Central robot (see "Where am I on the Internet?" earlier in this chapter). But, trust us, your incoming mail volume will pick up as people find where you are. If it doesn't, try subscribing to a few mailing lists (see Chapter 16). We delete 90 percent of the mail we receive after we read it, and we still have thousands of saved messages.

Replying to a message

Another thing you can do when a message is open on your screen is send a reply message. You start this process by giving the reply command. Your e-mail program then opens a new outgoing message automatically addressed to the sender or senders of the original message with the subject line filled in. The subject is the subject of the original message with the word *Re* placed in front. (*Re* is short for *regarding* or, for the Latin speakers among us, *in re*.)

Many e-mail programs also include the text of the original message in the body of the reply. To set off your reply, a right angle bracket (>), colon (:), or tab indentation appears in front of every line of the original message. This reformatting is called *quoting* the original message.

When messages bounce back and forth a number of times, the quoted text can get quite complicated, with three, four, or even five angle brackets in front of some lines, forming a kind of high-tech court transcript. Computer types, who are used to puzzling out complex program files, may find this angle bracket build-up acceptable. Many others find it very tedious and confusing.

Edit the quoted text in a reply message so that it is clear and no longer than necessary to remind the original sender of what you are replying to.

Forwarding and redirecting (bouncing) mail

Another option you have when a message is open is to *forward* it to someone else. The forwarded message indicates that it came from you. The text of the message you are forwarding often appears in a quoted format. Usually, you can add your own comments to the forwarded message.

Redirecting a message — also called bouncing a message — is a lot like forwarding one, only the mail is sent as though it came from the original person directly. The message isn't quoted and the sender and reply-to information is left intact. This way, if the new recipient of the mail wants to reply, the response goes to the original sender, not to you just because you passed it on.

Forwarding a message says, "I think you might be interested in this." Bouncing a message says, "This should have been sent to you."

Forwarding or redirecting e-mail along to someone else is easy and cheap. It's one of the handiest things about e-mail, and at the same time it can make you very unpopular if misused. It's handy because you can easily pass along a message to someone who needs to know. It can get you a reputation as a pain-in-the-modem if you send out floods of messages to recipients who would just as soon not hear about yet another important cause or bon mot. So please, please think a little about whether you will really be making your e-mail friends' day by forwarding that message to all of them. Better still, ask them: "From time to time, I get interesting e-mail on the plight of the Antarctic phytoplankton. Would you like me to send it on to you?"

Inspect the list of recipients carefully when forwarding mail. Some mail addresses are really mailing lists that redistribute messages to many other people. Make sure you know where your e-mail is going.

Filters

You can easily get inundated with incoming mail, especially if you subscribe to automated mailing lists (see Chapter 16). Not only can you take a long time to slog through hundreds of incoming e-mail messages every day, but you can easily miss the one important message in all that dreck. To help you deal with this problem, some mailers offer a feature called *filters*.

Filters are sets of rules that you create in your mailer program. When your mailer gets new incoming mail, it uses those rules to sort your mail into different piles based on who sent the mail and what the subject is, sort of like what an efficient secretary used to do back in the twentieth century. The piles of messages then show up in different incoming mailboxes. Some filters also highlight key messages on the incoming message list with colors or priority codes.

You can ask your mailer program to put e-mail from mailing lists into separate mailboxes for each list. Mail whose subject mentions a project you are working on can go into yet another box. And, of course, mail from your boss or significant other can be given the priority it deserves.

Headers: The basics

Headers are the seemingly indecipherable lines of text that appear at the beginning of every incoming e-mail message (some mailer programs display headers at the end of a message). The most common format for headers is that used on the Internet. Other mail systems have their own format for headers, but the information is usually pretty much the same.

```
From cb@dummies.net Tue Jan 28 15:09:17 1997
Mime-Version: 1.0
Content-Type: text/plain; charset="us-ascii"
Date: Tue, 28 Jan 1997 16:09:17 +0100
To: agr@dummies.net (Arnold G Reinhold)
From: cb@dummies.net (Carol Baroudi)
```

Subject: Josh's homework. Table 3-1 is a guide to what the most important parts of an Internet mail header mean.

Table 3-1	The Parts of an Internet Mail Header
Header	**Description**
Subject:	Describes the message (strongly recommended)
To:	Lists recipients of the message (at least one required)
Cc:	Lists "carbon copy" recipients (optional)
Bcc:	Lists "blind carbon copy" recipients; these recipients' names are not sent with message (optional, use with care)
From:	Address of message author (required and filled in automatically)

(continued)

Table 3-1 *(continued)*

Header	Description
Reply-To:	Address where replies should be sent if different from the From line (optional)
Date:	Time and date the message was sent (required, filled in automatically)
Expires:	Date after which message expires (optional, rarely used)
Message-ID:	Unique machine-generated identifier for the message (required, filled in automatically)
Mime-Version:	Version of MIME being used (see "Sound! Pictures! Action!" in this chapter)
Content-Type:	What MIME data format is being used (see "Sound! Pictures! Action!" in this chapter)
Content-transfer-encoding:	How MIME is transmitting the message (see "Sound! Pictures! Action!" in this chapter)
Lines:	Number of lines of text in the message (optional, filled in automatically)

Note: Many other optional header lines exist — none of them are of great importance.

A picture is worth a million bytes

Sooner or later, plain old everyday e-mail is not going to be good enough for you. Someone's going to send you a picture you just have to see, or you're going to want to send something cool to your new e-mail pen pal. Some mail systems can handle graphics and other non-text data right in the message body. Sometimes the entire message is in a special format (such as MIME, which we talk about soon), and sometimes people *attach* things to their mail.

Getting attached

To exchange computer files such as computer programs, drawings, photographs, and video clips using electronic mail, you may need to send or receive them as *attachments*. The e-mail message acts sort of like a cover letter with a package. You have to unwrap the attachment separately.

Attachments come in many flavors. You may or may not have the software you need to read the package you receive, but Chapter 15 tells you how to know what you're looking at and what your likely next step is toward making it comprehensible.

Meanwhile, we tell you now about MIME, a convention for including stuff other than plain text in e-mail messages. MIME stands for multipurpose Internet mail extensions, by the way.

Sound! Pictures! Action!

MIME supports a long list of kinds of stuff, ranging from slightly formatted text using characters (such as *emphasis* for *emphasis*) up through color pictures, full-motion video, and high-fidelity sound. The group that designed MIME had enough sense to realize that not everyone has a computer that can handle all the fancy high-end stuff, so a single MIME message can contain alternative forms of the same thing, such as beautifully formatted, typeset text for people with fancy video screens and plain text for people on simple terminals. Because MIME also handles nested messages, a single MIME message might contain a document and a couple of illustrations to go with it.

All kinds of computer data links exist out there in networkland, and some of them are hostile, or at best unhelpful, to one another. About the only thing they agree on is text. So MIME disguises all of its fancy formats as plain old text (at least it looks like text to computers. To us it looks more like QW&IIdfhfFX97/$@).You can recognize a MIME message by looking for special mail headers that look something like this:

```
MIME-version: 1.0
Content-type: TEXT/PLAIN; CHARSET=US-ASCII
Content-transfer-encoding: 7BIT
```

The first line says that the message is using Version 1.0 of the MIME standard (the only version defined so far). The second line says that this particular message contains just text. The third line says that the text is represented in the message as the simplest kind of text that's out there (computers are so dim that even this isn't obvious to them). Different kinds of messages use different Content-type headers.

- If you are using a mail program that is MIME-compliant, you'll know when you have a MIME message because, as you're reading your mail, a window pops up all of a sudden with a picture or some formatted text, or perhaps your computer begins singing the message to you (remember singing telegrams?). Eudora, Netscape, and Pine are MIME-compliant, and America Online can send and receive MIME mail.

- If your mail program doesn't know about MIME and you get a MIME-ized message, it shows up as a large message in your mailbox. If it contains text, it might be readable as is, give or take some ugly punctuation. The sound and pictures, on the other hand, are totally hopeless because they are just binary digitized versions of the images and not any sort of text approximation.

✔ If you get a picture or sound MIME message and your mailer doesn't automatically handle it, clunky but usable methods may exist for saving the message to a file and extracting the contents with separate programs. Consult your Internet service provider's help desk.

Chapter 4

The Finer Points of E-Mail

*I*n the previous chapters, we covered the basics of e-mail — sending and receiving messages and filing them away. Now it's time to talk about the subtler issues, like what to write and how to write it. We address those questions in this chapter. We also address addresses one more time, to tell you more than you probably want to know about domain names and what they mean, and to introduce the Evil Empire of e-mail, X.400.

The Psychology of E-Mail

We humans have evolved many methods to communicate in person: speech, eye contact, body language, touch. And, we have invented many more ways to communicate over distance: letters, telegrams, telephone, fax, and now e-mail. Each has its own power and limitations. Many of e-mail's strengths are also its limitations:

✔ E-mail's speed discourages thoughtful replies.

✔ Its low cost can lessen its impact.

✔ Its textual basis makes it hard to catch nuance and inflection.

✔ In volume, it's easy to overlook.

Marshall McLuhan told us that the medium is the message. The message of e-mail can be casual, flip, cold, shot-from-the-hip, matter-of-fact. All you need to get your messages to stand out above the clutter is a little thought and a little effort and, most of all, a little empathy: How would you feel if you received the message you are about to send?

E-Mail Etiquette

Before you alienate your friends and your would-be friends with insensitive messages, take some hints from our years of e-mail experience. Our advice applies to *all* your e-mail, be it to friend, family, or coworker. It applies quadruply to messages you send to hundreds of complete strangers via mailing lists, where the only impression you make is with your e-mail.

If you use e-mail for any length of time, you *will* get a message from someone that just makes you seethe with rage.

```
To: you
From: The Boss


When will the Simson contract be ready?


Boss
```

Doesn't he know you were in the office until 3 a.m. this morning working on the stupid thing? Doesn't he realize it would have been done already if he had told you last week about those changes Simson requested? Doesn't he know you were planning to take your kids to a ball game this afternoon?

Well, your boss was just getting ready for his boss's staff meeting and needed to know what to say if the subject came up. What seemed to him like a harmless request for a status update sent you over the edge. It might have been more palatable if he had written

```
To: you
From: The Boss


  Thanks for the extra effort on the Simson contract. Could
  you give me an idea when you think you'll have it done? I
  need an estimate for Sue's 10 am meeting.


Boss
```

Our dictionary defines *etiquette* as proper behavior or courtesy. The speed and impersonal nature of e-mail make respecting social conventions even more important. Here are a few suggestions regarding more effective e-mail style:

- ✔ Watch your tone. E-mail can seem brusque even when you don't intend it to be. Try to read it from the recipient's point of view before sending.

- ✔ Avoid foul language. Just because Senator Exon is trying to ban dirty words on the Internet doesn't mean you have to use them.

✔ Don't send messages full of pointless and excessive outrage — what we netoids call a *flame*. For example:

```
you bozos are going to tell me what to say?
```

✔ Irony and sarcasm are easy to miss without the raised eyebrow. Double-check your humor. Sometimes, adding a *smiley* helps to let your reader in on the joke. For example:

```
you bozos are going to tell me what to say?   ;-)
```

✔ Sending text entirely in capital letters is considered SHOUTING.

✔ When in doubt about your message's tone, save the message overnight and read it again in the morning before you send it, or ask someone else to read it over before you send it. Many's the message we wrote and later threw away unsent.

✔ If you do get involved in a vitriolic exchange of messages, known as a *flame war,* the best way to stop is to let the other guy have the last word.

✔ Your Subject line should tell the recipient as much as possible about your message, without getting too long. "Don't park in the back lot this Thursday" is much better than "Parking Announcement."

✔ Check your spelling. You may have to use a word processor if your mailer lacks a spell check feature. Typos can twist the meaning of your message so badly that you end up saying exactly what you didn't want to say. And proofread it again. A spell checker makes sure that your message consists of 100-percent actual words, butt it doesn't sea too it that there the words ewe wanted two use.

✔ Remember that e-mail is not particularly private and that a glitch can cause the system to deliver your mail to the wrong recipient on the wrong system (like your boss or your kids).

✔ Don't pass on chain letters. Here are some common examples that have made the rounds several times by now:

- A dying boy who wants lots of greeting cards (he's not and he doesn't).

- They want to tax modems (the proposal was squelched in 1987).

- A "Good-news" computer virus that infects via e-mail — it's a hoax.

✔ Make money fast just by putting your name at the bottom of the list and forwarding this message to 10 friends. (These schemes are invariably illegal, guaranteed to annoy your friends, and a waste of time and money.)

✔ If you don't get a response from someone to whom you sent e-mail, or if the response is very different from the one you expected, politely ask for clarification:

```
I sent you a note about your chapter. Did you get a
        chance to look at it?
```

or

```
Yikes, maybe I wasn't making myself clear. What I meant
        to say was . . .
```

Or pick up the phone and call if it's appropriate. Try to nip e-mail misunderstandings in the bud. Never blame the other person. Assume that your message wasn't clear or that the message never got there. If you have to blame something, start with the technology.

Subjects and Kings

General W. G. Pagonis was in charge of all the logistics for the 1991 Gulf War — moving all the equipment and supplies for 600,000 soldiers to Saudi Arabia in six months, getting everything ready for battle, and then moving the stuff back out when the war was over. The general used an eccentric management style: All messages to him from people in his command had to be written on a 3-by-5 inch index card. If he wanted more, he'd ask. The idea was simple and powerful. Confining subordinates to a 3-by-5 card made people think about what they wanted to say, and the general could listen to comments from many more of his troops because each message was so short.

A friend of ours, who was working for Harvard Business School Press at the time, read about Gen. Pagonis in a news magazine. She thought a book by him would sell, but she had no mutual contact. So she wrote a note on an index card and mailed it to him. His book, *Moving Mountains,* was published in 1992.

Important people who are hooked up to e-mail get tons of messages each day. They simply cannot read them all. All they will ever read of most messages is the subject line, and then the messages are bounced to a subordinate or trashed. If you want your message read, make that subject line work for you. Think of Gen. Pagonis's 3-by-5 cards. You've got about 60 characters to get their attention.

Sign on the Dotted Line

E-mail doesn't leave a lot of room for artistic creativity. One place where people do try to add a special touch to their e-mail is the signature. Many people turn their signatures into a personal letterhead, or letterfoot, to be more accurate. Here's John's signature, for example:

```
Regards,
John R. Levine, Trumansburg NY
Primary perpetrator of "The Internet for Dummies"
and Information Superhighwayman wanna-be
```

Typing a fancy signature like that into each message you send would be a pain. Fortunately, almost all e-mail programs let you set up a special file called a *signature* file. Text in the signature file will automatically plop down at the end of all your outgoing messages. The only problem is that people sometimes get carried away, filling their signature with whole paragraphs lifted from their favorite book, or page-long *ASCII art*, pictures drawn in letters, numbers, and special characters. Here's an example of an ASCII art signature:

```
                                 _...._'_'_..._
                     ================================
        ,_____._/'    '_..._____..._'
       (_____||_) . . ,_'
       /  /.-'       '/   Michael Mathiesen
       '_____._- - - - _/     phantom@nevada.edu
           '_____.'
```

In the old days, overly long signatures were blamed for clogging up the Internet. The rule used to be that you should keep your signature to four lines or fewer. This is still not a bad policy. Long signatures are still a problem on articles bound for mailing lists and newsgroup postings that get sent and resent thousands of times as they make their way around the globe. But we've seen obnoxious one-line signatures and we've seen ten-line sigs that made us smile. And with all the graphics on the World Wide Web, e-mail is just not that big a burden on the Internet anymore. We're not your mother. Just keep your signature in good taste, and remember that your regular correspondents are going to see your signature dozens if not hundreds of times.

While most e-mail programs let you turn off the automatic signature feature, you probably won't remember to do so when you send that one message to someone you really want to impress.

Managing Addresses

Many e-mail programs include handy little features built in to help you manage the many e-mail addresses that you have to handle. Some let you make up a short nickname or alias that you can use instead of typing in a long, awkward Internet address. Others let you set up an e-mail address book inside the mailer. You can then select your recipient from a pull-down list or other graphical gimmick.

Another useful feature that some mailers offer is mailing lists. These are not as complex as the automated mailing list systems we describe in Chapter 16. They are a simple way to assign a name to a set of e-mail addresses: everyone in the department, say, or everyone working on the Simson account. These kinds of mailing lists can be very handy.

If your mailer does not have these features and you can't upgrade to one that does, don't despair. You can use a database program or even a word processor to manage your e-mail list. Just create a text document and type in the addresses you use one to a line, like this:

```
letters@globe.com        Boston Globe, letters to the editor
news07b@aol.com          Channel 7 News Boston
president@whitehouse.gov Bill Clinton
root@whitehouse.gov      Hillary Rodham Clinton
email2@dummies.net       Dummies Central
info@idgbooks.com        IDG Books
70277.2052@compuserve.com Rush Limbaugh
wesun@npr.org    National Public Radio Sunday Edition
scitimes@nytimes.com Science editor, New York Times
```

When you want an address, just open your e-mail list in your word processor, copy the address you want, and paste it into your mailer's To field. You can even set up a simple mailing list by typing all the addresses in a single group:

```
Media list:
letters@globe.com, news07b@aol.com,
70277.2052@compuserve.com,
wesun@npr.org, scitimes@nytimes.com
```

Finally, don't forget to let people know about your e-mail address. Many people remember to put it on their business card, but what about your stationery, fax cover sheets, and even answering machine message? (We think tattoos are excessive.) In Chapter 14, we tell you how to find someone else's e-mail address. Some of the resources described there are good places to list your e-mail address.

It's 3 p.m. Do You Know Where Your E-Mail Is?

In Chapter 3, we warned you to take a close look at the address fields of your message before you click the Send button. If your message says something you wouldn't want everybody in the company to read, you need to be extra careful, particularly if you are writing a reply message. Don't simply verify that every address in the To, cc, and bcc fields points to someone you want to see what you are saying. You also have to think about where each recipient might forward your message, and then think about where each of *those* recipients might ship it. Clicking that Forward button is easy. E-mail that you send to three colleagues in the morning can be all over the building and in half your branch offices by that afternoon.

Putting a note in your message saying "For your eyes only" or "Don't forward this to Meg" only compounds the problem. Meg will be even more annoyed, and the forwarder might not have sent her a bcc if you hadn't reminded him. Office politics can get nasty.

The best way to protect yourself is never to write an e-mail message that would make you squirm if it were posted next to the office water cooler. If you have to write something negative about someone's performance or pet idea, write it in such a way that you could still look the subject in the eye if he or she ever got hold of it. Better yet, send the subject a copy in advance asking for comments before you send it on. Acting like a mensch can take the sting out of your criticism.

If you really need to communicate confidentially, send it to just one address and, if possible, encrypt it. See Chapters 17 and 18 for more information about encryption.

Reading Your Mail Offline

Here's an idea that can save you enough money to pay for this book: If you are using a mail service that charges by the hour for connect time, you may be able to read and compose your e-mail offline. Many of the value-added services, as well as mailers like Eudora and Netscape Navigator, let you do this easily. You just log in, retrieve your mail, and log out again. You can then read your messages, reply to whichever ones need answers, and create new messages without having to worry about online charges or hogging the phone. You save your outgoing mail in an outbox. After you are finished, just log in again and send your outgoing messages. That's all there is to it.

If you're using a shell account or a service that doesn't let you easily download your mail, you can still pinch a few pennies. For shell users, your terminal emulator, that program that connects you to your provider, often logs your whole session. When you've finished reading your mail, you in fact have a giant transcript of everything you just read. Save any lengthy replying you have to do until after you've disconnected. Compose your responses in text files that you can later cut and paste into an outgoing message.

Likewise, while you're connected to your provider, you can copy mail that you're reading into a text file on your machine and then save the replying for when you're off the meter.

Abbreviations, Smileys, and Emoticons

E-mail users have used a variety of techniques to liven up their messages. One of the simplest is *emphasis*. Because bold and italics are *not* universally available options, e-mail convention is to bracket words you want to **stand out** with asterisks or underscore characters. Here is how you might include the above sentence in an e-mail message:

```
Because bold and italics are *not* universally available
options, e-mail convention is to bracket words you want to
_stand out_ with asterisks or underscore characters.
```

Other techniques used to liven up e-mail are abbreviations, smileys, and emoticons.

Abbreviations, smileys, and emoticons are the e-mail equivalent of slang, so you probably shouldn't use them in formal messages. If you use abbreviations and smileys, use them sparingly. Don't do this:

```
FYI WRT smileys FAQ:
IMNSHO e-mail users have **no** self-
discipline! AFIK YMMV :-> ROTFL NRN
BTW, seen any new TLAs? TIA
TTFN CUL 8-)
::clicks on _send_ button::
```

Abbreviations

Abbreviations serve several purposes in e-mail. They help prevent repetitive stress injury by cutting down on typing. They conserve scarce electrons by making transmitted messages shorter. Perhaps the most important function they perform is to let people know that you are part of the club. We think they are over-used and often stupid, and the club is stupid too. But you should know what the most common ones mean. Table 4-1 shows some of the most widely used abbreviations.

EUOMUNA (E-mail users often make up new abbreviations)! No list of e-mail abbreviations can ever be complete.

Table 4-1	Commonly Used Abbreviations
Abbreviation	*What It Means*
AFAIK	As far as I know
AKA	Also known as
BFN	Bye for now
BTW	By the way
CUL	See you later
FAQ	Frequently asked questions (actually a list of answers)
FYI	For your information
HNN	Hey nonny nonny or Hey nonny no
IMHO	In my humble opinion
IMNSHO	In my not so humble opinion
IMO	In my opinion
NRN	No response necessary
LOL	Laughing out loud
RSN	Real soon now (don't count on it)
ROTFL	Rolling on the floor, laughing
ROTFLOL	Rolling on the floor, laughing out loud
RTFM	Read the manual (you should have looked it up yourself)
SNAFU	Situation normal, all fouled up
TIA	Thanks in advance
TLA	Three-letter acronym
TTFN	Ta ta for now (good-bye)
WRT	With respect to
WYSIWYG	What you see is what you get
YMMV	Your mileage may vary
73	Best regards (from ham radio)
88	Love and kisses (from ham radio)

Smileys and other emoticons

Not long after you start getting e-mail, you begin to wonder if people have gone a little crazy with the punctuation keys. You start seeing unmatched parentheses and oddball colons and semicolons, and you start to wonder what you're missing. Well, if you bend your head to the left as far as you can manage, you'll often see a kind of smiling (or frowning) face known as a *smiley*. Smileys come in an infinite number of flavors, but Table 4-2 shows you some common ones to give you the idea.

Table 4-2	Smileys
Smiley	*What It Means*
:-)	The basic smiley
;-)	Winking smiley. "Don't hit me for what I just said!"
:-(	Frowning smiley
:->	Sarcastic smiley
:-p	Smiley with its tongue stuck out (nyah nyah)
:-@	Screaming smiley
:-o	Uh oh! smiley
8-)	Wearing sunglasses smiley
::-)	Wears glasses normally smiley

Lots, lots more are out there. If you have access to the World Wide Web, you can find long lists of smileys at `http://net.dummies.net/smileys`. Most of these smileys are not in circulation among e-mail users, but they are very entertaining if you are in a properly silly mood.

Smileys are part of a bigger class of e-mail paraphernalia known as *emoticons*. How's that for a nineties word? Emoticons are stylized conventions, developed in e-mail and in forums, chat rooms, and newsgroups, that try to bring subtlety of inflection and tone to written communications. We tend to want to type the way we talk, but our tone of voice doesn't come across the wire. Emoticons help bridge the gap and soften the harshness of less-than-polished text. Here are a few emoticons outside of the smiley category:

_\,,/	I love you (from American Sign Language)
`<g>` or `<grin>`	Same as :-)
`<sigh>`	Sigh!
`::`	Action markers, as in `::removes cat from key-board::`

Action markers can be useful to those of you planning your online wedding or other theatrical venture.

More about Addresses

As we said in Chapter 3, addresses are the hardest part of e-mail *and* the most important. So here is some more information on this scintillating topic that never ceases to amuse us. For example, did you know that you can learn a lot about where a piece of e-mail comes from by looking at its domain name? Did you know you can own a domain name of your very own for only $50 a year? And if you ever ran into an X.400 address, would you know what to do with it? We suggest you glance through this section so you know what's here, and then use it as a reference when you need it.

Domain names

The part of an Internet address that comes after the at-sign (@) is the *host name. Hosts* are just computer systems that are attached to the Internet — for example, `xuxa.iecc.com`.

Notice that host names have several parts strung together with periods. You decode a host name from right to left:

- The rightmost part of a name is its *zone* or *top-level domain name* (in the example, `com`).
- To the zone's left (`iecc`) is the name of the company, school, or organization. This is sometimes called the *second-level* domain name.
- The part to the left of the organization name (`xuxa`) identifies a particular computer within the organization.

In large organizations, host names can be further subdivided by site or department.

A partial name is known as a *domain.* For example, `xuxa` is in the `iecc.com` and `com` domains.

Who said that?

Forging e-mail return addresses is not all that hard, and people sometimes leave their logged-in computers unattended, allowing spurious mail to be sent. So if you get a totally off-the-wall message that seems out of character for the sender, somebody else may have forged it as a prank.

Many people on the Internet adopt fictional personas. The lonely flight attendant you are corresponding with may really be a 15-year-old boy. A famous *New Yorker* cartoon shows a mutt at a computer terminal, thinking "On the Internet, no one knows you're a dog."

Not every mail address has an actual person behind it. Some are for mailing lists (see Chapter 16), and some are *robots*. Mail robots have become popular as a way to query databases and retrieve files.

Don't zone out now

Three categories of zone, or top-level domain, names are in common use:

✔ Organizational

✔ Geographic

✔ Other

Organizational zone names

If the zone is three letters long, it is an *organizational name*. The three-letter code indicates the type of organization, and the part just before the zone indicates the specific organization.

Table 4-3 describes the organizational names currently in use.

Table 4-3	Organizational Names in E-Mail Addresses
Zone	*Type of Organization*
com	Commercial organization
edu	Educational institution
gov	U.S. federal government body or department
int	International organization (e.g., NATO, U.N. agencies, and so on)
mil	U.S. military site (the site can be anywhere in the world)
net	Networking organization
org	Anything that doesn't fit elsewhere, such as a not-for-profit group

Most systems that use the organizational names gov and mil are in the United States.

Brand new zones

Seven additional top-level domain names will soon be added to those already in use. The new names, which should be available by late-1997, are

firm	for businesses
store	for businesses offering goods to purchase
web	for organizations emphasizing activities related to the World Wide Web
arts	for organizations emphasizing cultural and entertainment activities
rec	for organizations emphasizing recreation and entertainment activities
info	for organizations providing information services
nom	for those wishing individual or personal names

Geographic zone names

If the zone name is two letters long, it is a *geographic name*. The two-letter code specifies a country, and the stuff in front of the zone name is specific to that country. For example, **ac** means academic in many countries.

The *us* domain, used by some schools and small organizations in the United States, is set up geographically. It is usually preceded by a two-letter state code. For example, John's machine that used to live in Cambridge, Massachusetts, is called `iecc.cambridge.ma.us`.

A host can have more than one name. John's machine is also known as `ivan.iecc.com`.

For the most part, geographic names use the two-letter country names that come from an International Standards Organization (ISO) standard. See Appendix A for a full list.

You may encounter a few other zones, including the following:

- **arpa:** Left over from the ARPANET, the Internet's predecessor
- **bitnet:** Unofficial zone used for mail to BITNET, a network of mostly IBM mainframes
- **uucp:** Unofficial zone used for mail to sites on a system called UUCP, a crufty old networking system that uses dial-up modems

X.400 addresses

In case you ever have to send mail to an X.400 system, here is a brief guide to X.400 addresses. X.400 is an e-mail standard that competes with the Internet's SMTP standard. Its main virtue is that it has been blessed by the United Nation's International Telecommunications Union, the same people who set the V.xx modem standards. X.400 is more popular in Europe than in the U.S., although the U.S. military, the people who invented the Internet, are basing their new worldwide command and control system on X.400 — your tax dollars at work. Some commercial e-mail systems such as Sprintmail also use X.400.

An X.400 address is a great deal more like a postal address than a phone number. X.400 addresses are made up of a bunch of different *attributes*. If you have enough of these attributes to single out one recipient, the mail should go through. If you don't, back it comes. The most common attributes and the codes used to represent them are

- **Given name (G):** The recipient's first name
- **Initials (I):** First or middle initial (or initials)
- **Surname (S):** The recipient's last name
- **Generational qualifier (GQ or Q):** Jr., III, and so on
- **Administration Domain Name (ADMD or A):** More or less the name of the mail system
- **Private Domain Name (PRMD or P):** More or less the name of a private system connected via a public ADMD
- **Organization (O):** The organization with which the recipient is affiliated
- **Organizational unit (OU):** The sub-organization with which the recipient is affiliated
- **Country (C):** A two-letter country code; see Appendix A
- **Domain Defined Attribute (D, DD or DDA):** Any code that identifies the recipient, such as username or account number

Write each attribute to include the code, followed by an equal sign (=), followed by the value of the attribute. Use the slash character (/) to separate attributes in an address.

For example, suppose you want to send e-mail to Samuel Tilden at Tammany Hall in the United States using Sprint's X.400 Telemail service, which is connected to the Internet via sprint.com. The address would be:

```
/G=Samuel/S=Tilden/O=TammanyHall/C=US/ADMD=TELEMAIL/
            @sprint.com
```

Grown men and women who are bright and well educated thought this up and actually proposed it as the world standard for e-mail addresses. It boggles the mind.

You are allowed to simplify an X.400 address when the only attribute needed is the recipient's name. Instead of

```
/G=Rutherford/I=B/S=Hayes/
```

you can write

```
Rutherford.B.Hayes
```

If someone tries to sell you a mail system based on X.400, throw that person out of your office.

Sending Mail from One Service to Another

Many value-added networks have their own mail-addressing schemes. Table 4-4 tells how to address Internet messages to these systems. In this table

- *Username* is the name that the recipient uses to log onto the system.

- *Usernum* is the recipient's numerical user ID.

- *Hostname* is the name of the particular computer within the remote network.

Table 4-4	E-Mail Addresses for Some Online Services	
System	*How to Address Messages*	*Notes*
America Online	*username*@aol.com	Leave out any spaces in the user name.
AT&T Mail	*username*@attmail.com	
AT&T Worldnet Service	*username*@worldnet.att.net	
BITNET	*username*@*hostname*.bitnet or *username*%*hostname*.bitnet@ mitvma.mit.edu or *username*%*hostname*.bitnet@ cunyvm.cuny.edu	

(continued)

Table 4-4 *(continued)*

System	How to Address Messages	Notes
CompuServe	*usernum.usernum*@compuserve.com	*usernum.usernum* is the numerical CompuServe ID with a period replacing the comma. For example, if the person's CompuServe ID is 71234,567, send mail to 71234.567@compuserve.com.
Delphi	*username*@delphi.com	
Easylink	*usernum*@eln.attmail.com	*usernum* is the 7-digit user ID number.
FIDONET	*firstname.lastname*@ p4.f3.n2.z1.fidonet.org or *firstname.lastname*@ f3.n2.z1.fidonet.org	Replace the numbers with parts of the person's Fido node number. For example, this user's Fido node number would be 1:2/3.4 or 1:2/3.
GEnie	*mailname*@genie.geis.com	*mailname* is based on the user's name, not the user's random login access name.
MCI Mail	*usernum*@mcimail.com	*usernum* is the person's numerical MCI mail address, usually written in the form 123-4567. You can leave out the hyphen.
Microsoft Network	*username*@msn.com	
Prodigy Classic	*usernum*@prodigy.com	The person's Prodigy account must be set up for Internet mail.
Sprintmail	/G=*firstname*/S=*lastname* /O=*orgname*/C=US/ ADMD=TELEMAIL/@sprint.com	
UUCP	*username*@*hostname*.uucp or *hostname*!*username* @internet_gateway	The first UUCP form works only for registered addresses. The most common gateway is uunet.uu.net.

Part II
Using Your Browser for E-Mail

The 5th Wave — By Rich Tennant

"WE SHOULD HAVE THIS FIXED IN VERSION 2."

In this part . . .

Some people would have you believe that the World Wide Web is the entire Internet. It's not, but to improve the illusion, the most popular Web programs, Netscape and Internet Explorer, come with e-mail programs. They're not great e-mail programs, but because everyone seems to have one or the other, they're instantly popular, so here they are.

Chapter 5

Netscape Mail: It's a Breath Mint AND a Floor Wax!

In This Chapter
▶ Getting Netscape
▶ Sending mail with Netscape
▶ Receiving mail with Netscape

*Y*es, this is the same Netscape that everyone uses to surf the World Wide Web (WWW). Versions of Netscape since 2.0 are adequate — if not superb — mail programs as well as Web browsers. Like Eudora, Netscape runs on your PC or Mac and downloads and uploads mail from and to your mail server.

We strongly prefer Eudora for mail, but because some people are stuck with Netscape, we discuss it here.

The people at Netscape apparently agreed with our opinion of their mail program because they completely changed it between Netscape 2.0 and 3.0, where it's part of the giant Navigator program, and Netscape 4.0, where it's now been extracted into a separate program called Messenger. If this chapter seems kind of schizophrenic, that's why. First we discuss the older Navigator mail system and then the new 4.0 Messenger system.

Setting Up Netscape Navigator Mail

We assume that you already have Netscape installed as a Web browser. If you don't, you might as well pick a better e-mail program, like Eudora. If Netscape is truly what you want, the installation is actually pretty simple. Under Windows 95, you get Netscape on a disk or download the enormous installation file from the Net, copy the installation file to an empty directory, and run it. The installation file expands into a bunch of files, and it then installs the rest of Netscape for you. On Windows 3.1, after you run the installation file, you may have to run the setup.exe that it extracted by double-clicking it in the File Manager. On a Macintosh, you just double-click the self-extracting archive (.sea) icon and then double-click the installer icon when it shows up.

Getting Netscape set up for use as a mail program is a little more complicated because, while you can go Web surfing without any further setup, to make Netscape a useful mail program, you have to fill it in on little details like your e-mail address. Fortunately, the setup is straightforward, though tedious.

1. Start Netscape.

2. Choose <u>W</u>indow⇨Netscape <u>M</u>ail.

Netscape will probably pop up an incomprehensible complaint about not being able to use a POP3 server. Yeah, we know, that's why we're here. Ignore it and click OK. You should see a screen like the one shown in Figure 5-1, with one sample welcome message waiting.

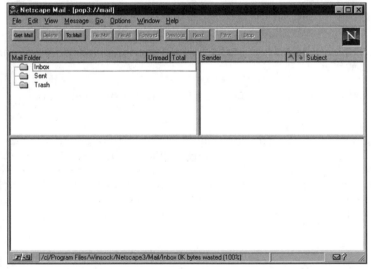

Figure 5-1:
Netscape Mail ready and waiting.

3. Choose <u>O</u>ptions⇨Mail and News Preferences. Select the tab called Servers.

You should see a screen like the one shown in Figure 5-2.

4. In the Outgoing Mail (SMTP) and Incoming Mail (POP) servers fields, enter the names of the computers that your Internet provider uses for outgoing and incoming mail.

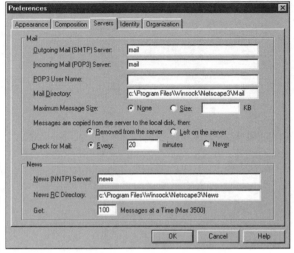

Figure 5-2:
Ready to set
up your
servers.

Your Internet providers should have given you the names when you signed up. Most likely, both names are the same.

5. Under POP User Name, enter your user name.

This is the name your provider assigned to you when you signed up.

You can leave the rest of the fields alone in this window. The fields may not be exactly the same as in the figure here; that's okay.

6. Select the Identity tab.

You should see a screen like the one shown in Figure 5-3.

7. After Your Name, enter the name you'd like to have shown in the return address on outgoing mail.

This is your actual name, like John Q. Public, not your e-mail address, which we discuss next.

8. After Your Email, enter your e-mail address.

This is generally your user name, the @ sign, and your provider's system name — something like `jqpublic@snarfflenet.com`.

9. Leave Reply-to Address blank.

The Reply-to Address defaults to your e-mail address, which is almost always right.

10. After Your Organization, enter any organization name that you'd like to have appear on outgoing mail. (Optional)

11. You can leave Signature File blank for now.

If you'd like, you can have a short (no more than four lines, please) signature automatically added to the end of each message. From Windows, run the Windows Notepad or Wordpad, type in the signature, and save it to a file named something like `\Netscape\Signature.txt`. Then enter that filename in the Signature File field. On the Mac, Netscape allows you to browse for a file. You can create the file with SimpleText or Eudora.

12. Click OK.

That's all the setup you need to do. You can twiddle with some of the other parameters later if you're feeling bored, but nothing else important needs to be changed.

Sending Mail with Netscape Navigator

The steps for sending mail from Netscape are almost identical to those for sending mail from Eudora (you are doing the same thing, after all):

1. Start Netscape.

2. Click the To: Mail button or choose File⇨New Mail Message.

This step opens a mail composing window, which looks like the window shown in Figure 5-4. If you're already looking at the Netscape Mail window, you can also press the New Mail button on the icon bar (the third button from the left).

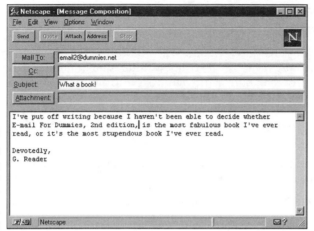

Figure 5-4:
Netscape's
ready for
you to enter
a message.

3. **Fill in the recipient's address (or addresses), indicate the subject, and type the message.**

4. **Click Send to send the message.**

That's the little flying envelope at the left end of the icon bar.

Netscape gives you the choice of sending mail immediately or stashing your mail in the Outbox and sending it later. If you have a dial-up account where you pay by the hour, composing all your mail and then connecting to your provider to send all the mail at once is invariably more economical.

You can switch between immediate and deferred mail sending in any message composition window. In that window, you can choose Immediate or Deferred from the Options menu. If you use deferred sending, outgoing mail is placed in a folder called Outbox until it's sent. You send your mail by choosing File⇨Send Mail in Outbox on the main menu or by pressing Ctrl+H.

Receiving Mail with Netscape Navigator

The Netscape Mail window has three parts. The upper-left part shows your list of mail folders, the upper-right shows the messages in the current folder, and the bottom part shows the current message. (This three-part window was introduced in the Agent and Free Agent net news programs and is becoming a standard.) You can adjust the sizes of the three parts of the windows by dragging the separating bars with the mouse.

To receive and read mail, follow these steps:

1. **Start Netscape.**

2. **Choose <u>W</u>indow⇨Netscape <u>M</u>ail.**

   This step opens the Netscape Mail window, which we saw in Figure 5-1. Netscape may try to retrieve any waiting mail immediately. If it doesn't, click the Get Mail button, the leftmost button on the icon bar. Incoming mail is filed in your INBOX folder. If you've never retrieved mail before, it'll ask you for your mailbox password on the mail server, which is generally the same password you use to connect to your Internet provider.

3. **Click the INBOX icon in the left column of the screen to see the messages in your Inbox.**

   The upper-right part of your screen shows the subject lines for incoming mail.

4. **Click each message to read it or click Next or Previous to read messages in order.**

After you have a message on the screen, you can click the Print, Delete, and other buttons to handle messages. We discuss the other functions, such as replying to and forwarding messages, a little later.

In the list of messages, two columns of inscrutable little icons are between the name of the message's author and the message's subject. The first column is a flag, which lets you mark a bunch of messages and then do something with all of them, like move them all to another folder. The second column is a little green hockey puck, which means that the message hasn't been read yet. Click the flag or puck column to turn the flag or puck on or off. Netscape shows a little dot that you can use as a target for your clicking. Marking a message as unread is a handy way to remind yourself that you still need to do something with a particular message.

Replying to messages

First, click the desired message. Then choose <u>M</u>essage⇨<u>R</u>eply, click the Reply button (it has an envelope with a bent arrow under it), or for the lazy, press Ctrl+R. Netscape opens a Message Composition window with the To: and Subject: fields all set and the original message loaded into the message body. Compose your reply and edit down the quoted material to the minimum needed to remind your correspondent what the discussion is about. Then click the Send button.

You can also use <u>M</u>essage⇨Reply to <u>A</u>ll or the Reply All button (the envelope with two bent arrows) to address the reply to all recipients of the original message, not just the sender.

Forwarding messages

When a message is on-screen, choose Message⇨Forward or click the Forward button, and Netscape opens a new window for your message. Netscape treats the old message as an attached file. You can't edit your old message, although you can add comments of your own to send along with it.

If you want to edit a message as you forward it, click Reply instead of Forward and then edit the To: field to address the message to the person to whom you wish to send the edited version.

Filing messages

Netscape lets you have as many mail folders as you want. To create a new mail folder, choose File⇨New Folder. Once you've created your folder, you can use the mouse to drag messages from the current folder to other folders. Hold down the Ctrl key while dragging to move rather than copying.

You can also move and copy messages by using the Message menu, but dragging is much more convenient.

Attaching files

In Netscape, you click the Attach button to send an attachment. Unlike most other mail programs, Netscape lets you attach any file or document you can describe with a *URL* (Uniform Resource Locator, the naming scheme used on the Web). Netscape gives you your choice of attaching a document by default (the last message or page you were looking at) or attaching a file. In the window that the Attach button opens, click Attach Location (URL) to attach a document, or click Attach File to attach a file. If you attach a file, you can click the Browse button to choose the file to attach. When you've decided what to attach, click OK to attach the file or document to the outgoing message and close the Attach window.

For incoming mail, Netscape displays any attachments that it knows how to display (Web pages and image files in the popular GIF and JPEG formats). For other kinds of attachments, it displays a little description of the file, which you click. After you click the file description, Netscape runs an appropriate display program if it knows of one, or Netscape asks you whether it should save the attachment to a file or configure a display program, which Netscape can then run to display it.

The Navigator Address Book

With Navigator, you can keep an address book of your favorite addresses. The easiest way to add an entry is to select a message from someone you want to add to the address book and then choose Message⇨Add to Address Book. Netscape opens an Address Book Properties window. Adjust the entry if needed and then click OK to add the entry to your address book. (You can leave the Nickname field blank because it's not very useful.)

Using your address book

Whenever you're creating a message, you can open the address book by clicking the Mail To: or Cc: buttons in the Message Composition window. You'll see a list of all of the entries in your address book. Click the one you want; then click one of the three buttons at the bottom of the address book, To:, Cc:, or Bcc:; and then click OK. The selected address is added to your message.

Editing and adding entries in the address book

You can edit entries in the address book by opening the Address Book window using Window⇨Address Book. To change an item, click the item and then choose Item⇨Properties.

To add a new entry, choose Item⇨Add User. This opens an empty Address Book Properties window into which you have to type the person's real name and e-mail address. Then click OK to add it.

If you double-click an entry, Netscape opens a Message Composition window addressed to that person.

Creating address lists

Netscape makes it possible — if not exactly easy — to make address lists. First, you have to have entries in your address book for everyone you want to have on your list. Create the entries using Item⇨Add User. Then create the list using Item⇨Add List. This opens an Address Book Properties window, suggesting the not-exactly-inspired list name of New Folder. Change the name to something better and click OK. (Don't enter any e-mail addresses yet.)

Now your list appears in the Address Book window as an empty folder. Drag in the addresses you want to have in the list. (**Note:** The addresses remain as independent entries as well.) If you have other lists, you can drag names from one list to another. Dragging a name off a list removes it from that list. Don't drag one list into another because that won't do what you want. Once you're happy with your addresses and lists, choose File⇨Close to close the Address Book window.

Threading Messages

One nice thing that Netscape Navigator can do is to *thread* your messages, which means to group related messages together based on the subjects and the reference lines that tell which message is a reply to what. Choose View⇨Sort⇨Thread Messages to turn on threading. In the View⇨Sort menu, you can choose other options to control the order in which messages or threads are displayed: by date, sender, subject, or message number.

Netscape Messenger

Once it became apparent that many users had figured out how to use Netscape Navigator mail, the developers at Netscape remedied this intolerable usability crisis by inventing an all-new and different mail program called Messenger that you have to figure out all over again.

Messenger handles both your e-mail and Usenet newsgroups, the Net's enormous distributed bulletin board system, and tries to make them look like one system, which we think causes more confusion than it solves. Because this is a book about e-mail, we won't mention Usenet any further than to point out that you can learn all about it in Chapter 11 of our *Internet For Dummies,* 4th Edition.

For your convenience, we've changed everything

The old Netscape Mail glommed the entire mail system into a single window. People didn't like that (it got kind of crowded), so Netscape overreacted and the new mail system uses a bunch of windows (a flock of windows? a pride of windows? a vision of windows? a crash of windows? well, there're a lot of them no matter what you call them). The mail windows fall into four categories:

✔ **Message Center:** There's one Message Center window. It lists all your mail and news folders.

✔ **Folder:** A Folder window lists all the messages in a single folder.

✔ **Message:** A Message window displays one message from one of your folders.

✔ **Composition:** A Composition window displays a message you're writing.

Normally, Messenger only opens a single window of each type.

Setting up Netscape Messenger

We have to admit they made setup a little easier. The first time you run Messenger, either from the Start menu or by clicking Communicator⇨ Message Center or Communicator⇨Messenger Mailbox, it pops up a wizard that leads you through the mail and news setup. The information you have to type in is the same as it was for Navigator Mail, discussed earlier in this chapter, but it's made clearer what items you have to type in. If your Internet provider preconfigured your software (as is often the case), you won't see the wizard, and Netscape will go directly to your mail.

Once you've gotten everything typed, you see the Message Center or Inbox Folder window.

Sending Mail with Messenger

The steps haven't changed much, although the screens look different.

1. **Start Messenger.**

2. **In the Message Center or any folder window, click New Msg.**

   You'll see a composition window like the one in Figure 5-5.

3. **Enter the recipient's address in the area that looks like blue-lined notebook paper.**

   You can put multiple recipients on multiple lines and click the To: blocks if you want some of them to be Cc: or Bcc: recipients.

4. **Enter the subject in the subject line.**

5. **Type the text of the message in the message area.**

   Avoid using any of the text formatting features, at least until you've read the sidebar "Rich text indigestion" in this chapter.

6. **Click Send to send the message.**

Rich text indigestion

Netscape offers a phantasmagoria of formatting tools, fonts, styles, bullets, boxes, you name it. Unfortunately, no mail program other than Netscape understands the HTML format codes it uses, so if you send formatted mail to someone who uses any other mail program, your recipient will see ugly format codes that make the message almost indecipherable.

When you try to send a formatted message, Netscape pops up a window asking whether you're sure your recipient can handle HTML mail. Unless you're 110-percent certain that he or she uses Netscape mail too, choose the option to discard the format codes and send the message. Your message may not be as beautiful, but at least it will be legible.

What's particularly annoying is that there is an enriched text standard for formatted mail that Eudora and many other mail programs use, but Netscape had to invent its own. Phooey!

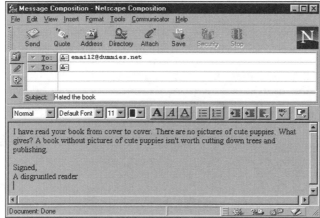

Figure 5-5:
Sending
a new
message.

Receiving Mail with Messenger

When you run Messenger, it attempts to retrieve any new mail into your mailbox. It usually pops up a box asking for your mail password, which is invariably the same as the login password you use to connect to your Internet provider.

Once the mail is received, it resides in your Inbox.

1. **Open the Inbox Folder window.**

   If the Message Center window is already open, double-click the Inbox entry.

In every Communicator window, there are four little icons at the bottom right. Click the second icon from the left, which looks like a little inbox, to go directly to your Inbox window.

2. **If Messenger hasn't just picked up your mail, click Get Msg to tell it to pick up any waiting mail.**

   The Inbox window shows one line per message. Unread messages are in bold type; messages you've read are in regular type.

3. **Double-click any message line to view the message.**

   If the message doesn't fit in the window, you can scroll it up and down.

4. **Click the Next button at the top of the window to switch to the next message you haven't read yet.**

   This lets you read all of your new mail quickly.

Replying to messages

In the Folder or Message window, click the Reply button, the one with the bent arrow pointing to the left. Netscape pops up a little menu giving you the choice of Reply to Sender (just the person who sent you the message) or Reply to All (the sender and all of the other recipients). Choose the appropriate one, and Netscape opens a Composition window with the To:, Cc:, and Subject: fields set, and the text of the original message quoted. Compose your reply and edit down the quoted material to the minimum needed to remind your correspondent what the discussion is about. Then click the Send button.

Forwarding messages

In the Folder or Message window, click the Forward button, the one with the bent arrow pointing to the right. Netscape opens a Composition window. You enter the address(es) to forward the message to and any comments you want to add, and then click Send to send it.

The observant user will note that there's darn little evidence of the message that you're trying to forward in the Composition window. If you click the little paper clip icon to the left of the recipient addresses (not the big paper clip icon at the top of the window), you'll see a reference to the attachment, in an obscure URL-like format that reminds Netscape which message it is. You can't edit the message you're forwarding; you can only send it as is.

If you want to forward a message and edit it in the process, click the New Msg rather than Forward button, enter the address(es) you want to forward the message to, and then click the Quote button at the top of the Composition window. This inserts a copy of the original message you can edit.

Filing messages

In the Folder or Message window, click the File button. Netscape drops down a list of folders, in which you click the one you'd like to file your message in.

To create a new folder (which you need to do before you can file anything there), go to the Message Center window and click New Folder. A window pops up in which you enter the name of your new folder and what existing folder to file it under. Usually you should file your new folder under the main Mail folder unless you want to create a hierarchy of folders.

Alternatively, get the Folder window and the Message Center on the screen. Drag the message from the Folder window into the Message Center window and drop it on the folder where you want to put it. Use Ctrl+click and drag to copy rather than move the message.

Attaching files

Netscape Messenger lets you attach files, messages, or Web pages to your outgoing mail. In the Message Composition window, click the large Attach icon with the paper clip. A menu pops up offering you the various attachment alternatives: Web pages, files, and a few other odds and ends. Pick the one you want and then enter the URL of the Web page or select a file.

In the Composition window, the list of attachments replaces the list of recipients. To get back to the list of recipients, click the little address box to the left of the attachments.

In incoming mail, Messenger displays attachments if they're of a type that it knows how to display, such as plain text, HTML pages, or GIF or JPEG images. Otherwise, it displays the attachment as a little box with an icon and a description of the attachment. Click the icon to run a program to handle the attachment.

The Messenger Address Book

Netscape has spiffed up their address book somewhat in Messenger.

The easiest way to add names to your address book is to copy them from an existing message. In the folder or message window, select Message⇨Add to Address Book. Netscape pops up a little window offering you the choice of adding just the sender or every address in the message including all of the other recipients.

To edit the address book, open the Address Book window by selecting Communicator⇨Address Book. Each address appears on a separate line. You can add new addresses by clicking the New Card button; edit existing addresses by clicking the address you want to change and then clicking Properties; or delete an entry by clicking the address and then the Delete button.

Using the address book while composing messages has a sort of ghostly simplicity. When you're entering an address, just start typing the person's name. As soon as you've typed enough to uniquely select an entry from your address book, Netscape displays the rest of the name in gray type. If that's the address you want, press Enter. If not, keep typing and the ghostly address goes away.

To create an address list, open the Address Book window and click New List. Netscape opens an Address List window. Enter the list name and, if you feel like it, a list nickname and description. (We think that a list that needs a description probably doesn't have the right name.) Then type in the names you want on the list using the same ghostly scheme we just described and click OK.

Netscape still insists that every name in an address list be entered directly in the address book as well. If you try to sneak a new address into a list, after you click OK, Netscape sternly rebukes you and gives you the choice of entering that address in your address book or discarding the rogue address. It's your call.

Chapter 6

Microsoft Internet Mail: Anything Netscape Can Do, We Can Do Better

· ·

In This Chapter

▶ Getting Microsoft Internet Mail and News

▶ Sending mail with Internet Mail

▶ Receiving mail with Internet Mail

· ·

*E*arly on, Microsoft probably expected everyone who used Windows 95 to send and receive their e-mail with Microsoft Exchange. Unfortunately, they overlooked one tiny point — Exchange is a horrible mail program for Internet users. This was a problem, but when they noticed that people were using a mail program from the Evil Blob of Silicon Valley (known to the rest of us as Netscape), they had to do something, and that something is Microsoft Internet Mail and News.

We still like Eudora better, but Microsoft's new program is a lot better for Internet users than Exchange is, both because it's easier to use and because it works well with Internet Explorer, Microsoft's Web browser.

Installing Internet Mail and News

There's no denying it — installing Internet Mail is a snap.

Internet Mail comes with another, separate program called Internet News, which handles Usenet news. We won't say any more about it here because this is an e-mail book.

Microsoft makes Internet Mail and News available for free. If you don't already have a copy but you do have a Web browser like Netscape or Internet Explorer available, you can download Mail and News from Microsoft's home page. Visit http://www.microsoft.com, follow the links to free downloadable software, and follow the instructions for downloading Mail and News for your particular system.

Once you have it downloaded:

1. **Run the Mail and News installation program.**

   Mail and News unpack themselves and install themselves into your computer.

2. **Follow the configuration instructions.**

   You have to enter your e-mail address, the names of your incoming and outgoing mail servers, and other routine mail system information described in Chapter 2.

Receiving Mail

1. **Start Internet Mail, either by running it directly from the Start menu or by clicking the Mail icon in Internet Explorer.**

   If this is the first time you've run Internet Mail, there's one message in your mailbox from your pals at Microsoft telling you what a fine idea it is to use their program. Use this message to practice deleting mail, described later.

2. **Click the Send and Receive button.**

   Internet Mail contacts your mail server and retrieves any waiting mail. Once you have mail in your mailbox, your screen resembles Figure 6-1, with the list of messages in the upper half of the window and one of the messages in the lower window. Messages you haven't read yet are listed in boldface.

3. **Scroll the list of messages up and down, and click any message you want to read.**

   The message appears in the lower part of the window. If you double-click a message, it appears in a separate window, which is easier to read.

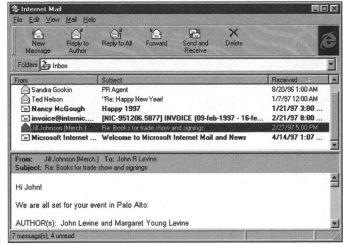

Figure 6-1:
Plenty of
mail, ready
to read.

Sending Mail

1. **Click New Message in Internet Mail.**

   A fresh message window appears, as shown in Figure 6-2.

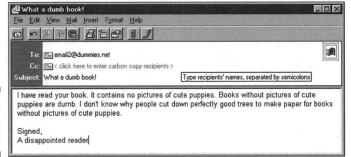

Figure 6-2:
Send us a
message.

2. **Type the recipient's address(es) in the To: and Cc: lines.**

   If you enter more than one address, you have to separate them with
   semicolons, not commas like every other mail program uses.

3. **Type the subject in the Subject: line.**

4. **Type your message in the message area.**

5. When you're done entering your message, click the Send icon, the little envelope at the left end of the toolbar.

This files your message in your Outbox. It won't actually be sent until the next time you click the Send and Receive button. A little window pops up to remind you of this; click OK.

You can create several messages while *not* connected to your Internet provider; then connect and click Send and Receive to send them all at once.

Other Mail Tricks

Microsoft provides the usual array of mail-handling features, just like Netscape does.

Deleting mail

In the main Mail window, click the message you want to delete and then click the Delete icon in the toolbar.

Replying to mail

In the main Mail window, click the message you want to reply to and then click either the Reply to Author or Reply to All button on the toolbar. Internet Mail creates a new message addressed to the author (or to the author and the rest of the recipients) with the text of the original message quoted. Be sure to edit down the quoted text to the minimum you need to remind people what the message is about.

Once you're done creating your reply, click the Send icon (the little envelope at the left end of the toolbar in the new message window) to file your reply in your Outbox. Click Send and Receive in the main Mail window when you want to send your message.

Forwarding mail

In the main Mail window, click the message you want to forward and then click the Forward button. Internet Mail creates a new message containing the text of the message you're forwarding. Enter the address(es) to which you are forwarding the message in the To: and Cc: lines. Add any comments you want to add to the message and then click the Send icon to file the new message in your Outbox. Click Send and Receive in the main Mail window when you want to send your message.

Filing mail

Internet Mail automatically creates four file folders: your Inbox and Outbox, a Sent Mail folder for mail that's been sent already, and a Deleted Message folder.

To create a new folder, select File⇨Folder⇨Create and type in the name of the new folder. Then click OK.

To see the messages in a particular folder, select the desired folder from the list in the Folders toolbar at the top of the main Mail window.

To file a message, in the main Mail window click the message you want to file, or click and drag to select multiple messages. Then select Mail⇨Move to or Mail⇨Copy to. A small menu appears listing all of your folders; click the one where you want to file your message(s).

Using Your Address Book

Internet Mail uses the standard Windows address book. If you already have address book entries that you use in other applications such as Word, you can share those entries with Mail. (The address book program isn't clairvoyant, so if you want to send e-mail to people already in your address book, you have to add their e-mail addresses.)

Adding e-mail addresses

The easiest way to add e-mail addresses to your address book is to copy them from incoming mail messages. To do so:

1. **In the main Mail window, double-click the desired message.**

   This opens the message in its own window.

2. **In the new window, select File⇨Add To Address Book.**

   Mail pops up a little list of all of the To and From addresses in the message.

3. **Click the address you want to add.**

You can also add a new address directly, in either the main Mail window or a message window.

1. **Click File⇨Address Book to open the address book.**

2. **Click New Contact.**

   This opens a Properties window.

3. **Fill in as much information as you want.**

   For a useful entry, you need at least the person's name and e-mail address.

4. **Click OK.**

Once you've created address book entries, you can edit any of them by double-clicking the little file card icon to the left of the person's name in the list of entries in the Address Book window.

In the Address Book window, if you put the mouse pointer on any of the entries and leave it there for a few seconds, you see a little box that describes that entry.

Using address book entries

You can select entries from the address book when you're sending mail.

1. **Create a message by clicking New Message or Forward.**

2. **In the New Message window, click the address card icon on the To: or Cc: line.**

   This opens the address book with two columns. The left column shows all the names in your address book, and the right column shows the addresses to which the message will be sent.

3. **Click the desired address in the left column and then click either the To or Cc button in the middle of the window.**

   You can repeat this step several times if you want to send the message to several people.

4. **Click OK.**

Part III
Using Online Services for E-Mail

"You know, I liked you a whole lot more on the Internet."

In this part . . .

We hear that a few people use online services like America Online and CompuServe (about 10 million, all told). In their quest to be all things to all people, they each have their own mail programs with their own peculiar quirks. So if you're an AOL or CompuServe user, read on.

Chapter 7

America Online Mail

In This Chapter

▶ Sending e-mail

▶ Creating your own messages

▶ Using FlashSessions to read your mail offline

merica Online (AOL, to its friends) is a widely used online service that includes Internet access. It comes with a nifty Windows-, DOS-, or Macintosh-based access program, so you can do lots of pointing and clicking and not so much typing of arcane commands. AOL has more than 8 million subscribers and is still growing. It offers an easy-to-use e-mail system that can get your message to AOL members or to any Internet account.

This chapter describes AOL software Version 3.0. AOL updates its software and the graphics that appear in its dialog boxes all the time, so your screen may not exactly match the figures in this chapter. If you decide to open an AOL account, or if you have trouble with your account, call 1-800-827-6364 (in the United States).

When we wrote this, AOL users were constantly running into busy signals, because so many AOL users were staying online for hours at a time and AOL didn't have enough phone lines. By the time you read this, AOL will probably have finished installing thousands of new phone lines and modems, so the situation should have cleared up. Before you consider signing up for an account, though, you might want to check with your friends who use AOL.

Mail It, AOL

America Online has a mail system through which AOL members can send messages to each other, as well as to the rest of the Internet. The messages can include attached files, too, which can be a very handy feature.

Your Internet address is your screen name (omitting any spaces) plus @aol.com. If your screen name is Hans Solo, for example, HansSolo@aol.com is your Internet address. To send a message to another AOL user, just address the message to the person's screen name. To send a message to someone with another type of account, address the message to the person's Internet e-mail address. (See Chapter 4.)

Checking for New Mail

When you sign onto AOL, it tells you whether you have any mail. On the left side of the Welcome! window you see either the message No New Mail or the message You Have Mail. Another way to tell whether mail is waiting for you is to look at the List Unread Mail icon on the toolbar — it's the far left one, a picture of a little mailbox. If the little red flag is *up,* you have mail.

Reading Your Mail

You probably *do* have mail, in fact, because every new member gets a nice note from the president of AOL. All members, old and new, tend to get lots of junk mail, too.

From the Welcome! window, you can click the You Have Mail icon to see your new mail.

To read your unread mail, follow these steps:

1. Click the leftmost icon on the toolbar, the one just below the word _File_.

This is the Read New Mail icon. Alternatively, you can choose Mail⇨Read New Mail from the menu or press Ctrl+R.

You see the New Mail dialog box, as shown in Figure 7-1. Each line on the list describes one incoming mail message with the date it was sent, the sender's e-mail address, and the subject.

2. To read a message, highlight it on the list and click Read or press Enter.

Or double-click the message. The text of your message appears in another cute little dialog box.

3. To reply to the message or forward it, see "Sending a reply" or "Forwarding a message" later in this chapter.

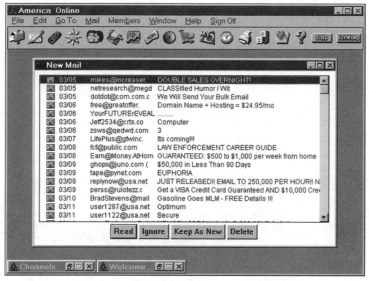

Figure 7-1:
Any new
mail?

4. **To see the next message, click the Next button.**

   If you are looking at the last message in your inbox, the Next button doesn't appear. (Makes sense!)

5. **When you finish, double-click the little box in the upper-left corner of each window you're finished with.**

From the New Mail window, you can choose not to read some of the messages (like all the junk mail). Select a message and click Delete to delete the message from your list immediately. Or click Ignore to mark the message as read.

Keeping messages

After you have read your mail, AOL keeps each message for a few days and then throws it away. If you want to keep a message around, select it from your list of mail and click the Keep As New button, or save the message on your computer, as described later in this chapter.

Once you've used the Ignore button to mark messages as read, AOL deletes them when it deletes the messages you really *have* read.

Sending a reply

To reply to a message you have received, display it as described in "Reading Your Mail" earlier in this chapter. To reply, follow these steps:

1. Click the Reply button.

You see a window like the one in Figure 7-2. The To address is already filled in with the address from which the original message came, and AOL suggests a subject line.

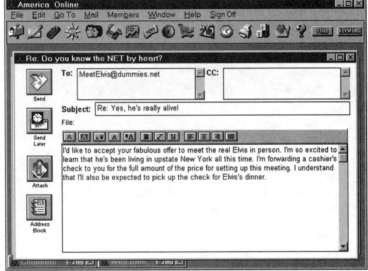

Figure 7-2:
When you reply to a message, AOL addresses it for you.

2. Type the text of your message in the box in the lower part of the window.

3. To send the message, click the Send icon.

Don't reply to really annoying messages right away. It pays to cool off after reading a brainless message some jerk just sent you.

Forwarding a message

To forward a message to someone else, display it as described in "Reading Your Mail," earlier in this chapter. Then click the Forward button, address the message, add any text you want (like "I know you are interested in geraniums, so I thought you might enjoy seeing this"), and click Send.

Composing a New Message

You don't have to reply to other messages — you can also *start* an exchange of messages, assuming that you know the e-mail address of the person you want to contact:

1. **Click the second icon from the left on the toolbar, the picture of a pencil and paper.**

   Alternatively, you can choose Mail⇨Compose Mail from the menu bar. Or just press Ctrl+M. You see the Compose Mail dialog box, which looks very much like the one you use when replying to or forwarding a message — see Figure 7-2.

2. **Enter the recipient's address in the To box.**

   For AOL members, just enter the screen name. For others on the Net, type the entire Internet address.

3. **In the cc box, enter the addresses of anyone to whom you want to send a copy.**

   You don't have to send a copy to yourself — AOL keeps copies of mail you have sent.

4. **Enter a brief subject line in the Subject box.**

5. **In the box with no name, type the text of your message.**

   Don't use the Tab key because it moves your cursor from one box to the next in the dialog box. You can press Enter, though, to begin a new paragraph.

   If you are sending a message to another AOL member, you can use the buttons along the top of the message box to format the text of your message. To find out what each button does, hold the mouse pointer over the button without clicking; the name of the button appears after a few seconds.

6. **When you like what you see, click the Send button.**

   AOL confirms that the mail is winging on its way.

7. **Click OK to make the message go away.**

Attaching a File to Your Message

If you want to send a file on your computer to someone as an e-mail message, AOL makes the process easy. When you are writing the message in the Compose Mail window, click the Attach button. You see the Attach File dialog box, which lets you choose any file from your PC. Select a file and click <u>O</u>pen. The file is included as a MIME attachment. Attachments work great for sending files to other AOL members and to anyone with an e-mail program, such as Eudora or Netscape, that can deal with MIME.

If you want to send a message to someone whose e-mail program can't handle MIME attachments, here's a way to include a text file with a mail message to anyone:

1. **Run your word processor, or any other program (like Windows Notepad) that can display the text you want to send.**

2. **Using that program, copy the text to the Clipboard.**

    In most programs, you copy by highlighting the text and choosing <u>E</u>dit⇨<u>C</u>opy from the menu. Most Windows programs let you copy highlighted text by pressing Ctrl+C or Ctrl+Ins.

3. **In America Online, begin a new message by replying to a message or by composing a new message.**

    (See "Sending a reply," "Forwarding a message," or "Composing a New Message" earlier in this chapter.)

4. **Place your cursor in the text box where you type the text of the message.**

5. **Choose <u>E</u>dit⇨<u>P</u>aste (or press Ctrl+V).**

    The text appears.

6. **Send your message as usual.**

In Windows, you *are* limited as to how much text you can copy at a time into the Clipboard, but it's big. If you have trouble, copy the text one piece at a time. This method works only for text, not for pictures or data files.

Saving a Message on Your Computer

If you get a message on AOL that you want to download to your computer, display it on the screen as described in the section "Reading Your Mail" earlier in this chapter. Then choose <u>F</u>ile⇨Save <u>A</u>s from the menu bar. AOL lets you choose the directory and filename in which to save the file on your computer. When you click <u>S</u>ave, it saves the e-mail message as a text file. Nice and easy!

AOL's Address Book

 AOL lets you make an address book of the e-mail addresses of your friends and coworkers. When you are composing a message, click the Address Book button on the Compose Mail window. You see the Address Book window.

In your address book, you can store addresses of your correspondents along with the nicknames you'd like to use for them — that is, what you'd like to type when you address mail to each person. For example, instead of typing *president@whitehouse.gov*, you can use the nickname *Bill*.

To add an address to your address book, click the Create button in the Address Book window. The Address Group window opens (a mysterious name for this window, unless you realize that you can use the address book for creating small mailing lists, too).

In the Group Name box, type the person's real name, or the name you'd like to type when addressing e-mail to the person. In the Screen Names box, type the person's AOL screen name or Internet address. To create a mailing list with one group name, enter a list of AOL screen names or Internet addresses in the Screen Names box. Click OK when you are done.

Using your address book to address a message is easy:

1. **Click the Address Book button in the Compose Mail window.**

   You see the address book.

2. **Select the person to whom you want to send the message, and click the To button.**

   The person's e-mail address appears in the To box in the Compose Mail window.

3. **Click OK in the Address Book window to make it go away.**

A Cheaper Way to Use AOL

AOL has a nice feature that lets you read your e-mail and newsgroup messages *offline* (when you are not connected to AOL). This feature, called *FlashSessions,* can save you big buckets of money if you pay for AOL by the hour or you have to pay per-minute charges for phone access. (***Note:*** FlashSessions are called *Automatic AOL* in the Macintosh version of AOL 3.0.)

FlashSessions lets you tell AOL to log in to your account, send e-mail messages you have composed, get the new mail, and log off as fast as it can.

You can also tell AOL to perform this series of steps at a preset time each day, such as in the middle of the night when your computer and telephone aren't doing anything else.

Setting up FlashSessions

Here's how to tell AOL that you want to use FlashSessions (you don't have to be connected to AOL while following these steps):

1. **Choose Mail⇨Set Up FlashSession from the menu bar.**

   You see the FlashSessions Walk-Through window, with lots of instructions.

2. **Follow the instructions and click OK when done.**

If you want to change the way your FlashSessions are configured, choose Mail⇨Set Up FlashSession again, then click the Walk Me Through button.

Composing e-mail offline

You can compose your e-mail when you are not connected to AOL. Run the AOL program, but don't connect. Then click the second icon on the toolbar (the Compose Mail button), choose Mail⇨Compose Mail from the menu bar, or press Ctrl+M. You see the Compose Mail dialog box. Address and write your e-mail message as usual. When you finish, click the Send Later button. AOL saves the message to be sent the next time you run a FlashSession.

Flashing on AOL

To run a FlashSession anytime, just choose Mail⇨Activate FlashSession Now. You see the Activate FlashSession Now dialog box. Click Begin to start the FlashSession.

Reading flashed mail

After you have used a FlashSession to download your e-mail, read it by choosing Mail⇨Read New Mail (or press Ctrl+R). To see a list of all the mail you've downloaded, not just your new mail, choose Mail⇨Read Incoming Mail. You can reply to mail and forward messages — click the Send Later icon when you finish editing the messages.

Chapter 8
CompuServe Mail

Introduction to CompuServe Mail

CompuServe caters to business and professional users and is a great source of technical information about computers, with support forums for hundreds of software and hardware vendors. Since CompuServe created easy-to-use access programs for Windows and Macs, a CompuServe account has become as user-friendly as some of the more recent online services, such as America Online and Prodigy.

CompuServe has a mail service for exchanging messages with other CompuServe users. The same mail service works for sending and receiving e-mail to and from Internet addresses. This chapter describes how to use CompuServe's mail.

CompuServe makes it easy to send attached files to other CompuServe users, but it's inconvenient and cumbersome to send attached files to the Internet.

 This chapter describes how to use CompuServe with version 3.0.1 of its software for Windows 95. If you are using WinCIM (Windows CompuServe Information Manager) for Windows 3.1 or MacCIM for the Mac, your screens will look a little different from those shown in this chapter.

My user ID is what?!

Unlike most other online services and Internet providers, CompuServe assigns a number to each user. Rather than an easy-to-remember username (such as ElvisLives or HeartThrob117), you get a number that looks like 77777,7777.

The exact number of digits varies, but your user ID is always a number with a bunch of digits and a comma somewhere in the middle. Users in the U.S. and Canada usually have numbers that begin with a 7, and overseas users usually have numbers that begin with 1. (This numbering scheme dates back to the stone age of computing, in the late 1960s. The numbers are base 8, by the way.)

Your Internet e-mail address is not the same as your CompuServe ID — you have to modify it to include the fact that it is a CompuServe account number. To figure out your e-mail address, change the comma in your user ID to a period and add @compuserve.com to the end. If your CompuServe ID is 77777,7777, for example, your Internet e-mail address is 77777.7777@compuserve.com.

Luckily, you can sign up for a name to use in place of the number in your e-mail address. Go to "register" and choose the username you'd like to use for your e-mail address. Once you have registered for a name, you can use that named followed by @compuserve.com for your e-mail address.

To sign up for a CompuServe account, get hold of one of its little disk packages (call 1-800-848-8199 in the U.S. or 614-457-8600 outside the U.S.). It contains a disk and instructions for installing it. Make sure that you have the right disk for your computer.

If you have trouble with the CompuServe software, call 1-800-944-9871 or 614-457-8600. These are voice, not modem, numbers.

Reading Your Mail the Cheap and Easy Way

The most efficient way to read your mail is offline, that is, while you're not connected to CompuServe. You don't have to pay for connect time while you are reading and composing messages. Here's how it works:

> ✔ You use the Mail⇨Send/Retrieve All Mail command. This command grabs all your mail and downloads it (copies it) from CompuServe into your In Basket, a storage area on your hard disk.

✔ You disconnect from CompuServe.

✔ While you're disconnected (and therefore not paying connect-time charges), you read your e-mail at a leisurely pace. You can even write replies or compose messages to other people. Messages you write appear on your list of outgoing messages, which is stored on your hard disk.

✔ When you finish reading your mail, you use the Mail⇨Send/Retrieve All Mail command again to send your outgoing messages and pick up any additional incoming messages.

The result is that you are online only long enough to download your incoming mail and upload your outgoing mail.

Ready to try it? Follow these steps:

1. **Run the CompuServe program but don't connect. Choose Mail⇨Send/ Retrieve All Mail.**

   The program displays the Progress Indicator window, so you can follow along as it dials CompuServe, logs on, grabs your mail, stores it in the In Basket on your hard disk, and hangs up. There! You stop paying connect charges.

2. **Close the Progress Indicator window by clicking the X button in the upper-right corner.**

3. **To read your messages, click the Mail Center button along the left side of the CompuServe window; then click the Read button along the top of the window (if it's not already selected).**

   You see a list of your messages, which looks like Figure 8-1. At the bottom of the CompuServe window is a message telling how many new messages await your perusal.

4. **To read a message, double-click it (or select it and click Open).**

   A message looks like Figure 8-2.

5. **To reply to the message, click the Reply button, compose a response, and click Send (if you want to connect to CompuServe and send it right now) or Send Later (to send the message the next time you connect to CompuServe).**

   When you reply to a message, CompuServe addresses the message for you. All you have to do is type your response.

6. **To forward the message to someone else, click Forward, address the message, and click Send or Send Later.**

Figure 8-1:
A list of
your
incoming
messages
— get out
your letter
opener!

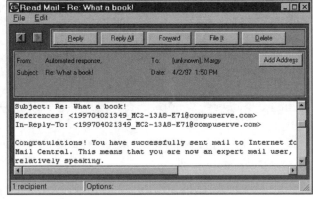

Figure 8-2:
After you
read a
message,
you can
reply to it,
forward it,
or file it (in
the circular
file, if you
want).

See the section "Using Your Little Black Book" later in this chapter to find out how to address a CompuServe message.

7. **To see the next message in your In Basket, click the right-pointing VCR-type button in the upper-left corner of the window.**

8. **To close a message, click the X button in the upper-right corner of the Message window or choose File⇨Close.**

9. **Compose any new messages by choosing Mail⇨Create Mail or by clicking the Create tab along the top of the CompuServe window. Then click the New button.**

10. **After you finish reading and composing mail, choose Mail⇨Send/ Retrieve All Mail.**

    The program calls CompuServe again, sends all your outgoing mail, and checks for any mail that has arrived since you last checked it.

You can see the messages that are waiting to be sent by clicking the Mail Center button along the left side of the CompuServe window and clicking the Create tab along the top of the window. If you want to change a message (perhaps you thought better of that snappy retort in a message to your boss), you can edit the message by highlighting it and clicking Open. To send all your outgoing messages right away, click Send All.

In addition to your lists of incoming and outgoing messages, CompuServe provides you with a filing cabinet in which to file your messages. After you read a message, you can click File It to store it in your filing cabinet. See that little yellow filing cabinet icon on the toolbar? Click it to see what's in your filing cabinet.

Reading Your Mail the Expensive and Easy Way

If you don't feel like dialing in twice to get and send your mail, you can read it while you're online. Go ahead, waste your money — we don't care! Use any of these methods:

- ✔ Click the Mail Center button along the left side of the CompuServe window. Then click the Read tab along the top of the window and click the Get Mail button.
- ✔ Choose Mail⇨Get New Mail command from the menu.
- ✔ Click the Go icon on the toolbar (the one with the green traffic light), type **mail**, and click OK.
- ✔ Click the little envelope icon along the bottom of the CompuServe window.

You see the same Mail Center windows we showed in the "Reading Your Mail the Cheap and Easy Way" section of this chapter.

When you are ready to hang up, click the Disconnect button on the toolbar (the handshake button) or choose Access⇨Disconnect.

Using Your Little Black Book

When you send mail to another CompuServe user, you address a message to that person's CompuServe ID (the one that looks like 77777,7777) or to the name the person registered to use for e-mail. When you send mail to someone on the Internet, you address the message to INTERNET:username@host.

For example, you can send a test message to us authors here at Dummies Central by addressing it to INTERNET:email2@dummies.net. (Our friendly robot will write back, and we authors will eventually read your message, too.) If you tell CompuServe that an address is on the Internet, the program will add the INTERNET: part for you.

Luckily, CompuServe would like to keep a list of the e-mail addresses that you use, so you can pick them off of lists instead of typing them each time you send e-mail. You don't have to be connected to CompuServe to use its little black book.

To start a brand new message, click the Mail Center button, the Create tab, and the New button. You see the Create Mail window, which looks very much like the window that displays messages you are reading (see Figure 8-1). Then click the Recipients button. You see the Message Recipient dialog box.

The Message Recipients dialog box shows the addresses to which this particular message is addressed. At the top are boxes for you to enter the recipient's Name and Address.

You can add an address to the list in two ways: typing it in and choosing it from the address book.

Send it to this guy

You can type the person's name into the Name box and the person's address into the Address box. Don't forget to type INTERNET: in front of Internet addresses (that is, any address that's not a CompuServe address). As you type the name, if the name is already in your address book, the address appears as if by magic in the Address box. (Isn't CompuServe wonderful?) Then click the Add to List button to add this person to your list of recipients for this message.

If the person's name *isn't* in your address book, CompuServe wants to know why. The Define Address Book Entry window pops up with the name and address of this new, unidentified person already filled in. If the information looks correct, click OK, and CompuServe adds the person to your address book, as well as to this message.

If you decide that you don't want to send the message to someone after all, choose his or her name from the list on the right and click Delete.

If you want to send a copy of the message to someone (or a blind copy), click the CC (or BCC) option. Then either choose an address from your address book or enter the person's information in the Name and Address boxes. In the list of recipients, each address is preceded by To:, CC:, or BC: to show how the message will be addressed to that person.

Lemme see that book

If you don't feel like typing addresses, or if you're pretty sure that the address to which you want to send your e-mail message is already in your CompuServe address book, you can ask CompuServe for help. Just click the Address Book button to tell CompuServe to display the Select Recipients window. Double-click the names of anyone you want to include in your message and then click OK when you are done.

Get the message?

When you finish addressing the message, click OK. The Create Mail dialog box opens, and you can enter the subject in the Subject box and the text of the message in the big box. When you finish, click Send Later to park the message in your list of outgoing messages until the next time you send messages to CompuServe, or click Send to connect to CompuServe and send it right away.

You can use the Windows Clipboard to copy text from another Windows program into a mail message. To include text from a word processing document, for example, select the text in your word processor, copy it to the Clipboard (in most programs you use the Edit⇨Copy command), place your cursor where you want the text to appear in your message, and choose Edit⇨Paste.

Send Along This File Too

The Create Mail dialog box lets you to attach a file to a message. If it's a text file, you can send it to anyone. If it's not text, you can send it only to other CompuServe users. (This limitation may change when CompuServe supports one of the standard methods of attaching non-text files to e-mail, such as uuencoding or MIME.)

To attach a file to a message, just click the Attach File button. (Actually, it's currently called the Attach File: 0 button, which means that zero files are attached so far.) You see the Open dialog box, which you use to find and select the file you want to attach. When you've highlighted the file, click the Open button. Then you see the Attach Files window listing the file that you just selected. Then click OK. Back on the Create Mail window. The Attach File button now says Attach File: 1. Send the e-mail message as usual.

When you receive a file attached to an e-mail message, you receive a separate message with the same subject line as the message to which it was attached. (Sounds to us like attached text files get detached, but as long they arrive, it sounds good to us.) The message announces that a file awaits your attention. After CompuServe asks you where to store the file, click Retrieve to download it to your computer.

If you want to practice mailing messages, go to the Practice Forum (click the Go icon, type **practice**, and click OK). Connect time is free while you're using this service, and the forum gives you someone to write to while you practice.

Part IV
Using *Real* E-Mail Programs

IF BOB DYLAN HAD PURSUED A CAREER IN COMPUTERS

"PUT HIM IN FRONT OF A TERMINAL AND HE'S A GENIUS, BUT OTHER-WISE THE GUY IS SUCH A BROODING, GLOOMY GUS HE'LL NEVER BREAK INTO MANAGEMENT."

In this part . . .

Yeah! *Real* e-mail users use *real* e-mail programs, programs that just do e-mail without all that fru-fru Web and online service stuff. (Are we a little biased? Who, us?) If you're a serious e-mail user, you'll want the extra flexibility of an e-mail program like Eudora. Or if you're on a limited budget, you'll want to check out Juno's free e-mail system. And there's lots more e-mail programs too, many of which we discuss. So read on and see what real e-mail users use.

Chapter 9

La Crème de la Crème: Eudora Light

● ●

In This Chapter

▶ Understanding Eudora Light

▶ Installing and configuring your own copy of Eudora

▶ Sending and receiving mail with Eudora

▶ Replying to and forwarding messages

▶ Saving money with Eudora

● ●

*E*udora is an easy-to-use mail-reading program from QUALCOMM, Inc., that works with Winsock and dial-up SLIP or PPP Internet accounts. Eudora runs under Windows and on the Mac OS and lets you write mail messages, read your mail, and reply to and store your messages in folders. It lets you define a standard signature, it deals beautifully with all kinds of attachments, and it has a good address book. What more could you want?

This chapter (and the next one, "Fancy Moves with Eudora Light") describe Eudora Light Version 3.0 for Windows 95. Eudora Pro, the commercial version, works similarly, as do the versions for Windows 3.1 and the Mac OS. If you use an older version of Eudora Light (like the widely used Version 1.5.4), consider upgrading to Version 3.0. You can download Eudora Light from the Eudora Web site (`http://www.eudora.com`) or you can load it from the CD-ROM in the back of this book.

Light Up Eudora Light

Eudora requires the following:

✔ A computer running Windows 95 or Windows NT (for the 32-bit version), or running Windows 3.1 or 3.11 or Windows for Workgroups (for the 16-bit version), or a Mac.

TIP

So who is Eudora, anyway?

According to the Eudora manual, the program's author was reading Eudora Welty's short story *Why I Live at the P.O.,* and he was inspired. It's nice to know that even nerds read some real books from time to time.

✔ An Internet connection that supports Winsock or MacTCP programs — for example, if you are connected to the Internet via Trumpet Winsock or Windows 95 Dial-Up Networking. You're in good shape if you have a PPP or SLIP account, like the accounts you get from AT&T WorldNet, Concentric, IBM Internet, or other Internet providers. You can't use Eudora with most UNIX shell accounts.

✔ An online service or Internet provider that provides a *POP server*, that is, a Post Office Protocol computer on the Internet that holds your mail for Eudora to pick up.

✔ At least 2MB of free disk space.

Installing Eudora

Eudora Light Version 3.0 is on the CD-ROM in the back of this book. Here's how to install the Windows 95 version:

1. **Insert the CD-ROM from the back of this book into your CD-ROM drive.**

   The installer program should start running by itself; if it does, skip ahead to Step 4.

2. **If the installer didn't run automagically, click the Start button, choose Run, type** d:\install **in the box that appears, and press Enter.**

   (If your CD-ROM isn't drive D, type the appropriate letter for the drive.) The installer program adds an installation program to your Start menu.

3. **Click the Start button and choose Programs⇨IDG Books Worldwide⇨ E-Mail For Dummies to start the installation program.**

4. **When you see the license agreement, read it and click Accept. On the next screen, click anywhere to continue.**

   You see the main menu listing the programs on the CD-ROM.

5. **Click the Communicating category and then the Eudora Light option, and then the Install button.**

   Eudora's installation program runs.

6. **Follow the prompts that appear on your screen, clicking the Next button to move from one screen to the next.**

7. **When Eudora is installed, click the Quit button to exit from the E-Mail For Dummies CD installation program.**

   Now you have a Eudora Light option on your StartÍPrograms menu.

If you use Windows 3.1, follow these steps:

1. **Insert the CD-ROM from the back of this book into your CD-ROM drive.**

2. **Choose File⇨Run from the Program Manager's menu, type** d:\install **in the box that appears, and press Enter.**

   (If your CD-ROM isn't drive D, type the appropriate letter for the drive.) The installer program adds a program group named IDG Books Worldwide to your Program Manager.

3. **Double-click the IDG Books Worldwide icon in Program Manager and then double-click the E-Mail For Dummies icon to start the installation program.**

4. **When you see the license agreement, read it and click Accept. On the next screen, click anywhere to continue.**

   You see the main menu, listing the programs on the CD-ROM.

5. **Click the Communicating category, then the Eudora Light option, and then the Install button.**

   Eudora's installation program runs.

6. **Follow the prompts that appear on your screen, clicking the Next button to move from one screen to the next.**

7. **When Eudora is installed, click the Quit button to exit from the E-Mail For Dummies CD installation program.**

   Now you have a Eudora Light icon in Program Manager.

Mac users can install Eudora by following these steps:

1. **Insert the CD-ROM from the back of this book into your CD-ROM drive.**

   An icon representing your CD-ROM drive appears on the desktop within a minute.

2. **Double-click the E-Mail For Dummies 2E icon to open a window revealing the CD-ROM'S contents.**

3. **Double-click the Read Me First document for any last-minute information. After you close this document, double-click the License Agreement for some interesting reading; close it when your done.**

4. **Back in the E-Mail For Dummies 2E window, double-click the Communicating folder. In the window that opens, double-click the Eudora Light folder.**

5. **Double-click the Eudora Light 3.1 Installer icon.**

6. **Follow the on-screen prompts to install Eudora Light.**

Filling in Eudora's blanks

After you install Eudora Light (or Eudora, for short), you have to tell it about yourself:

1. **Click the Start button and choose Programs⇨Eudora Light if you use Windows 95. Windows 3.1 and Mac users can double-click the Eudora icon to run the program.**

   You see the Eudora Light window with the Options dialog box on top of it (see Figure 9-1). If you don't see this dialog box, choose Tools⇨Options from the menu. The left side of this dialog box has a column of icons. When you click an icon, the settings in the rest of the dialog box change.

2. **In the POP Account box, enter your e-mail address.**

   This is usually your login account on your Internet provider's computer, but it doesn't have to be — it's wherever you receive mail.

3. **In the Real name box, enter your real name as you want it to appear in parentheses next to your e-mail address.**

4. **Click the Hosts icon in the list of icons on the left side of the Options dialog box.**

   A new bunch of boxes appears in the Options dialog box. Your POP account setting is already filled in with the e-mail address you typed in Step 2.

5. In the SMTP box, enter the name of the Internet host computer to which you send your mail (your mail *gateway*).

If you're not sure, ask your Internet provider. Your mail gateway's name may be the same as the part of your POP account after the at-sign (@).

6. Click the Checking Mail icon on the left side of the dialog box.

You see a bunch of settings that control how often to check for incoming messages and what to do with them.

7. Click the Save password box so that a check appears in its box.

This setting tells Eudora to ask you for your Internet password the first time it checks your mail and to store your password for future mail checks. If this setting isn't selected, you have to type your password each time you check your mail.

Skip this step if someone might sneak up to your computer and secretly check your mail when you're off refilling your coffee mug.

8. Click the Sending Mail icon on the left side of the dialog box.

Yet more settings appear.

9. Click the Immediate send box to remove the check.

You just told Eudora not to send each message as you write it. Instead, you plan to write a few messages and then send them in a batch. This arrangement saves on Internet connect-time.

10. Click the Attachments icon on the left side of the dialog box.

You may have to scroll down the column icons to bring the Attachments icon into view.

11. Click the large Attachment Directory button (which is currently blank), choose the directory in which you'd like to store attached files, and click the Use Directory button.

The directory name you just chose appears on the Attachment Directory button. If you skip this step, each time you receive an attached file, Eudora asks where to put it.

Leave everything else as it is (for now). You may want to change some settings later, but these should do for now.

12. Click OK to save these settings.

The Options dialog box disappears, leaving you with a rather blank-looking Eudora Light window.

Eudora now knows enough about you to send and retrieve your e-mail messages from the Internet. If you need to change your settings later, choose Tools⇨Options from the menu.

The first time you exit from Eudora, or check your mail, Eudora will ask if you want to register. Do so! Qualcomm is doing a wonderful thing for the Internet community by giving away such an excellent e-mail program. We'd like to encourage them.

Eusing Eudora

Before we get into the details, we have a few words about how to use Eudora: Eudora displays lots of windows, including mailboxes that show lists of messages, message windows that show the text of one message, composition windows for writing your own messages, and other windows. Eudora happily lets you display lots of windows at a time, and you can switch among them.

Eudora has a cute row of icons on its toolbar. If you can't guess what a button does, position the mouse pointer on the button and keep it there for a few seconds. A label appears telling you the name of the button.

When you start Eudora, its window usually isn't totally empty. Down the left side of the window you usually see a list of your Eudora *mailboxes*. Mailboxes are places to stash messages, and you start out with several:

- ✔ **In:** Contains your incoming messages.
- ✔ **Out:** Contains messages waiting to be sent and messages you've already sent.
- ✔ **Trash:** Contains messages you've deleted, until you take out the trash.

We cover how to make more mailboxes, to store messages by topic or person, in Chapter 10.

Hello Out There!

To try Eudora out, send yourself a message. It's the fastest way to find out whether things are working.

Here's how to send a message:

1. **Click the New Message button on the toolbar, or choose Message⇨New Message from the menu bar, or press Ctrl+N.**

The New Message button is the one that looks like two pieces of paper and a pencil. You see a window entitled No Recipient (because you haven't told Eudora yet who the message is for).

The top part of this window contains the message headers — the "envelope" for the message. Your e-mail address already appears on the From line of the headers. The bottom part of this window is where you type the text of the message.

2. **Click to the right of the To label in the message headers. Then type the e-mail address to which you want to send a message.**

   To send a test message to yourself, type your own e-mail address.

   If you want to send the message to more than one person, you can enter more than one Internet address. Just separate the addresses by commas. We talk about using an address book to address your messages in Chapter 10.

3. **Click to the right of the Subject label and type the subject of your message.**

   You can also press the Tab key to move from the To line to the Subject line. As always, make the subject as specific as possible.

4. **If you want to send anyone copies or blind copies, enter the address (or addresses) in the Cc or Bcc fields.**

   Blind copies are copies of a message that are sent to someone without the other recipients knowing it. Blind copies are especially useful in industrial espionage.

   Skip the Attached line in the headers; we get to attachments in a minute.

5. **Below the gray line, type the text of your message.**

   You don't have to press Enter at the end of every line — Eudora word-wraps to make your message look nice.

6. **To send your message, click the Queue or Send button, whichever button appears in the upper-right corner of the message headers.**

   If you set up Eudora to send all messages immediately (using the Immediate send option in the Options dialog box), Eudora shows a Send button rather than a Queue button at the right end of the toolbar for the message.

   When you click the Queue or Send button, your message disappears. Don't worry; Eudora hasn't lost it!

TIP

What are all those buttons?

At the top of the message window, Eudora displays a row of interesting-looking boxes and buttons. You can use them to control a bunch of cool things about your messages. Here they are, from left to right:

✔ **Priority:** This small blank box controls the priority of the message. If you click the button to the right of the box, you can see the list of priorities. This setting is usually blank, which means that the message has a normal (not urgent or boring) priority.

✔ **Signature:** This box usually says "Standard" and controls whether your signature file is automatically placed at the end of the message. Click the button to the right of the box to switch to your alternate signature or to no signature. See the section "Kilroy Was Here" later in this chapter for information on how to create your own standard and alternate signatures.

✔ **Encoding:** This box usually says "MIME" and controls the way Eudora attaches files to your message if the file contains something other than text. See Chapter 10 for information on attaching files to a message.

✔ **QP (Quoted-Printable):** Usually pressed (selected), this button controls the way Eudora attaches text files to your message. Just leave it pressed.

✔ **Text as Attachment:** This button tells Eudora more about how to handle attached text files. When this button is pressed (as it usually is), attached text files are sent as separate files. When this button isn't pressed, the text in the file is placed at the end of the message.

✔ **Word Wrap:** This button is usually pressed, telling Eudora to word-wrap so that you don't have to press Enter at the end of every line.

✔ **Tabs in Body:** Selecting this button tells Eudora to type spaces when you press the Tab key in the body of the message. If this button isn't selected, the Tab key moves you to the next field in the window (usually the To field). Leave it selected.

✔ **Keep Copies:** Pressing this button tells Eudora to keep a copy of your messages in your outbox. Leave it pressed; sometimes you need to refer to a copy of a message you've sent.

✔ **Queue** or **Send:** Click this button when you are done composing your message. (The next section describes how you control which button you see.)

When Does Eudora Send the Message?

Eudora can hold your messages in a *queue* (just imagine all those messages standing patiently in line) and send them on your signal. Or Eudora can send your messages as soon as you finish writing them — it's your choice. Use the Immediate send option in the Options dialog box to control when Eudora sends out messages that you compose.

You can save connect-time with your Internet provider if you do as much message reading and writing as possible when you are not connected, and then connect to the Internet and send your messages in a group. If sending a message ties up your PC for a minute or two, you may prefer to keep your messages in a queue and send them every few hours.

When we told you how to set up Eudora in the "Light Up Eudora Light" section earlier in this chapter, you turned off the Immediate send option in the Options dialog box. Turning the setting off tells Eudora to hold your messages in a queue.

If Eudora is set up to hold outgoing messages in a queue, nothing seems to happen when you click the Queue button. To send the messages in the queue, press Ctrl+T (or choose File⇨Send Queued Messages from the menu). If you chose the Send on check option in the Options dialog box (you probably did — it's the default), Eudora sends your queued messages whenever you check your incoming mail, too.

What if you want to see your queue? Easy — double-click the Out mailbox on the mailbox list on the left side of the Eudora Light window. If you don't see a mailbox list, choose Mailbox⇨Out from the menu bar. A window named Out appears, listing the messages you've sent or in the queue to be sent.

If you want to save a message and send it later, choose File⇨Save from the menu bar. Then close the window. The message is saved in your outbox but not queued for sending, so you can edit and send it later.

Here Comes Your Mail!

Well, you've sent mail, but how about getting the mail that's coming to you? How about the test message you sent earlier, for example?

Getting the mail

Here's how to get your incoming messages from your mail server:

1. **Click the Check Mail button on the toolbar, press Ctrl+M, or choose File⇨Check Mail from the menu.**

   The first time you check your mail, Eudora asks for your password.

Testing, testing

If you are testing Eudora and you're not yet sure that you plan to use it, you can tell Eudora *not* to delete the messages after it downloads them to your computer. Then you can use another mail program to download the messages again. Of course, once you start using Eudora, we're sure that you'll love it!

To tell Eudora to leave incoming messages on your mail server, choose Tools⇨Options from the menu, click the Checking Mail icon, click the Leave mail on server setting so that an × appears, and click OK. Now Eudora retrieves your mail as usual, but it doesn't delete it from your mailbox at your mail server, where your

mail is held. The good thing about this arrangement is that if you screw up retrieving your mail, you can download it again. When you get Eudora working as you would like, be sure to turn the Leave mail on server setting off.

If your provider has an extremely old mail server program, each time you check your mail you may get all the old messages in your mailbox as well as the new ones. If this happens to you, tell your provider to get a newer mail server. (Qualcomm, the people who wrote Eudora, give away a nice one called qpopper.)

2. **Type the password to the computer where you get your mail (your mail server). Press Enter or click the OK button.**

   The password appears as a row of asterisks when you type it, so type carefully.

   Eudora connects to your mail server, grabs your mail, and copies it to your PC. You see a Progress window showing a series of messages as it does so. The Progress window first shows Eudora logging in to your POP server (that is, your mail server), and then it shows the subject line of each message.

   When Eudora is done downloading your incoming messages, you see a message saying that you have new mail, and you may hear a cute tune. If you don't have any messages, you get an apologetic message telling you so.

3. **Click OK to make the message go away.**

   You see a new window called In with a list of your incoming messages, if any.

If the In window doesn't appear automatically, you can open the In window at any time by choosing Mailbox⇨In from the menu.

Reading the mail

The In window shows the contents of your In mailbox — messages you haven't read yet. You see one message per line, with the name of the person who sent it (you, in the case of your test message), when it was sent, the number of pages, and the subject. In the leftmost column, you see a black dot or bullet for messages you haven't yet read, or a blank for messages that you have read but haven't replied to or deleted.

To read a message, double-click it in the In window. You see a message window like the one shown in Figure 9-1.

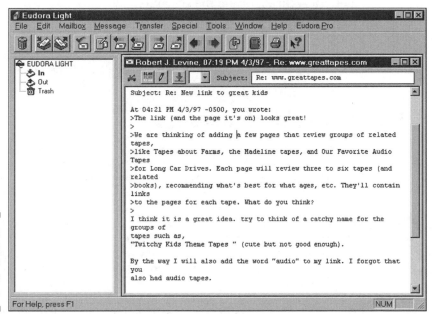

Figure 9-1:
A message
from the
outside
world.

When you are looking at a message, you can easily reply to the message, delete it, forward it to someone else with your comments, or redirect it to someone else — just read on to find out how.

Sending your response

To reply to a message:

1. **Select the message in the In mailbox (or any mailbox, for that matter) by clicking it once, or display the message by double-clicking it.**

2. **Click the Reply button on the toolbar (the one with one envelope flying leftward), choose Message⇨Reply from the menu bar, or press Ctrl+R.**

    Eudora shows you a message window so that you can compose your reply. Eudora fills in the address of the person you are replying to and copies the subject from the original message. The text of the message you are replying to appears in the body of the message, with each line preceded by a >.

3. **Delete all but the important parts of the quoted original message.**

    If you are responding to a particular point in the original message, leave just that point. Be sure to delete the most boring parts of the original message — headers and the signature.

4. **Write and send the message as usual.**

After you reply to a message, an *R* appears in the leftmost column of the In window, so you know that you have already dealt with the message.

Getting rid of messages

You can delete a message that you have already read. With a message on-screen or selected from a mailbox, click the Delete Message(s) button on the toolbar (the trash can), choose Message⇨Delete from the menu bar, or press Ctrl+D.

If you delete a message by accident, you can dig it out of the trash. Double-click the Trash mailbox on the list of mailboxes, or choose Mailbox⇨Trash from the menu. You see the Trash mailbox with all your deleted messages. Drag the message from the Trash mailbox back to your In mailbox and then close the Trash window.

To get rid of the messages in your Trash mailbox (so they don't fester there forever), choose Special⇨Empty Trash from the menu. Or choose Tools⇨ Options from the menu, click the Miscellaneous icon (it's at the very bottom of the column of icons), click the Empty Trash when exiting setting so that you see a check in its box, and click OK. Now when you choose File⇨Exit, Eudora takes out the trash.

Moving along to the next message

When you have read a message, you can close the message window to see the In window again. Then double-click another message to read it.

You can also press Alt+Down-arrow key to move to the next message.

Committing a message to paper

To print a message, select the message from the mailbox or display the message on the screen. Then click the Print button on the toolbar, press Ctrl+P, or choose File⇨Print from the menu bar. You see a Print dialog box that lets you choose which pages to print and how many copies. Click OK when you have made your choices.

Sharing a message with friends

To forward a message to someone else:

1. **Select the message in the In mailbox (or any mailbox, for that matter) by clicking it once, or display the message by double-clicking it.**

2. **Click the Forward button on the toolbar (the one with an envelope flying rightward) or choose Message⇨Forward from the menu bar.**

   Eudora shows you a new message window. The text of the original message appears, indented by the > character (this character shows that you are repeating information you received from someone else). Delete the parts that won't be interesting to the person you're forwarding the message to, and add your own comments at the end (or anywhere).

3. **Type the address of the person to whom you want to forward the message just to the right of the To label.**

   If you want to forward the message to more than one person, you can enter more than one Internet address separated by commas.

4. **Send the message as usual by clicking the Queue or Send button.**

After you forward a message, an *F* appears in the leftmost column of the mailbox window next to the message you forwarded.

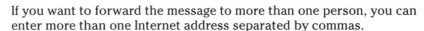

Oops! This message isn't for me!

Redirecting a message is a nicety that most mail programs don't do. If you feel that you got a piece of mail in error and you want to pass it along to its proper recipient, you can redirect it:

1. **Select the message in the In mailbox (or any mailbox, for that matter) by clicking it once, or display the message by double-clicking it.**

2. **Click the Redirect button (the envelope flying up and to the right) or choose Message⇨Redirect from the menu bar.**

   Eudora displays the message in a new message window, but redirecting doesn't indent the text the way forwarding does. Also, the message is from the person who originally sent it, not from you.

3. **Enter the address to which you want to redirect the message.**

4. **Send it as usual.**

After you redirect a message, a *D* appears in the leftmost column of the mailbox containing the original message. This letter suggests that you are free to delete it now.

Saving Money with Eudora

You can use Eudora when you are not connected to the Internet. This is a great advantage because it lets you read your mail and concoct responses at your leisure, without worrying about how much money you're spending on connect-time to your Internet provider.

Checking mail automatically

Wouldn't it be nice if Eudora could automagically check your mail every half hour? It can!

Choose Tools⇨Options from the menu, click the Checking Mail icon, and type a number of minutes in the Check for mail every box. Then click OK. Eudora checks your mail automatically at the interval you entered.

If you are not always connected to the Internet, automatic mail-checking can be terrific. If all goes well, Eudora tells your Internet software to connect to your Internet account, gets your incoming messages, sends your outgoing messages, and hangs up — perfect! You're connected to the Internet only long enough to grab your messages.

On the other hand, you'll be making a bunch of phone calls if you check your e-mail every half hour. Another possibility is to tell Eudora to check your mail only when you tell it — read on.

Getting set to save money

Here is how to set up Eudora to minimize your connect time:

1. **Choose Tools⇨Options from the menu.**

   You see the Options dialog box.

2. **Click the Checking Mail icon. Enter a zero in the Check for mail every box.**

   This tells Eudora not to check for mail except when you tell it to.

3. **Click the Sending Mail icon. Don't choose Immediate send.**

   That is, click the little box to remove the check. This setting tells Eudora not to send each message as soon as you have written it. Instead, Eudora waits until you give the word.

4. **Select the Send on check box, so that a check appears in it.**

   This setting tells Eudora that while it is checking for new mail, it can send any mail that is waiting to be sent.

5. **Click OK.**

Now Eudora is configured to let you read and write your e-mail when you are not connected to your Internet account.

Checking your mail frugally

When you want to read and respond to your e-mail, follow these steps:

1. **Run Eudora.**

2. **Look at your In mailbox to see whether you want to respond to any messages. Also compose any new messages you want to send (by clicking the New Message button on the toolbar, pressing Ctrl+N, or choosing the Message⇨New Message command).**

3. **Click the Check Mail button on the toolbar, choose File⇨Check Mail from the menu, or press Ctrl+M.**

   Eudora tells your Internet connection program (usually Dial-Up Networking, if you use Windows 95) to connect to your Internet provider. A Progress window tells you as Eudora gets your new messages and sends your messages that are queued up, waiting to be sent. Then your computer hangs up.

If your computer doesn't automatically connect to the Internet, run your usual connection program (like Trumpet Winsock or Dial-Up Networking), log in, and then try checking your mail again. When your mail has arrived, tell your connection program to hang up.

4. **Click OK to clear any box that tells you about new mail (or that tells you that you don't have any).**

5. **Read your new messages.**

They appear at the bottom of your In mailbox with a bullet in the leftmost column. Read them, compose replies, delete boring ones, move good ones into other mailboxes, or whatever.

6. **When you are finished with your incoming messages and ready to send the messages you've written, click the Check Mail button again.**

If you chose the Se_n_d on check box in the Settings dialog box, as we suggested, this step both checks for new mail and sends your queued outgoing mail.

As in Step 3, if your computer doesn't connect automatically, run the connection program, log in, and then click the Check Mail button in Eudora. When Eudora is done sending and receiving messages, disconnect.

Kilroy Was Here

You can make a signature that Eudora can automatically add to the end of messages you send. A signature usually consists of your full name, your e-mail address, perhaps your mailing address or phone number, and maybe some pithy saying. Long, flowery signatures are a bad idea because people get tired of seeing them after the first time.

Eudora lets you create two signatures: a standard signature and an alternate. For example, you can use your standard signature for the business-related messages that make up the bulk of your e-mail. You can use the alternate signature for the messages you send to friends and post to the Domestic Poultry mailing list, discussing your pet chickens.

Creating your own personal signature

To make a signature, follow these steps:

1. **Choose _T_ools⇨_S_ignatures⇨Standard to edit your standard signature (logically enough).**

You see a totally blank window, unless you've created a signature before (in which case you see your existing signature).

2. Type the text of your signature in the window, as shown in Figure 9-2.

Figure 9-2:
A signature appears at the bottom of messages you send so that you don't have to type this stuff over and over.

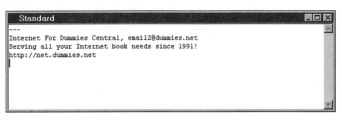

```
Standard                                                    _ □ ✕
---
Internet For Dummies Central, email2@dummies.net
Serving all your Internet book needs since 1991!
http://net.dummies.net
```

3. Click the Close button in the upper-right corner of the window to close it.

Eudora asks whether you want to save the changes to your signature.

4. Click Yes.

Eudora remembers this signature forever or until you change it.

To make an alternate signature, choose Tools➪Signatures➪Alternate from the menu.

Your signature can be as long as you want. Some people think that it's incredibly clever to have a signature about 30 lines long with little pictures, quotations, political comments, 14 phone numbers, some fax numbers, a home address, a business address, and a summer address. They are wrong — long signatures are just obnoxious. The rule of thumb is that a signature should be as short as possible and never longer than four lines. We manage to get a name, e-mail addresses, and a pithy comment ("Space aliens are stealing American jobs." — MIT Econ Professor) into 3 lines and, by golly, you can, too.

Signing with a flourish

To add your signature to a message, take a look at the window in which you are composing the message. Click the second box from the left on the toolbar in the message window (the box that usually says "Standard"). You can choose to include the standard signature, the alternate signature, or no signature at all.

That's not all Eudora Light can do — read Chapter 10 for more!

Chapter 10

Fancy Moves with Eudora Light

. . . .

In This Chapter

▶ Sending and receiving files with Eudora

▶ Using Eudora's address book

▶ Keeping important messages in mailboxes and folders

▶ Sorting your incoming messages into mailboxes automatically

▶ Getting Eudora Pro

. . . .

Chapter 9 explains how to install Eudora and start using it as your e-mail program. We think you'll agree that it's easy and pleasant to use — we've been using Eudora for several years and still love her. This chapter explains more fun things that you can do with Eudora.

May I Have a File, Please?

When you send a message, you may want to include a file that you have stored on your PC. Such a file is called an *attachment* (not an emotional attachment, just an attachment). You can attach a word-processing document, a graphics file, or anything that can be stored in a file on your computer.

When you attach a file, think about the person who will receive the file. What is this person going to do with it? If you send a Microsoft Word for Windows document, the person on the other end must have the same program or a program that can read that type of document. If you correspond with folks on different types of computers — especially UNIX and mainframe folks — they may be out of luck. You may want to find out beforehand which types of files your correspondent can deal with.

The Internet uses three different methods to attach files to e-mail messages: MIME, uuencoding, and BinHex. See Chapter 15 for details on how they differ. In most cases, MIME's the one you want.

Attaching a file

To attach a file to a message, follow these steps:

1. **Compose the message as usual.**

   You can compose a new message using the New Message button on the toolbar, or you can reply to or forward a message. You can attach a file to any message you send with Eudora.

2. **Click the Attach File button from the toolbar (the one with the paper clip). Or choose <u>M</u>essage⇨Attac<u>h</u> File from the menu bar or press Ctrl+H.**

   You see the Attach File dialog box, which lets you indicate the exact file you have in mind.

3. **Choose the folder and filename of the file to attach and click <u>O</u>pen.**

   No, you don't want to open the file. You want to attach it, but that's the button to click anyway. The folder and filename appear in the header of the message on the Attached line.

4. **Send your message as usual.**

The contents of the attached file don't appear as part of the message. The file is "stapled" to the message but remains separate.

If you drag a file from the Windows File Manager, My Computer, or Windows Explorer into Eudora, the file is attached to the message you're composing.

If you change your mind about attaching the document, click the filename in the message header and press the Del key to delete it.

You might think that rather than use the <u>M</u>essage⇨Attac<u>h</u> Document command, you can just type the folder and filename of the file you want to attach right into the Attached line of the header of your message. But no! Eudora doesn't let you do this (and we don't know why not).

Eudora can't send attached files using uuencoding. For that, you have to upgrade to Eudora Pro.

Including information from a document

Another way to send information from a word-processing document as an e-mail message is to copy the text from your word-processing program into Eudora. When you copy text into a message, the text appears as part of the text of the message, not as an attachment.

In your word processor, highlight the text you want and copy it to the Clipboard (by choosing Edit⇨Copy). In Eudora, start a new message and put your cursor where you want the text to appear. Choose Edit⇨Paste (or press Ctrl+V) to copy it from the Clipboard.

Getting an attached file

When Eudora retrieves your mail from your mail server, it notices immediately whether an incoming message has an attachment. If you previously told Eudora where to store all attachments, it will store the attached file there. If you have never told Eudora where to put attached files, Eudora stops in its tracks and displays a Save Attachment dialog box. This dialog box lets you decide in which folder to put the incoming file. Of course, because you can't see the message yet, you may not know what the file contains, so it can be hard to decide where it should go. You may be able to guess by its original filename, which Eudora shows you.

Eudora automatically decodes the attached file by using BinHex or MIME as appropriate, so it appears just as it did when it left the sender's computer.

If you don't want to be bothered every time Eudora gets an attached file, you can tell Eudora in advance which folder to put attachments in. Choose Tools⇨Options from the menu bar so that you see the Options dialog box. Click the Attachments icon in the left-hand column (you may need to scroll the icons down to see it) and then click the big Attachment Directory button. Eudora displays a dialog box that lets you choose the folder. Click the Use Directory button after you have chosen it. The folder name now appears right in the big button (strangely enough). Click OK.

From now on, Eudora files all attachments in that folder. You are still notified when attachments arrive because the messages to which they are attached show up in your In mailbox.

When you open a message to which a file is attached, you see a line like this:

```
Attachment Converted: C:\DOWNLOAD\MEGPIX.GIF
```

This line says that the message has an attachment, that the attachment was successfully downloaded, decoded, and stored, and where the resulting file is and what it's called.

Eudora Light can't deal with uuencoded files. If someone sends you a file attachment with uuencoding, Eudora Light doesn't know what to do with it, so it just displays the uuencoded file as part of the e-mail message. The text of the uuencoded file looks like a 15-month-old has been pounding on the keyboard with the Caps Lock key on (we know this from direct experience with a 15-month-old) except that each line begins with an *M*. If you get a uuencoded file, either tell the person who sent you the file to send it again using BinHex or MIME, or upgrade to Eudora Pro.

Macintosh users might want to get a copy of Jeff Strobel's shareware utility UULite. Contact `jstrobel@world.std.com`. This program saved our you-know-whats when we were writing this book!

Eudora's Little Black Book

Typing Internet addresses can be annoying with all the strange punctuation. Even more annoying is having to type lists of addresses when you want to send a message to a bunch of people. To avoid this annoyance, you can use Eudora's *nickname* feature, stored in its Address Book.

What's in a nickname?

A nickname is a short name you can use instead of typing an entire Internet address. If you intend to send a great deal of mail to Dummies Central, for example, it can be a pain to type `email2@dummies.net` over and over. It's much nicer to type `Dummies` instead.

No problem! Eudora lets you make up as many nicknames as you want and stores them forever in your Eudora Address Book. A nickname can be short for one Internet address or for a whole list of them. To look at your Address Book and fool with nicknames, click the Address Book button on the toolbar (the little green book), choose Tools⇨Address Book, or press Ctrl+L. You see the Address Book window.

The box on the left lists all the nicknames (Address Book entries) you have created. One of these nicknames is highlighted, and the right side of the Address Book window shows the details of that entry. When the Address(es) tab is selected, the box shows the actual Internet address (or addresses) for the entry. Click the Notes tab to see, edit, or enter notes about the person or group of people.

When you are done using the Address Book window, close it. If you made any changes to your nicknames list, Eudora asks whether it should save the changes. Click Yes.

Making a nickname

To make a nickname, follow these steps:

1. **Click the New button in the Address Book window.**

   You see the New Nickname dialog box.

2. **Type the nickname you want to create. For example, type** Dummies.

3. **Click OK.**

   The New Nickname dialog box goes away and you return to the Nicknames window. The new nickname appears on the Nickname list.

4. **Click the Address(es) tab and type the actual Internet address to use for this nickname.**

   If this nickname is for a group, enter a list of addresses separated by commas, or press Enter after each entry.

5. **Click the Notes tab and enter any notes about the nickname.**

   If you know which mail program the person (or people) use, note it here because you might need to know this when you're sending attached files. You may also want to enter any alternative e-mail addresses that people might have (many folks have several).

6. **Repeat these steps for all the nicknames you want to create.**

It is okay to separate the addresses for a list of people by pressing Enter after each address when you type in the Address(es) box. But you cannot do this anywhere else in Eudora. Instead, you have to separate the addresses by commas.

When you are reading a message from someone you correspond with, it's easy to make a nickname. Choose Special⇨Make Address Book Entry from the menu or press Ctrl+K. Eudora asks what you want to call the nickname. When you enter a name and click OK, Eudora creates a nickname for the person who sent you the message, and you never have to type the address again.

For people who you write to a lot, you can take an extra step: Add the person's name to your *recipient list*. The names on your recipient list appear when you choose Message⇨New Message To from the menu, and you can choose any of the names off the recipient list with your mouse. For example, if the nickname *Bill* is on your recipient list, you can create a new message to Bill by choosing Message⇨New Message To⇨Bill from the menu. To add someone to your recipient list, click the Recipient List box on the Address Book when the person's name is displayed.

Using a nickname

We like to keep the Address Book window open so that we can choose names off the list whenever we want to create a new message. When you are composing a message and you want to send it to someone with a nickname, choose the person from the list in the Address Book window and click the To button. The nickname appears in the To field in the message that you are composing.

You can start a new message even more easily, in fact: In the Address Book window, choose the person to send the message to and click the To button. Eudora figures that you want to start a new message to that person and opens a new message window with the nickname in the To field.

You can choose more than one nickname from the Address Book list if you want. Click one of the nicknames and then Ctrl+click each additional name you want to use.

File It, Eudora

If you are like us, you want to save a certain number of your messages. To keep them organized, we like to save them in different groups, which Eudora calls *mailboxes*. Eudora comes with three mailboxes: In, Out, and Trash, which we told you about in Chapter 9.

You can create your own mailboxes (for example, one for personal messages, one for a discussion of your department's budget, one for project planning messages, and one for messages about the football pool). After you have made a mailbox and put messages in it, you can read the messages, reply to them, delete them, or move them to other mailboxes exactly as you would if they were in your In mailbox.

Eudora likes to display a list of your mailboxes on the left side of the Eudora window. You can make this mailbox list wider or narrower by using the mouse to drag the vertical window edge to the left or right. If you don't want to see the mailbox list at all, drag its vertical border all the way to the left. You can always open the list back up by dragging its edge back over to the right.

What are those funky-looking numbers?

In the lower-left corner of a mailbox window, you see a box that says something like *5/10K/135K*. This is Eudora's cryptic way of telling you that five messages are in the mailbox (the first number), they take up 10K of disk space (the second number), and that junk lying around in the mailbox takes 135K of disk space (the third number). To tell Eudora to get rid of the junk, click the box (it's really a button). Eudora takes out the trash, and the third number shrinks to zero.

Opening a mailbox

To look at a mailbox, double-click its name on the mailbox list at the left side of the Eudora window. Alternatively, choose Mailbox from the menu bar to see a menu that contains all your mailboxes, and then choose a mailbox. Either way, a window for that mailbox opens. For example, to look at the trash, double-click Trash in the mailbox list or choose Mailbox⇨Trash.

Your In (incoming) and Out (outgoing) mailboxes also have their own icons on the toolbar. Clicking the second icon on the toolbar (the one with a red incoming arrow) opens your In mailbox, while the third icon (the one with a blue outgoing arrow) opens your Out mailbox.

When you open your Out mailbox, messages that have already been sent appear with an *S* in the leftmost column. Those that are queued for sending are marked with a *Q*.

Make me a mailbox

To create a new mailbox and move a message into it, follow these steps:

1. **In the In window or any other mailbox window, select the message you want to put in the new mailbox by clicking it.**

   Alternatively, you can display the message by double-clicking it.

2. **Choose Transfer⇨New from the menu.**

   You see the New Mailbox dialog box, as shown in Figure 10-1.

Figure 10-1:
Making
a new
mailbox to
hold your
fascinating
messages.

3. Type the mailbox name in the box.

The name can contain spaces. Capitalize it nicely so that it will look good on your menus and windows.

4. Click OK.

Eudora makes the new mailbox and moves the chosen message into it.

Your new mailbox now appears on both the Mailbox and Transfer menus. To see the new mailbox, choose Mailbox from the menu and then choose the mailbox name. To move a message into the new mailbox, select or view the message, choose Transfer from the menu, and choose the mailbox name. What a convenient system!

If you want to set up a bunch of mailboxes without moving messages into them, choose Mailbox⇨New from the menu.

Saving a message in a mailbox

Once you've created a mailbox, here's the easiest way to file a message there: drag it. That is, drag the message from its location in the In mailbox (or wherever the message is now) to the mailbox name in the mailbox list on the left side of the Eudora window. Eudora moves the message to the mailbox you chose.

Saving a message in a text file

What if you want to use the text of a message in a document that you are writing? Saving a message from Eudora into a text file is easy. Either view the message or choose it from the mailbox where it lives. Then choose File⇨Save As from the menu bar. You see a Save As dialog box that lets you decide which folder to put the file in and which filename to use. When you click Save, Eudora makes the file.

Alternatively, run your word processor. Display the message in Eudora, highlight the part of the text that you want to use in your document, and choose Edit➪Copy from the Eudora menu (or press Ctrl+C) to copy it to the Windows Clipboard. Switch to your word processor and paste the Clipboard text into your document by choosing Edit➪Paste from the menu bar.

For organizing lots of mail, use folders

We really like mailboxes. Mailboxes are great for saving all your interesting mail by topic or by sender. However, if you set up more than 12 mailboxes, the Mailbox and Transfer menus get rather long. What to do? Organize your mailboxes into *folders*.

A folder is a collection of mailboxes with a name. For example, if you have mail about three different projects that you are accepting bids on, you can make a folder named *Bids* containing one mailbox for each project. We've got a folder named *Books* with a mailbox for each book we've written containing e-mail messages about writing arrangements, corrections to be made, and so on. (No complaint messages, of course.)

To create folders, move mailboxes into folders, get rid of mailboxes you don't use any more, and rename mailboxes, use the mailbox list at the left side of the Eudora Light window.

You can use the mailbox list to do lots of things, including deleting and renaming mailboxes, creating folders, and moving mailboxes into and out of folders. The next few sections tell you all about these tasks.

Fold me a folder

You can create mailboxes from the Mailboxes window by choosing Mailbox➪New. You see the same dialog box that appeared in the section "Make me a mailbox" earlier in this chapter. You can use the same dialog box for making folders. Here's one way to make a folder and put some mailboxes into it.

1. **Choose Mailbox➪New from the menu.**

   You see the New Mailbox dialog box.

2. **Type the name for the new folder in the box.**

   Use capitalization and spaces so that the folder name will look nice on the Mailbox and Transfer menus.

3. **Click the <u>M</u>ake it a folder check box so that it contains a check.**

4. **Click <u>O</u>K.**

   Eudora shows the folder on the mailbox list (with a cute little yellow folder icon) and then displays the New Mailbox dialog box again so that you can create a mailbox in your new folder.

5. **Create a mailbox that you want to put into the folder.**

   Type the mailbox name and click <u>O</u>K. If you've already got a mailbox or two to move into the folder, click <u>C</u>ancel instead. When Eudora creates a mailbox, it appears with a little rural mailbox icon on the mailbox list.

Another way to create a new folder or mailbox is to right-click the EUDORA LIGHT entry at the top of the mailbox list and then choose <u>N</u>ew from the menu that appears. The New Mailbox window appear where you can create the folder or mailbox as usual. If you want to create a mailbox in a folder, right-click the folder name and choose <u>N</u>ew.

What is in this folder?

You can use the mailbox list to see what mailboxes are in a folder. To "open" a folder, double-click the folder name or click the little plus sign to the left of the folder name. The plus sign switches to a minus sign and Eudora displays the mailboxes in the folder. To "close" the folder, click the minus sign or double-click the folder name. The list of its contents vanishes.

Stuff that mailbox into a folder

You can move mailboxes from one folder to another, or out of any folder, using the mailbox list. To move a mailbox into a folder, drag it to its new location on the mailbox list. To move a mailbox out of any folder, drag it to the EUDORA LIGHT entry at the top of the list.

Shuffling Messages Automagically Using Filters

Until the latest version of Eudora Light came out, you had to buy Eudora Pro to get the coolest feature of all: message filtering. *Filtering* lets you tell Eudora to sort your incoming mail into mailboxes.

If you belong to e-mail mailing lists, filtering is a terrific way to sort messages from each mailing list into separate mailboxes. Mailing list messages make so much more sense when read as a group, rather than mixed together with your personal messages. Another benefit of sorting out your mailing list messages is that your In mailbox contains only messages that are actually addressed to *you*.

To make, edit, or delete filters, you use the Filters window, displayed by choosing Tools⇨Filters from the menu. Figure 10-2 shows the Filters window.

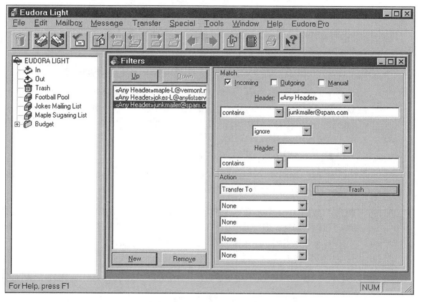

Figure 10-2:
Each filter tells Eudora to transfer a set of incoming messages to a different mailbox (or to the trash).

When you create a filter, you tell Eudora how to recognize the messages you want to filter and what you want to do with them. For example, you can tell Eudora that you want to filter all the messages that contain the characters *JOKES-L* anywhere in the headers, so that the filter applies to all messages from the JOKES-L mailing list. Then you can tell Eudora to transfer these incoming messages to your Jokes Mailing List mailbox.

You can create as many filters as you want. You can make one filter that sticks your JOKES-L messages in one mailbox, puts messages from your box in a mailbox named *The Boss Says*, and throws away messages from an advertiser who won't leave you alone. (Yes, a filter can move messages right into the Trash mailbox.) If you upgrade to Eudora Pro, filters can also print messages automatically or forward them to someone else.

Filter it, please

To make a new filter, follow these steps:

1. **Display the Filters window by choosing <u>T</u>ools⇨<u>F</u>ilters; then click the <u>N</u>ew button.**

   A filter called *Untitled* appears in the list of filters at the left side of the Filters window. The rest of the window contains the settings for this new filter. At this point, they are all blank. Leave the Match option set to Incoming so that Eudora filters your incoming messages.

   The settings about the filter are in two groups: the Match settings in the top half of the window and the Action settings in the bottom half of the window.

2. **Click in the <u>H</u>eader box and choose Any Header.**

   For most filters, you can tell Eudora to look in all the headers for a set of characters that identifies the messages you want. Usually, you can leave the next box, which says *Contains*, alone, to tell Eudora that you want all messages whose headers contain the text that you type in the following box.

3. **Click in the blank box to the right of the box that says *Contains* and type the text that identifies messages to be filtered.**

   For example, if you want to filter all messages from the Maple Sugaring mailing list (a group that discusses the fine points of collecting and boiling down maple tree sap into syrup), you can type the mailing list's address in the box.

4. **Leave the rest of the settings in the Match part of the window alone.**

   The Ignore box and the three boxes below it allow you to specify a second way to identify messages to be filtered. Leave the box that says *Ignore* alone when you want to specify just one way of identifying messages.

5. **In the Action part of the Filters window, all the boxes say *None*. Click the first of the boxes and choose <u>T</u>ransfer To from the menu that appears.**

   This setting tells Eudora to transfer all the messages that match the text you typed in Step 3 out of the In mailbox and into a different mailbox. But which mailbox?

   The box you clicked now says *TransferTo* and a large button labeled *In* appears next to it.

6. Click the In button and choose the mailbox to transfer the messages into. If you want to create a new mailbox to contain the messages, choose <u>N</u>ew and create a mailbox as usual.

The name of the mailbox you chose (or created) now appears as the name of the button.

Leave the rest of the *None* boxes alone. You've created a filter — the list of filters now contains an entry for this filter.

Fooling with filters

The next time you receive mail, the messages you specified should automatically be transferred to the mailboxes you selected. If the filters didn't work, open the Filters window and check the settings for the filters. To see the settings for a filter, click the filter on the list at the left side of the Filters window. That filter's settings appear in the rest of the Filters window, and you can change them if they don't work.

Be sure that the <u>I</u>ncoming box is checked for each filter so that Eudora uses the filter on your incoming messages.

You can create more filters by clicking the <u>N</u>ew button again. You can delete an existing filter by selecting it from the list and clicking the Remo<u>v</u>e button. When you are done fooling with filters, close the Filters window. Eudora asks whether you want to save your changes; click <u>Y</u>es.

You'll Love Her Big Sister, Eudora Pro

The commercial version of Eudora, Eudora Pro, works just like Eudora Light, with a bunch of extra features, including these:

✔ You can send attached files using uuencoding. If you need to send files to folks whose e-mail programs can't deal with MIME or BinHex attachments, this feature is worth the price of the program.

✔ Eudora Pro's filters are not limited to transferring messages to mailboxes. Your filters can also open filtered messages on your screen, print messages, forward messages to someone else, or reply to messages.

✔ A built-in spell-checker makes it easier to send literate-looking messages. Just click the Check Spelling button on the toolbar.

If you find that you like the program and use it frequently, think about buying Eudora Pro. It's not very expensive. After all, if everyone uses the shareware version and nobody buys the real thing, the software division of Qualcomm (who wrote it) will go down the tubes, and the program will never be updated. Be a good citizen of the Internet and buy the software you use. (End of commercial announcement.)

Chapter 11

E-Mail à la Carte:
Free E-Mail with Juno

In This Chapter

▶ Getting Juno

▶ Running Juno

▶ Putting Juno to work

Contributed by Alison Barrows

*J*uno is one of the first of a new kind of e-mail service — free (or, almost-free) e-mail that is funded by advertisers. Juno only runs on PC-compatible systems running Windows 3.1 or higher and requires a 9,600-baud modem. And there's one tiny catch — you have to look at ads every time you look at e-mail. But the trade-off could be worth it.

Once upon a time, Juno had free 800 numbers you could use to get your mail. They now have 400 access numbers in different cities around the U.S., so if you're a toll call away, Juno isn't exactly free. (In this case you might want to shop around for a local Internet service provider — some have e-mail-only accounts that may cost less than your phone bill for "free" e-mail.)

Juno is accessed through it's own network — you can't pick up mail using an existing PPP or SLIP connection. To date, Juno has signed up more than two million subscribers. To ensure that they can keep up with demand, Juno, from time to time, limits the number of new subscribers they sign up in a given month.

So How Do I Get Free E-Mail?

In order to take advantage of Juno's free e-mail you have to get their software. There are a number of ways to do this:

- ✔ You can download the software from their Web site: http://www.juno.com.

- ✔ If you know someone who already uses Juno, you can make a copy of his or her Juno disk. Juno encourages people to copy their software and pass it to their friends.

- ✔ You can call Juno at 800-654-JUNO to order the software, though in this case, Juno may ask you to cover the cost of processing your order and producing and shipping the disk. (As of May 1997, Juno is charging $8.82 for this service.)

Juno is happy to have you share their software, so if you have a friend willing to download it for you, that may be the quickest way to get the software.

Getting Up and Running with Juno

Once you have the software, you have to install it and set up an account. If you downloaded the Juno software, you now have a file called junoinst.exe on your hard drive. Double-click the file in My computer or Explorer to begin installing the software. If you ordered the software, begin the installation by following the directions that come with the disk.

Once you've started the installation process, windows appear to tell you what you are doing (installing Juno) and to ask you where to put the files. (The default folder should be fine, unless you have a compelling reason to change it.) It then installs the files you need to run Juno.

Once Juno is installed, you need to set up a user profile. Start Juno by clicking the Start button and choosing Programs⇨Juno. To create a new account, click the Create New Account button.

As you go through the screens of the setup process, click the Next button at the bottom of the window. If you need to return to a screen you've left, click the Back button.

Before you can begin the sign-up process you must agree to the service agreement by typing "yes" in the box. On the next screen, Juno asks you for your name, address, and phone number. To move from one field to the next, click the Tab key on your keyboard. Juno also needs information about your phone service; to change a marked option, click the option that you want to pick.

Juno asks you how to set up your modem: You can either set it up manually or let the installation program set it up. Click the Automatic Modem Set-Up button unless you need to set up the modem manually. You may have to pick your modem from a list of possibilities.

After your modem has been identified, you see the E-mail Address and Password window, where you are asked to pick an e-mail address and type a password. You need to type your password twice to be sure that you typed it exactly as you intended. You also need to remember this password, so write it down and put it someplace safe. Click the Activate Account button to start your Juno account.

Since more than two million people have already signed up to use Juno, your first choice of e-mail names may not be available, and you will see a window that tells you that you must pick a different name and suggests one that is available. Click OK to return to the E-mail Address and Password window, where you can type a new e-mail name and click the Activate Account button to see if the name is available. You may wish to use the suggested name or provide something more memorable (names with numbers are not particularly easy to remember). You may want to try a combination of your names and initials, choose a nickname, or pick a fictional or historical name that will be easy for you and your e-mail friends to remember.

Once you have found an e-mail address that is unique, Juno tells you that your account has been successfully created. Now is a good time to write down both your new e-mail address and the password you used.

Think you're done? Well, not quite. Now you have to choose the dial-in number to to pick up your mail from Juno. On the Select Local Access Number screen, you type your phone number (or your computer's phone number if you got it its own). Then click the Select Main Access Number to see access numbers local to you. Choose a local number and click OK to return to the Select Main Access Number screen. Answer the other two questions on this screen and click the Next button to choose a backup number.

The last step requires that you answer 18 questions so that Juno can target the ads it shows you. When you get to the end of the questions, click the Finish button. After displaying a couple of informational dialog boxes, you're finally ready to read and create e-mail with Juno.

Jump-Starting Juno

After you've set up your account, actually sending and receiving mail using Juno is absurdly easy.

Running Juno

To open Juno click the Start button and choose Programs⇨Juno (that's if you're using Windows 95 — if you're using Windows 3.1*x*, double-click the Juno icon). Juno asks you to choose or confirm your e-mail name and enter your password. (If multiple Juno accounts are accessed from your computer, you can choose the account by clicking the down arrow next to the Name box.)

The Welcome to Juno dialog box gives you the two options you saw when you first opened Juno to create your account, as well as some additional ones. If you want to use Juno to read and write mail, just check that your e-mail name is correct, type your password, and click O̲K or press Enter. You'll rarely if ever use the other options on this dialog box.

Do you see the check box labeled Enter Password Automatically? Are you tempted to click it so that you never have to enter your password again? If you click that check box, anyone using your computer can send e-mail with your name on it — and he or she can read and delete your mail.

Getting your mail

Juno is an *offline* e-mail package, which means that you are not connected to the mail server except when you choose to send or pick up e-mail. Juno does not automatically pick up your mail for you — you have to tell it when to dial in to see if you have new mail.

When Juno first opens, it displays the Check for New Mail dialog box, which asks you if you want to check for new mail. Click Y̲es to dial into Juno and pick up new mail. Click N̲o if you want to create new mail or read messages you have already received. Either way (although you may have to wait for Juno to dial in to pick up mail), you see the window in Figure 11-1.

You can only get your mail if you're not using your modem for anything else, which means that you can't be dialed in to an Internet service provider or be using fax software (even if it's only waiting for an incoming fax). But when your modem is free, picking up your mail is easy. You can either open Juno and click the Y̲es when it asks you if you want to check for new mail, or you can click the G̲et New Mail button on the Read tab when Juno is open. Also, when you send mail, Juno picks up new mail.

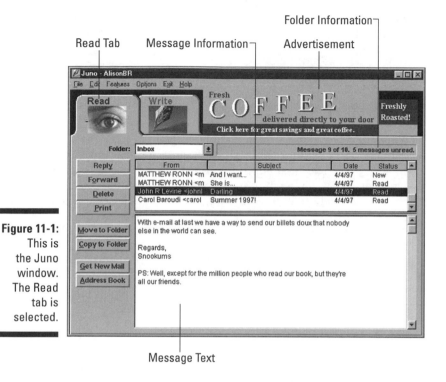

Read Tab   Message Information⌐   Advertisement   Folder Information⌐

Figure 11-1:
This is
the Juno
window.
The Read
tab is
selected.

Message Text

The Juno window

The first thing you notice about the Juno window is the huge tabs with full-color pictures: the Read and Write tabs. The next thing you notice is the advertisement. Remember? This is why you're getting free e-mail.

The Read tab shows you information about e-mail messages in your Inbox or in another folder. Near the top of the window is the message information including the name of the person who sent the message, the subject of the message, the date it was sent, and whether you've read it. A drop-down list displays the names of the folders. Often, as in Figure 11-1, you'll want to read the messages in the Inbox. To the right of the folder name is summary information about the folder — how many messages are in it, and how many have not been read. You also see which message is selected ("Message 9 of 10," for example).

The text of the selected message appears at the bottom of the window. To view a different message, click the message information in the top window. You can change the size of the two panes by clicking and dragging the divider between the message information pane and the message text pane.

After you've read a message, there are some things you may want to do with it: Respond to it (*reply,* in e-mail terms), forward it to someone else, or file it for future use.

Replying to a Message

To reply to a message, click the Repl_y button. The Reply Settings dialog box appears to ask you two questions. Decide if you want to send the reply to the sender only or to all the people who received the original message. You also need to decide if you want to include the text of the original message in the reply or not. If you do include the original text, each line of the original text is preceded with >. Make sure the lines that you write do not start with >. Type the reply and then click the _Send Mail message.

For more about the options you see when you click the _Send Mail button, see the section "Writing a Message," later in this chapter.

Forwarding a Message

To forward a message, click the F_orward button. Provide the address or alias of the person you're forwarding the message to. You can add to the message if you wish (telling the person why they might be interested in the message is always a good idea). Click the _Send Mail button to send the message.

Tossing Messages

To delete a message, select the message and press the Del key, or click the _Delete button on the Read tab. When you choose to delete a message, it is permanently deleted, not simply moved to a Wastebasket or Deleted folder as with some other e-mail packages.

Filing Your Messages

If you like to keep messages, you probably want to create folders to store them in. The Inbox is best used for incoming messages or messages that need a response. Other messages should be deleted or moved to a folder.

As you consider creating folders, think about how to logically file your mail so that you can find it later. (If you don't think you'll need to find it later, you should probably delete it.) Juno does not support hierarchical folder structures, so you can't create a folder within a folder.

Creating a new folder

You can create a new folder by choosing File➪Create folder and typing the name of the folder in the New folder name box on the Create Folder dialog box. You can also create a new folder as you copy or move a message to a folder. See the next section for details.

Moving a message to a folder

Move a message to a folder by selecting the message and clicking the Move to Folder button. The Move to Folder dialog box appears. Here, you can either select an exising folder or create a new one by typing a new folder name in the Move Message into box. Click OK to move the message to the selected folder.

If you prefer, you can *copy* a message to a folder by clicking the Copy to Folder button. The steps are exactly the same, except you end up with copies of the message in two places: the original folder (probably the Inbox) and the folder you selected on the Copy to Folder dialog box.

Viewing the contents of a folder

Once you've moved messages to folders, you have to take an additional step to see them again. Use the Folder box on the Read tab: Click the down arrow and choose the folder you want to view.

Writing a Message

Click the Write tab (shown in Figure 11-2) to create a message. Notice that the pictures on the tabs change: The Write tab changes from a pen to a pen writing a squiggly line, and the Read tab changes from an open eye to a closed eye.

Filling in the details

The Write tab of the Juno window consists of a number of boxes: To, Cc, Subject, and Message. You can use the mouse or the Tab key to move from one box to another. (The exception is the Message box. Once the cursor is in the Message box, pressing the Tab key moves the cursor to the next tab stop, not to the next box.) You must fill in the To box to send a message; the others are optional (which means that, yes, you can send an empty message, something done mostly by mistake).

The first step to creating a message is to address it. (Well, actually, you don't have to do this first, but if you don't know whom the message is for, why write it?) You must supply an Internet e-mail address or an alias for the person you want to send the message to in the To box. (See the section "Working with Addresses" later in this chapter if you need help.) If you're sending the message to more than one person, separate addresses in the To box with commas. To send a copy of the message to someone, provide his or her alias or e-mail address in the Cc box.

Next, provide a Subject for the message. The subject should tell the recipient what the message is about and should make it easy to find the information later if the message is filed.

Then write your message in the Message box. You can send the message by clicking the Send Mail button, but read on for some things you might do with your message before sending it.

Checking the spelling of a message

To check spelling before sending an outgoing message, click the Spell Check button after writing the message. If Juno finds misspelled words in the message, it displays the Spell Check window.

You can replace a misspelled word with a word in the Suggestions box by selecting the correctly spelled word and clicking the Replace button. If the correctly spelled word does not appear in the Suggestions box, type it into the Replace with box. If the word is actually correctly spelled, click Ignore All, or click the Dictionary button to add the word to the dictionary. You can also choose to Ignore the word just once, Replace All instances of the misspelled word with the selected word in the Suggestions box, or Cancel the spell check.

Filing a draft message

You may be working on a message that you're not ready to send — maybe you have to double-check the address of the recipient or check some facts. To save a draft copy of a message, choose File⇨Save draft of message or press Ctrl+S. The Save Message Draft dialog box appears, telling you your message has been saved. Click OK to do a new task in Juno. The message disappears from the Write tab.

When you're ready to work on the message again, choose File⇨Retrieved saved draft or press Ctrl+R. The Retrieve from Draft dialog box appears. Select the message you want to work on and click OK. The message appears on the Write tab.

Sending a message

Remember that Juno is an offline e-mail package, which means that you only dial in to the server for brief periods. To send a message, you have to dial in. However, if you're writing a bunch of messages, you don't have to dial in to the server as you finish each one. Instead, you can collect finished messages in the Outbox and send them all at once.

To send a message, click the Send Mail button on the Write tab. Juno displays the Send Mail dialog box.

You have two choices: You can store the message in your Outbox and send it later (by clicking the Put Message in Outbox button), or you can dial in and send it now (by clicking the Get and Send Mail Now button). There are advantages and disadvantages to each option: If you put the mail in your

Outbox, you can edit it if you change your mind about anything you wrote; however, you have to remember to actually send it (although Juno helps you with that). If you send the message right away, you don't have to worry about forgetting to send it, but you can't edit it again, and you have to wait for Juno to send your message and check for new mail before you can do anything else with your computer.

One of the most important advantages of putting messages in the Outbox is being able to edit them. If you need to edit a message in the Outbox, choose File⇨Retrieve message from Outbox or press Ctrl+E. The Retrieve from Outbox dialog box appears. Choose the message you want to edit and click OK. The message is displayed on the Write tab.

To send messages stored in the Outbox you can

- ✔ Click the Send Mail button on the Write tab and click the Get and Send Mail Now button on the Send Mail dialog box.

- ✔ Click the Get New Mail button on the Read tab and then click the Get and Send Mail button.

Saving a copy of messages you write

By default, messages you send are not available to you to read after they've been sent. If you want to save a copy of all outgoing mail, choose Options⇨Automatically save all sent mail. (When this option is selected, it appears on the menu with a check mark.)

To see mail you have sent, click the Read tab, click the arrow next to the folder name, and choose Sent.

Changing your mind about a message

If you change your mind about sending a message you've written, you can delete it. How you do so depends on where the message is.

- ✔ If the message is displayed on the Write tab, click the Clear button to delete it. You see the Clear Message dialog box, which asks you if you're sure you want to delete the message. Click Yes.

- ✔ If you saved a draft of the message, choose File⇨Retrieve saved draft from the menu. Select the message on the Retrieve from Draft dialog box and click the Delete button. Click Yes when Juno asks if you're sure you want to delete the message.

> ✔ If the message is in the Outbox, choose File⇨Retrieve message from Outbox. Select the message on the Retrieve from Outbox dialog box and click the Delete button. Click Yes when Juno asks if you're sure you want to delete the message.

If the message has already been sent, you're out of luck.

Working with Addresses

Always having to type an Internet address into the To box on the Write tab gets old fast, as does trying to remember e-mail addresses. And you may want to create a group of addresses, called a *Mailing List,* so that you can send a message to the whole group without having to name each recipient individually. Fortunately, Juno has an address book to make managing your e-mail addresses easier.

Adding a name to the address book

To open the address book, click the Address Book button on the Read tab. You may see a dialog box with some introductory information about the address book. You can click the check box at the bottom of the dialog box if you don't want to see this box in the future. Once you get past the informational dialog box, you see the address book, shown in Figure 11-3.

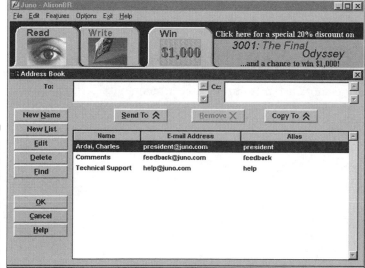

Figure 11-3:
The Juno Address Book lists a person's name, alias, and e-mail address.

The address book lists people by name, e-mail address, and alias. You can sort by any of these three categories by clicking the gray bar at the top of the column. (In other words, if you want to sort the address book by e-mail address, click the gray bar that reads E-Mail Address.) An alias is a kind of nickname — you can send messages to people by using their aliases in the To box on the Write tab if you have entered their e-mail addresses in the address book.

To add a name to the address book, click the New Name button. You see the New Name dialog box, where you fill in the First Name, Last Name, E-Mail address, and Alias of the person you are adding. When you have finished typing the information, click the OK button to add the new information to the address book. Juno asks you if you would like to add another entry to the address book. Click Yes to see the blank New Name dialog box, or click No to return to the address book.

Using the address book to address a message

The reason the address book is convenient is because it gives you some shortcuts to use when you're addressing messages. Once you have some names in the address book, you can use aliases in the To box instead of typing full addresses. If you don't remember an alias, you can click the Address Book button, select the person you want to send a message to, and click the Send To or Copy To button. When you've added the people that you want to send the message to in the To and Cc boxes, click the OK button to write the message.

Dealing with Attachments

Juno does not currently support file attachments. Keep an eye out for messages from Juno about updates of the software. Maybe they will implement this feature in the future.

Chapter 12

UNIX Mail: Pine

- -

In This Chapter

▶ Dealing with UNIX, if you absolutely must

▶ Using Pine, the latest, greatest UNIX e-mail program

▶ Fiddling with other UNIX mail features, like automatic mail forwarding

- -

*W*e assume that you have a very good reason for choosing to use a UNIX shell provider. Either you had no choice at all (UNIX shell accounts are the only accounts available to you either economically or geographically), or your perverse nature propels you toward the obscure, arcane, user-hostile environments where Men are Men but *Nerds are Kings*.

Getting Your Shell Account

One reason you might be using a UNIX system may be that you have access through school or work, and that's what's available. If that's the case, signing up, if not automatic, is probably pretty straightforward. Look for somebody with the title System Administrator.

If you have to pay for your shell account, try to find a service with real service. UNIX Internet providers are widely available, and most major cities have them now. If you're a first-time user, you probably will want to call the provider and talk to a live human being to get your account set up and learn the appropriate settings for your communications software. If the person on the other end of the phone is less than helpful, look for another service.

Shell Shock: Getting Connected

Unlike commercial online service providers that give you a disk with their software all configured and installed and ready to stick into your machine, UNIX shell providers tend to resemble secured posts with armed sentries waiting for you to provide the secret password before they blow your head off. Getting connected is not always that bad, but it can seem that way.

Shell providers assume that you have some kind of communications package installed and that you know how to set it up to dial in to an account. Maybe you do, and maybe you don't. If you're not an experienced computer user, we strongly suggest that you find a friend who is experienced or else get help from whomever sold you your computer. Even experienced computer users sometimes have difficulty with this part.

If you don't have any friends or if you're the first kid on your block to try to do this, we highly recommend *Modems For Dummies,* 3rd Edition, by Tina Rathbone (IDG Books Worldwide, Inc.). You don't need all 464 pages, but chances are that she'll answer most of your questions. The 464 pages attest to the fact that getting set up is not so easy, and because we have to stop writing this book at some point, we don't cover it all here.

Your modem probably came with some communications software, and that software probably came with a manual. Can you find it? We're not necessarily saying that it will help, but it probably won't hurt. Windows 3.1 users can use the Windows Terminal program that comes as a standard part of Windows. (It's not great, but it'll do.) Windows 95 users can fire up HyperTerminal (click the Start button and choose Programs⇨Accessories⇨HyperTerminal). Mac users can use Mac Terminal, MicroPhone, or whatever software came with their modem.

Using some combination of friends, sales support, manuals, and prayer, people really do manage to get themselves connected. You'll know you're there when

 ✔ You choose P̲hone⇨D̲ial (or your package's equivalent) and you hear your modem dialing a number (if your modem has a speaker — not all of them do).

 ✔ You see intelligible text displayed on your screen.

 ✔ When you type your response, what you think you're typing appears on-screen as you type it, with a little tolerance for typos and hidden passwords.

That's it. Congratulations — the really hard part is over.

Yikes! It's UNIX

If you have a UNIX shell account, you have to deal, unfortunately, with UNIX. For the purpose of this chapter, we assume that you don't know how to use UNIX already. When you use the Internet through a UNIX shell provider, the more UNIX you know, the better. So if you want to make your Internet life more fun, learn more UNIX. Get a copy of *UNIX For Dummies,* 3rd Edition, brought to you by people you know and trust (and published by IDG Books Worldwide, Inc.).

We'll assume that you know how to log in, up to the point that you are faced with one of the most daunting sights in all of computerdom: the UNIX prompt.

It's waiting for you

The UNIX prompt is UNIX's way of telling you that it is waiting breathlessly for you to type a command. UNIX prompts vary — in fact, you can change it to *Yes, great one?* if you are in the mood. Your UNIX prompt is usually a single character, like *$* or *%*. UNIX aficionados can tell a lot about what kind of UNIX you use just from the prompt, but you don't have to worry about varieties of UNIX if all you want to do is deal with your e-mail.

If you're a Mac or Windows user, put away your mouse. Dial-up UNIX is a mouse-free environment, and trying to use it will only frustrate you. When we talk about putting your cursor somewhere in a UNIX program, we mean use the arrow keys or navigation keys inside the program to move the cursor. Pointing and clicking your mouse won't move the cursor. Sorry.

Telling it what to do

To give UNIX a command, you wait until you see the UNIX prompt, type the command exactly right, and press the Return or Enter key. (We call it Enter in this chapter.) To type a command exactly right, you have to type the correct character, correctly capitalized — UNIX makes a big distinction between capital and small letters. If we tell you to type **pine** and you type **PINE**, it's not going to work. Hint: Most UNIX commands are in lowercase.

Here are some rules that apply to typing UNIX commands:

- ✔ If you make a typing mistake, press the Backspace key, or try Delete or Ctrl+H.

- ✔ To cancel the entire command before you have pressed Enter, press Ctrl+U, or try Ctrl+K. The command disappears.

- ✔ When you finish typing the command, press the Enter or Return key. (Okay, we said that already.)

- ✔ If you type a command that UNIX doesn't know, or if you mistype a command, you see a message saying that UNIX couldn't find the command.

✔ Don't type any extra spaces in the middle of commands. Do, however, type a space *after* the command and any other information that we tell you to type on the command line.

✔ If you're stuck, type **help**. Not all UNIX systems have a help command, but it's worth a try. All UNIX systems have online manuals, accessible via the **man** command, but they are written in Afghani, so forget about them unless you're extremely desperate.

✔ Many UNIX shell account providers have created files with lots of useful information for new users. Make sure that you read everything your provider or system administrator suggests before you take the next step.

✔ If you're really stuck, send an e-mail message to staff. If you're even stucker than that, call your Internet provider or system administrator on the phone and pose your question as calmly as possible to a real person.

Pico?? What's that?

To write an e-mail message, you use a text editing program. One very common text editor in the world of UNIX is Pico, an easy, friendly, and all-around preferable text editor voted "best of breed" by the authors of this book.

If you're not sure whether your UNIX system has the Pico editor, type the following command when you see the UNIX prompt: pico.

Don't forget to press Enter. If you get an error message, Pico is not available. If you see a screen with a line that starts *UW PICO(tm)* at the top, you're in! Press Ctrl+X to leave Pico.

If you don't have Pico, you're going to need help learning one of the tougher UNIX editors like emacs or vi. If you find yourself in this pickle, ask your system administrator if he or she could get you a copy of pico. If not, you might want to invest in *UNIX For Dummies,* which could help you with a lot more than editing text.

Pico for dummies

When you are in Pico, you can just type along merrily, using the arrow keys to move around as needed. When you are done typing your message, press Ctrl+X to leave. If you haven't already saved your message, Pico asks you if you want to do so.

Table 12-1 lists some particularly useful Pico commands.

Table 12-1	Particular Pico Commands
Keystrokes	*What They Do*
Ctrl+A	Moves to the beginning of the line
Ctrl+D	Deletes the current character
Ctrl+E	Moves to the end of the line
Ctrl+G	Gets help
Ctrl+O	Saves your text
Ctrl+T	Checks your spelling
Ctrl+X	Exits

Using Pine to Read Your Mail

Way before the Internet became chic, folks used e-mail on networks of UNIX workstations, so UNIX e-mail lore runs deep. The easiest e-mail program you can find on a UNIX system (in our opinion) is Pine. The folks at the University of Washington in Seattle created Pine, which began as a mutant version of Elm, at the time the best available e-mail program, making it even easier to use than Elm. A particularly neat thing about Pine is that it can handle an extended version of mail called *MIME,* which lets you include all kinds of files with your messages.

If your system doesn't have Pine, complain to your Internet provider or system administrator (and tell him or her we sent you). Because Pine is available for free, it's available on lots of UNIX-based systems, including most Internet shell providers. Assure your Internet provider or system administrator that you will be back 10 times a day with questions if you can't use Pine.

Pine originally stood for *Pine is nearly elm,* but now its authors, pumped up with self-esteem (not misplaced), proudly say that it stands for *Pine is NOT elm.*

Do you have mail ?

You can tell whether you have messages in your mailbox because UNIX displays this message when you log in:

```
You have mail.
```

Running Pine

To run Pine, just type **pine** and press Enter. You see a screen like the one in Figure 12-1.

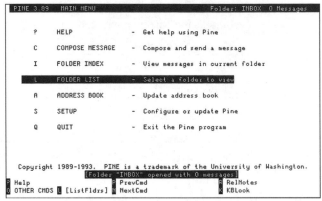

```
PINE 3.89   MAIN MENU                        Folder: INBOX  0 Messages

        ?     HELP              - Get help using Pine

        C     COMPOSE MESSAGE   - Compose and send a message

        I     FOLDER INDEX      - View messages in current folder

        L     FOLDER LIST       - Select a folder to view

        A     ADDRESS BOOK      - Update address book

        S     SETUP             - Configure or update Pine

        Q     QUIT              - Exit the Pine program


        Copyright 1989-1993.  PINE is a trademark of the University of Washington.
                        [Folder "INBOX" opened with 0 messages]
? Help                        P PrevCmd                      R RelNotes
O OTHER CMDS L [ListFldrs] N NextCmd                         K KBLock
```

Figure 12-1: Pine shows you a nice, simple menu.

Figure 12-1 shows you Pine's *main menu,* with a list of its favorite commands. Pine uses one-letter commands. Notice that one of the commands is highlighted. You can also choose commands by moving the highlight (pressing the up- and down-arrow keys) and then pressing Enter. Toward the bottom of the screen, Pine tells you how many messages are in your inbox.

If you are using UNIX by way of a communications program, watch out for which terminal type your program is emulating. Pine works fine if your program emulates a VT100 terminal but not so well if it emulates an ANSI terminal. You can usually change which terminal type your program emulates. From the UNIX prompt, type **set TERM = vt100** or **export TERM=vt100**. (If one doesn't work, try the other.)

Leaving Pine

After you finish using Pine, press q to quit. Pine asks whether you really, really want to quit (it's so sure that you just pressed q accidentally). Press y to leave. If you have left messages in your inbox that you have read but not deleted, Pine asks whether you want to move the messages to the read-messages folder — press y or n. If you deleted messages, it asks whether you want them to be expunged (really deleted) now — again, press y or n. Finally, you leave.

Sending messages

You're in Pine and you're ready to send some e-mail. No problem. Pine ordinarily runs the Pico text editor unless you or someone else has configured it otherwise. To send a message, follow these steps:

1. **Press c to compose a new message.**

   Pine displays a screen with prompts for To (the address to send the message to), Cc (addresses to send copies of the message to), Attchmnt (names of files to attach to the message), and Subject (the subject line).

   You can move from blank to blank by pressing the Tab key or the up-and down-arrow keys. You type the text of the message underneath the line that says — Message Text —.

   At the bottom of the screen is a list of the control keys you can use. (The caret in front of a letter means that you press Ctrl with the letter — for example, ^G means that you press Ctrl+G.)

2. **Enter the addresses on the To and Cc lines and the subject on the Subject line.**

   You can enter several addresses on the same line by separating them with commas.

3. **If you want to attach a file to the message, enter the filename in the Attchmnt (attachment) blank.**

   Alternatively, you can press Ctrl+J to tell Pine that you want to attach a file. It prompts you for the filename. The file has to be on your UNIX account. It can't be on the PC or Mac that you use to dial in to your UNIX account — you have to upload the file to your UNIX account before you can attach it to a message.

4. **Type the text of the message.**

5. **When you are ready to send the message, press Ctrl+X. Pine asks whether you really want to send it — just press y.**

   Pine sends the message and displays the main menu again.

   If you decide not to send the message after all, you can press Ctrl+C to cancel it.

Here are some cool things you can do while you are writing your message:

   ✔ For lots of helpful information about how to use Pine, you can press Ctrl+G. Pine has complete online help.

✔ You can even check the spelling of your message — just press Ctrl+T. Pine checks all the words in your message against its dictionary and highlights each word it can't find.

✔ You can include text from a text file. Move your cursor where you want the text to appear and press Ctrl+R. If you use Pine on a shell Internet provider, you have to upload the file from your own computer to the provider before you can include it. One way you can get around the upload is to open the file, select all the text, copy it, and then return to Pine and paste in the text you just copied.

Reading your messages

At the top of the main menu is a status line, and at the right end of it Pine tells you which folder you are viewing and how many messages it has (more on folders in a minute). Your *inbox* folder contains incoming messages you haven't read.

To read your incoming messages:

1. **Press i to see the messages in the current folder.**

   (This step assumes that you haven't changed to another folder. We cover how to change folders in "Looking in a folder" in this chapter.)

   Pine displays a list of messages. You see one line of information per message, beginning with a + if the message was sent directly to you (not cc'd, for example). The next character is N for new messages you haven't read, D for messages you've deleted, and A for messages you have answered.

   You also see a message number, the date the message was sent, who sent it, how big it is (in characters), and the subject.

2. **To read a message, highlight it.**

   You can press the up- and down-arrow keys or p (for previous) and n (for next).

3. **When you've highlighted the message you want to read, press v to view it.**

   Pine displays the text of the message.

When you are looking at a message, here are some things you can do:

✔ Forward the message to someone else by pressing f. You see the regular Pine screen for composing a message with the text of the original message included in the text of this message.

✔ Reply to the person who sent the message by pressing r. Pine automatically addresses the message to the person who sent the original one.

✔ Delete the message by pressing d. The message doesn't disappear right away, but it is marked with a D on the list of messages. When you exit from Pine, your deleted messages really get deleted. If you change your mind, you can undelete a message by pressing u.

✔ Move to the next message by pressing n. Or move back to the previous one by pressing p.

✔ Return to Pine's main menu by pressing m.

✔ Press ? to see Pine's online help.

Take a look at the list of commands at the bottom of the screen. Whenever you see O OTHER CMDS, more commands are available than can fit on the menu. Press o to see more commands.

Saving messages

Pine lets you create many folders in which to put your messages so that you can save them in an organized manner. To save a message in a folder, press s when you are looking at it or when it is highlighted on the list of messages.

If you save a message to a folder that doesn't exist, Pine asks whether you want to create that folder. Press y to do so. After you move a message to a folder, Pine automatically deletes it from your inbox. Very tidy.

Looking in a folder

After you've put messages in folders, you may want to look at them later. When you see Pine's main menu, you can press l (the lowercase letter *L*) to select which folder to view. Pine automatically makes several folders for you, including the ones in this list:

✔ **INBOX:** Your incoming messages; messages remain here until you delete or move them

✔ **sent-mail:** Messages you've sent

✔ **saved-messages:** A place to save messages before you send them

Highlight the one you want and press Enter. Pine lists the messages in the folder.

What printer?

If you are dialing in to a shell Internet provider to run Pine, pressing y to print your message usually doesn't work. The reason is that Pine is running on your provider's UNIX computer and the message would print on a printer connected to that computer, which is probably nowhere near where you are.

Here is the normal way to print a message on your own computer:

1. Save the message as a text file.

2. Download the file, using whichever method works with your Internet provider.

3. Print it from your own computer.

What a drag — but wait! If you use Procomm or Kermit on a PC, or MacKermit or VersaTerm on a Macintosh, you are in luck. These programs are so smart that Pine can tell them to print directly on your computer's printer after you tell Pine to display the message. Ask a local Pine expert to set you up for direct printing on your PC.

You can make more folders by moving messages into them (as described in the previous section, "Saving messages").

Saving messages as text

If you want to use the text of a message elsewhere or download it to your own computer, save it in a text file first:

1. View the message or highlight it on the list of messages.

2. Press e.

Pine asks for the filename in which to save the message. (It puts the file in your home directory.)

3. Enter the filename and press Enter.

That's it — Pine copies the text into a file.

Printing messages

To print a message, press y when you are viewing the message or when the message is highlighted on the list of messages.

Creating your own address book

It can certainly be annoying to type long, complicated Internet addresses. Let Pine do it for you — set up an address book.

When you press a at the Pine menu, you switch to *address book mode* (it even says ADDRESS BOOK at the top of the screen). If you have already entered some addresses, Pine lists them.

When you finish fooling with your address book, press m to return to Pine's main menu.

To create an entry in your address book when you are in address book mode:

1. **Press a.**

   Pine asks for the full name of the person.

2. **Type the person's last name, a comma, and then the first name, and press Enter.**

   Pine asks for a nickname (the name you type when you address mail).

3. **Type the nickname. (Make it short but easy to remember.)**

   Finally, Pine asks for the person's e-mail address.

4. **Enter the e-mail address just as you would when you address a message.**

Pine stores the entry in your address book and lists it on the address book screen.

If you make a mistake, you can edit an entry later. Just highlight it on the list of addresses and press e to edit it.

You can also create an address book entry directory from the address of a message. If you are looking at a message from someone whose address you want to save, just press t. Pine prompts you for the person's full name (it might even suggest it, if it's part of the message header), nickname, and e-mail address. (Pine suggests the address of the sender of the current message.)

Attaching files to messages

You may want to send the following two types of files along with a message:

✔ Text files, composed entirely of plain text characters

✔ Other files, such as word-processing documents, spreadsheets, or graphics files

E-mail can include only plain characters, so if you want to send something other than text, you have to convert it into text temporarily, send it, and have the recipient unconvert it. Luckily, Pine does most of this for you using a system called MIME (_m_ultipurpose _I_nternet _m_ail _e_xtension). MIME remembers not only the name of the attached file but also what type of file it is.

Before sending an attached file to someone, make sure that he or she can decode it at the other end. Not all mail readers can understand and decode MIME attachments. Windows and Mac mail programs, such as Eudora and Pine can, but most versions of elm and the ancient UNIX `mail` program cannot. So ask your intended recipient first!

Including text in your message

If you want to send a text file to someone, you can include it as part of the text of the message. When you are composing the message, move the cursor to where you want the file to appear. Then press Ctrl+R and type the name of the file. The text appears in your message.

Attaching files

To attach one or more files to a message (by using MIME):

1. **Compose a message as usual.**

   It contains any text you want to send along with the file (or files).

2. **Press Ctrl+J to tell Pine that you want to attach a file.**

3. **When Pine asks for the filename, type it.**

   If the file isn't in your home directory, type in the full pathname.

4. **When Pine asks for an attachment comment, enter a short description of the file.**

   Depending on the mail reading program that your recipient uses, this description may show up somewhere.

   Pine displays the filename and description on the `Attchmnt` line of the screen. Pine also numbers this attachment 1 (in case you want to attach other files, too).

5. **Repeat Steps 2 through 4 for each file you want to attach.**

6. **Send the file as usual.**

Decoding attached messages

When you receive a message that contains MIME attachments, the message begins with a list of the attachments like the following:

```
Parts/attachments:
  1 Shown    5 lines Text
  2 OK    478 lines Text, "Table of contents"
  3 OK  1926 lines Text, "Draft of Chapter 2"
```

Then comes the text that was typed in the message. Following the text are instructions for viewing each attachment, similar to the following:

```
[Part 2, "Table of contents" Text 478 lines]
[Not Shown. Use the "V" command to view or save this part]
```

If the attached file consists of nothing but plain text, Pine can show it to you. Press v to view an attachment. Pine asks which attachment you want to see. Actually, what it lists as attachment 1 is the text of the message. The first attached file is attachment 2.

Type a number.

If you press v to view the attachment, Pine displays it on the screen.

If you press s to save the attachment as a file, Pine asks for the filename to use. It suggests the name the file had when it was originally attached to the message.

When you finish looking at the attachment, press e to exit from the viewer.

If the attached file consists of other information, such as a word-processing document or a graphics file, save it and then look at it using the appropriate program.

Other Cool Stuff about UNIX Mail

Here are some other UNIX mail tricks that you can use.

Sign here

You can make a *signature file,* a file that contains text for your mail program to include at the end of every message. The file must be called `.signature` and be in your home directory.

Use your text editor (remember Pico, emacs, and vi?) to make a signature file. Keep it short (no more than four lines long), and include your name, your e-mail address, other address information you want everyone to know, and (if there's room) a pithy or philosophical message that characterizes you.

To create or edit a file with a text editor, type the name of the file on the command line. For example, to create or edit the signature file using the Pico editor, type `pico.signature`.

After you've created a signature file, you don't have to type your signature at the end of every message. To test it, send a message to yourself and see how the signature looks. The signature appears at the bottom of the message when you compose it. To omit the signature information from a message, just delete it.

Forward, mail!

If you have several accounts, you may enjoy collecting all your incoming e-mail in one account and reading it all at the same time. UNIX makes this easy. To tell UNIX to forward all of your mail to another account, use a text editor to make a file named `.forward` in your home directory. (Yes, the name starts with a dot.) The file must contain one line of text, the e-mail address to which you want to forward your mail.

As soon as this file exists, your incoming mail starts bouncing along to the forwarding address. To turn off forwarding, delete the `.forward` file or rename it (as, say, `forward` without the dot).

Sorry, I'm gone

When you are on vacation, your e-mail can pile up alarmingly. And folks who have never met you in person may not realize that you are going to be gone for a week at your mountain-top meditation retreat. If you'd like to let everyone know that you are gone, and when you'll be back, you can use the *vacation program.*

To run the vacation program, write a form letter that you'd like to be sent in response to any mail you receive. Store the message in a text file in your home directory called `.vacation.msg`. It might say something like

```
Thanks for your e-mail, but I'm meditating
16 hours a day high atop Mt. Monadnock. I'll
be back on Thursday the 8th, at which time
I'll sift through my mountains of e-mail and
eventually get back to you.
```

Then, type

```
vacation -i
```

This command initializes your *vacation database* that tracks who's sent you mail. Finally, you have to arrange to pass your mail to the vacation program. Create a file called `.forward` that contains

```
\yourname, "|/usr/bin/vacation"
```

Instead of *yourname*, put your user name. This file tells the mail system to deliver incoming mail to your regular mailbox as normal and also to call the vacation program for each incoming message.

Each time a mail message arrives for you, the vacation program replies with your canned response. If the person's already received the canned response within the past week, it doesn't send it again.

When you get back from vacation, delete the `.forward` file to turn off the vacation program. Then start working your way through the messages stored in your incoming mailbox.

Your Automatic Secretary

If you get a lot of mail, you'll probably find that wading through all of your incoming mail starts to become a chore. One thing you can do is arrange to sort your incoming mail into folders based on the sender and subject. This lets you deal with mail one category at a time and also lets you decide which incoming mailboxes to read and when.

Before you try setting up mail sorting, ask your system administrator whether he or she has installed the widely used *procmail* mail sorting system as the standard mail delivery program. If not, the instructions that follow won't work. You can still arrange to sort mail, but setup is considerably harder. See our *Internet Secrets* for the gruesome details.

Setting up to sort incoming mail involves two steps:

- ✔ Creating the incoming mailboxes
- ✔ Defining the sorting criteria

You create the incoming mailboxes in Pine, and you create a file of "rules" for procmail to control the sorting criteria.

Making the mailboxes

To create the mailboxes

1. **Run Pine and press L to see the list of message folders.**

2. **Move the cursor to INBOX.**

3. **Press A to add a new mailbox.**

4. **Pine asks the name of the server to use.**

   Press Enter to tell it to use the very computer that you're logged into.

5. **Pine asks for the name of the folder to add.**

   This folder name is actually the name of the file to use. Generally, you want to put all of your mail folders in your mail directory, so if you want to call the folder *fred*, type `mail/fred` to put it in the mail directory.

   UNIX filenames should consist of lowercase letters, digits, and underscores. (You can use other characters, but confusion can ensue.)

6. **Pine asks for the folder's nickname.**

   This is the name that Pine will use to refer to the folder. You can type any characters you want — for example `Fred Smith` if that's who the mail will be from.

That's it. You can create as many incoming folders as you want. If you decide you don't want one of your folders, just move the cursor to its name and press d.

Saying what to sort

This part is a little trickier. You have to create a pattern file for procmail, a program written by a German guy who evidently believed that using any more characters than are absolutely necessary is a terrible waste of time.

The pattern file is called `.procmailrc`. You create or edit it by typing `pico .procmailrc`.

The file consists of *recipes,* each of which identifies a category of mail and what to do with it. Here's a typical recipe:

```
:0
* From:.*fred@flint
mail/fred
```

The `:0` marks the first line of a recipe (we said he didn't like to waste characters).

The second line starts with an asterisk to mark it as a *pattern*. Procmail scans the headers of each incoming message to see if the pattern matches. Patterns can be extremely complicated (they're the same as the ones used by the *egrep* program, if you know what that is), but for most purposes, you can get by with only a little knowledge of patternology. The most important thing to know is that `.U` is a wild card that matches anything. So, for example, the preceding pattern matches any line that contains `From:` and also `fred@flint`.

The third line says in what file to save matching messages. Use the same folder name (not nickname) you gave to Pine.

A real `.procmailrc` file usually contains several recipes, and also some comments to remind you what your sorting criteria are supposed to mean:

```
# identify mail from Fred
:0
* From:.*fred@flint
mail/fred

# this sorts by the subject
:0
* Subject:.*meeting
mail/meeting

# this sorts by who the mail is addressed to, usually
# the best way to identify mail to mailing lists
:0
* To:.*bread-bakers
mail/bread
```

Using multiple folders

Once you've created your multiple folders, Pine makes them easy to use. After you open your inbox, you can use the Tab key to find the next new message. When no more new messages are in the current folder, Tab looks through the rest of your incoming folders for new mail, so you just Tab your way through until Pine tells you that you have no new mail.

Each time Pine finds a folder with new mail, it asks you whether you want to look in that folder or continue looking in other folders, so you're in charge of when you read what.

Incoming folders work the same as any other folders, so you can save messages from one folder into another the same way we discussed in "Saving messages" (earlier in the chapter), using the S key.

One minor disadvantage of multiple incoming folders is that UNIX only reports "You have mail" when you have mail in your main inbox. You have to use Pine to look and see if you have mail in any other incoming folder.

Chapter 13
Other Popular E-Mail Programs

· ·

In This Chapter

▶ Outlook 97

▶ Microsoft Exchange

▶ Pegasus

· ·

Contributed by Alison Barrows

*T*here are many other e-mail packages in the world. In this chapter, we cover how to do all the basic e-mail tasks with some of the most common e-mail packages.

Outlook 97

Outlook 97 is the newest addition to Microsoft's family of e-mail products. It follows in the footsteps of Microsoft Mail and Exchange, which are covered later in this chapter. Outlook 97 comes with Office 97, but you can also buy it separately. Outlook is more than just an e-mail program. It also stores addresses (the snail mail type), phone numbers, and tasks, and it keeps track of appointments, among other things. Its e-mail capabilities are impressive. Even though Outlook is a multifeatured product, Microsoft didn't skimp on e-mail features. We cover how to use some of Outlook's more basic e-mail features in this section.

You may use Outlook because you use a Microsoft Mail system at work and you graduated up from Microsoft Mail or Exchange. However, Outlook works with any POP mail server, meaning that you can use it if you have an e-mail account with a SLIP or PPP Internet connection.

Looking out an Outlook window

Figure 13-1 shows a view of Outlook. The bar on the left is the Outlook bar. It contains icons for your Inbox and Calendar, as well as other tasks you may do in Outlook. The number in parentheses next to the Inbox is the number of unread e-mail messages in your inbox. In the figure, the left side of the Outlook window shows the contents of the Inbox. You know it's the Inbox because it's labeled. That label is also called the Folder Banner and can be used to display other Outlook folders.

In Figure 13-1, some messages are displayed with *AutoPreview,* which displays the first three lines of unread messages. Messages that have not been read are displayed in bold and with an unopened envelope to their left. Messages with attachments (like the first message in the figure) appear with a paper clip. The second message in the figure is a meeting request — the sender has to be using Outlook or Exchange to send a meeting request. The third message was marked urgent by the sender; however, it's only a warning about the bogus Good Times "virus." Messages that have been read appear in normal type with an open envelope to their left.

E-mailing with Outlook

Basic e-mail tasks are pretty straightforward in Outlook:

┌Outlook Bar   Folder Banner

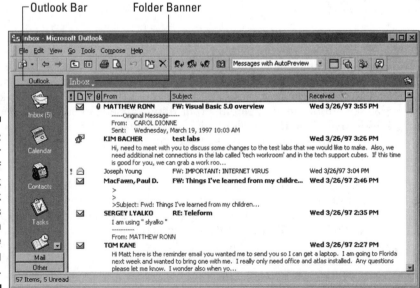

Figure 13-1:
Your
version of
Outlook
might look
like this
when
you're
reading
your mail.

- **Creating and sending a new e-mail message:** Create a new message by clicking the Create New Message button, the first button on the toolbar, or pressing Ctrl+N. (If you are not in the Inbox or another mail folder, use the drop-down list on the first toolbar button to choose <u>M</u>ail Message). Outlook spawns a whole separate message window — a window that gets its own button on the Windows 95 taskbar. Fill the To and Subject fields and write the message. Send it by clicking the <u>S</u>end button, the first button on the message window toolbar.

- **Reading a message:** Open a message to read it by double-clicking the message in the Outlook window. When you have finished reading a message, you can close the message window or use the Previous Item or Next Item button to view another message.

- **Replying to a message:** Reply to a message by selecting it and clicking the Reply button, the first of three buttons with human heads on them. When you use this method, the reply goes only to the sender of the original message. To reply to all the people who received the original message, click the Reply to All button, which is to the right of the Reply button. You can also reply to a message when it is open (that is, you're reading it) by clicking the <u>R</u>eply button on the message window toolbar.

- **Forwarding a message:** Forward a message by selecting it or opening it and clicking the Forward button.

- **Printing a message:** Print a message by selecting it or opening it and clicking the Print button. To use options on the Print dialog box, choose <u>F</u>ile⇨<u>P</u>rint to display the Print dialog box.

- **Deleting a message:** Delete a message by selecting it and pressing the Del key or clicking the Delete button on the toolbar. When a message is deleted, it goes into the folder called Deleted. If you deleted the message by mistake, you can move it out of the Deleted folder. Deleted messages remain in the Deleted folder until you empty the folder. (Right-click the Deleted icon on the Outlook Bar and choose Empty "Deleted Items" Folder.)

   If you checked the Empty the Deleted Items folder upon exiting option on the General tab of the Options dialog box, the Deleted Items folder will be emptied each time you close Outlook.

You can use Word as your e-mail editor when you use Outlook. This allows you to take advantage of the automatic spell-checking and formatting features (although a recipient must have Outlook or another e-mail package that reads rich text e-mail messages to see the formatting). If you have Word and you're not already using it as your editor, choose <u>T</u>ools⇨<u>O</u>ptions, click the E-Mail tab, and click the Use Microsoft <u>W</u>ord as the e-mail editor option so that a check mark appears in the check box.

Outlook allows you to file messages in different folders. You can move a message to a folder by selecting the message and clicking the Move to Folder button on the toolbar. Alternatively, right-click the message and choose <u>M</u>ove to Folder from the shortcut menu. Double-click the folder you want to move the message to in the Move Items window. You can create a new folder at any time by choosing <u>F</u>ile➪<u>N</u>ew Folder from the menu.

If you like to see the folder structure all of the time, click the fifth button on the toolbar, the Folder List button. You can then view the contents of any folder by clicking the folder name in the folder list. Another way to display the contents of another folder is to click the Folder banner and choose a folder from the drop-down list.

Working with attachments

Outlook can handle both MIME and uuencoded attachments. Attachments appear in messages as icons. To attach a file to a message, create the message, put the cursor where you want the icon for the attached file to appear, and click the Insert File button on the message window toolbar (it looks like a paper clip) to display the Insert File dialog box. Alternatively, choose <u>I</u>nsert➪<u>Fi</u>le from the menu to display the Insert File dialog box. Make sure that the As attac<u>h</u>ment option is checked. Double-click the file you want to attach to the message and send the message as usual. Another option is to skip all the steps you just read and drag the file you want to attach from My Computer or Windows Explorer and drop it in the message window.

An alternative to sending a file with a message is to *link* the file to the message. A linked message is not included in the message, so it doesn't take up hard disk space. Instead, double-clicking the icon for a linked file opens a file in a specified location. Linking is a better option than including the file in the message when

- ✔ You are sending a large file to a number of people
- ✔ All of the recipients have access to a network drive or some other shared resource where you can store the file you want them to have.

To link a file, follow the steps for attaching a file. On the Insert File dialog box, click the Lin<u>k</u> to file option so that a check mark appears.

When you receive a message with a file attached or linked to it, you will see an icon in the message. To open the attachment, double-click the icon. To save the attachment without opening it, right-click the icon and choose <u>S</u>ave As from the shortcut menu. Edit the file and folder names if necessary, and click OK.

Outlook is reluctant to tell you if you're sending MIME or uuencoded attachments. By default it uses MIME. If you need to send a uuencoded attachment or need to be sure which kind of attachment you're sending, follow these steps:

1. **Choose Tools➪Services from the menu to display the Services dialog box.**

2. **Select Internet Mail on the Services tab.**

   If you don't see Internet Mail in the list box called "The following information services are set up in this profile," you may need to add it.

3. **Click the Properties button to display the Internet Mail dialog box.**

4. **Click the Message Format button to display the Message Format dialog box.**

   If the Use Mime when sending messages option has a check mark, then attachments are being sent with MIME; otherwise, message attachments are uuencoded.

5. **Click OK to close each dialog box and return to the Outlook window.**

Exchange

The e-mail capabilities of Exchange are very similar to those of Outlook and Microsoft Mail — not surprising since they are all Microsoft e-mail products. Exchange comes with Windows 95. You may use it to read your MSN mail or because your company uses a Microsoft Mail server. You can use Exchange to handle e-mail from many different sources, including a POP mail server.

Exchanging windows

Figure 13-2 shows a view of the Exchange Inbox. You can also set Exchange up to display the folder structure as well as the contents of the folder. Just click the Show/Hide Folder List button, the second button on the toolbar.

Like Outlook, an unread message appears in bold with a closed envelope, and read messages appear next to an open envelope in regular type. Exchange uses a paper clip next to the message information to indicate that an attachment is included with the message.

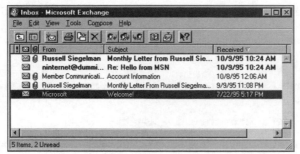

Figure 13-2:
The
Microsoft
Exchange
Inbox.

Exchanging e-mail

If you've used Microsoft Mail, you'll find all the basic tasks in Exchange quite familiar. If you're new to Exchange, here's how to get started:

✔ **Creating and sending a new e-mail message:** Create a new message by clicking the New Message button, the third button on the toolbar. Exchange opens a separate message. Fill the To and Subject fields and write the message. Send it by clicking the Send button, the first button on the message window toolbar.

✔ **Reading a message:** Read a message by double-clicking it.

✔ **Replying to a message:** Reply to a message by selecting it and clicking the Reply button. When you use this method, the reply goes only to the sender of the original message. To reply to all the people who received the original message, click the Reply to All button.

✔ **Forwarding a message:** Forward a message by selecting it and clicking the Forward button.

✔ **Printing a message:** Print a message by selecting it and choosing File⇨Print or pressing Ctrl+P.

✔ **Deleting a message:** Delete a message by selecting it and pressing the Del key or clicking the Delete button at the top of the window. When a message is deleted, it goes into the Deleted Items folder, which is another folder to hold mail. You can undelete it by clicking the Deleted Items folder to display the message and moving the message to another folder. By default, the Deleted Items folder is emptied when you right-click the folder name and choosing Empty Folder from the shortcut menu. Exchange can also be set up to empty the Deleted Items folder each time Exchange is closed.

Like most e-mail packages, Exchange allows you to file messages in different folders. You can move a message to a folder by right-clicking the message in the Exchange window and choosing Move from the shortcut menu.

Double-click the folder you want to move the message to in the Move window. You can also drag a message from the right side of the window to a folder on the left side of the window to move it.

To create a new folder, choose File⇨New Folder and name the folder. Exchange creates a hierarchical folder structure — the folder you create will be a subfolder of the folder that is selected.

Exchanging attachments

Exchange supports both MIME and uuencoded attachments, but be warned: If you use the Microsoft Mail server, you will only be able to send and receive uuencoded attachments. You can tell when a message has an attachment because you see a paper clip next to the message information. An attachment appears as an icon in a message. Open an attachment by double-clicking the icon in the message. Save the attachment on your hard disk (or on a floppy, if you prefer), by choosing File⇨Save Attachments from the message window menu.

To send an attachment with a message, begin composing the message, place your cursor where you want the attachment icon to appear and click the Insert File button in the message window. Choose the file you want to attach and click the OK button to add the icon to the message. You can also drag the file from My Computer or Windows Explorer and drop it in the message window to attach it to the message.

Pegasus

Pegasus is a very popular, free e-mail package much like Eudora Light. For simple activities, Eudora is generally considered an easier package to use. Pegasus, however, has filtering features that the free version of Eudora lacks. Pegasus also sends and retrieves mail in the background. In other words, you can continue to read and create e-mail messages at the same time as Pegasus is sending or retrieving messages. To use Pegasus to send and retrieve e-mail, you need an Internet connection and an e-mail account on a POP server. The current version of Pegasus is 2.5.

If you like Pegasus and would like to support its continuing development, you can order the manuals for $35. For information on ordering the manuals, click the second to last button on the Pegasus toolbar — the one with the dollar sign on it.

Pegasus windows

The Pegasus window looks something like Figure 13-3. Figure 13-3 shows the New Mail Folder window in the top-left corner, partially covered by a message window in the bottom-right corner. Notice that a myriad of buttons are visible. The main toolbar near the top of the window contains a whopping twenty buttons, and larger buttons appear at the top of each window within the Pegasus window.

The New Mail Folder window displays information about messages that have been received. Messages that have been read display a check mark next to them. Messages that you have composed a reply to appear with a blue dot to their left (though none are shown in the figure).

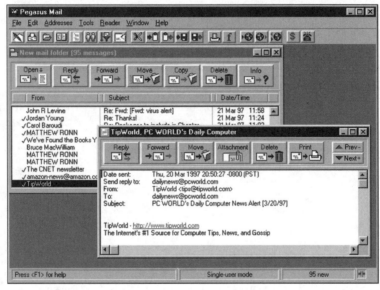

Figure 13-3:
A typical
Pegasus
window,
with the
New Mail
Folder
window and
a message
window
displayed.

The Pegasus window has its own toolbar. However, many of the windows you use within Pegasus, such as folder windows and message windows, also have their own toolbars.

Pegasus's online help is fairly comprehensive. Display the help index by choosing Help⇨Help index.

E-mailing with Pegasus

Pegasus performs the standard e-mail functions that you would expect to be able to do with any e-mail package. Here are the specifics:

- **Creating and sending a new e-mail message:** Create a new message by clicking the Compose a New Mail Message button, the first button on the main toolbar. When you've provided the address or alias for the person to send the message to in the To field, filled in the Subj field, and written your message (and read it for accuracy), send it by clicking the Send button on the message window. To check your message for accurate spelling, click the Check Spelling button in the message window (it's at the far right near the top, and is labeled abc).

- **Reading a message:** Read a message by double-clicking it or by selecting it in the Folder window and clicking the Open button at the top of the folder window.

- **Replying to a message:** Reply to a message by selecting it in the Folder window and clicking the Reply button. You can also open the message and click the Reply button in the message window. The Reply Options dialog box appears. Click check boxes to add or delete options — the options you want to use need a check mark next to them. Click the OK button to display the message window.

- **Forwarding a message:** Forward a message by selecting it in the Folder window and clicking the Forward button or by opening the message and clicking the Forward button. The Forward Message to dialog box appears. Fill in the Forward to text box with the address or alias of the person you want to forward the message to. To edit the message, click the Edit the message before forwarding check box so that a check mark appears. Otherwise, the message is forwarded as soon as you click the Forward button.

- **Printing a message:** Print a message by opening it and clicking the Print button on the message toolbar. You can print a window (such as the New Mail Folder window) by clicking the Print the Current Window button on the main toolbar.

- **Deleting a message:** Delete a message by selecting it and pressing the Del key or clicking the Delete button at the top of the Folder window. Once a message is deleted, it cannot be retrieved (unless you have a backup somewhere).

Pegasus also allows you to file messages in different folders. You can move a message to a folder by selecting the message and clicking the Move button on the folder toolbar. The Select a Folder dialog box appears.

You can do the following:

- ✔ Move the message to an existing folder by double-clicking the folder name or selecting the folder and clicking the Open button.
- ✔ Move the message to a new folder by clicking the New button, naming the folder, and clicking OK.

To view other folders, choose File⇨Mail folders or press Ctrl+L. You see the Folders dialog box. Here, double-click a folder name to open the folder.

Pegasus is happy to let you work offline. Just choose File⇨Enter offline mode to work offline. When you're done, choose File⇨Leave offline mode.

Pegasus attachments

Pegasus can send all three kinds of attachments: MIME, uuencoded, and BinHex. To send an attachment with an e-mail message, click the Attachment tab on the message window.

When you receive a message with an attachment, it appears in the Folder window with a small black box to the left of the message information. When you open the message, information about the attachment appears at the bottom of the message window. You can choose to open the attachment or save it on a disk by clicking the Open or Save button.

Part V
Advanced E-Mail Topics

The 5th Wave   By Rich Tennant

"I don't care if you <u>do</u> have a coalition of kids from 19 countries backing you up; I'm still not buying you an ISDN line."

In this part . . .

Sending and receiving e-mail is *part* of the fun. But how do you know who to send mail to? Or how do you send them your favorite files full of off-color jokes, er, we mean, highly productive business documents? How about finding people with similar interests on mailing lists, or keeping your mail private? It's all *right* here. We even have one chapter in this section for those eager for the technical details, but you can skip it and we'll never know. And as a special bonus, we include a chapter on surfing the Internet (a little) via e-mail.

Chapter 14

How to Find Someone's E-Mail Address

Where Is Everybody, Anyway?

You might have figured out one minor problem keeping you from sending e-mail to all your friends: You don't know their addresses. In this chapter, we show you lots of different ways to look for addresses. But we save you the trouble of reading the rest of the chapter by starting out with the easiest, most reliable way to find out people's e-mail addresses:

Call them and ask.

Pretty low-tech, huh? For some reason, this way seems to be absolutely the last thing people want to do. But try it first. If you know or can find out the phone number, calling and asking is much easier than any other method.

They won't mind if you give them the finger

One of the most useful commands, if you generally know where someone receives mail, is *finger*. On most UNIX shell provider systems, you can use finger to find out who is logged in right now and to ask about particular users. Most other service providers support the finger command; check with the help desk to find out if yours is one.

TIP

What if you don't know your own address?

For people who've *always* known their e-mail address, not knowing your own address seems impossible. But it happens frequently — usually because someone's using a private e-mail system that has a gateway to the outside world that provides instructions for how to send messages to the outside but no hint about how outsiders send stuff in. Fortunately, the solution is usually easy: Send a message to your friend and tell your friend to reply to your message. All messages have return addresses, and all but the absolutely cruddiest of mail gateways put on a usable return address. Don't be surprised if the address has a great deal of strange punctuation. After a few gateways, you always seem to end up with things like this:

```
"blurch::John.C.Calhoun"%farp@
    slimemail.com
```

Usually, if you type the strange address back in, it works, so don't worry about it.

You can find out your own address this way by sending a message to our ever-vigilant mail robot at email2@dummies.net, which will send you back a note telling you what the return address in your message was. The human authors see those messages as well, so feel free to add a few words telling us whether you like the book.

Fingering from UNIX

To run finger from a shell prompt, simply type **finger** *username@hostname* and press Enter. For example, to finger someone whose e-mail address is elvis@bluesuede.org, you would type this line: finger elvis@bluesuede.org.

You get back something like the following:

```
Login name: elvis     In real life: Elvis A. Presley
Directory: /usr/elvis     Shell: /bin/sh
On since Jun 30 16:03:13 on vt01  1 day 9 hours
Idle Time
Project: Working on "Hound Dog"
Plan:
Write many songs, become famous.
```

The exact format of the response varies a great deal from one system to another because fiddling with the finger program is a bad habit of many UNIX system hackers.

Fingering with Eudora

If you don't have a UNIX shell account but do use SLIP or PPP, have no fear. The Windows and Mac versions of Eudora can finger people for you. In Eudora Versions 1.*x* and 2.*x*, choose Window⇨Ph (or press Ctrl+U) to open the Finger window. In Eudora 3.*x*, choose Tools⇨Directory Services. Type the address you want to finger in the Command box and the name of the server where you want to check, and click Finger. The results appear in the big text box. Press Ctrl+F4 to close the Finger window.

Using finger works only if the fingeree's Internet provider runs a program called (intriguingly enough) a *finger server*. It doesn't hurt to try; the worst that will happen is a "Connection refused" message.

The giant finger

Some places, universities in particular, have attached their `finger` programs to organizational directories. If you finger `levine@bu.edu` (Boston University), for example, you get the following response:

```
[bu.edu]
 There were 55 matches to your request.

E-mail addresses and telephone numbers are
only displayed when a query matches one
individual. To obtain additional information
on a particular individual, inquire again
with the index_id.
```

The finger program then lists all the matches. It gives the actual mail address (or occasionally some other ID code) for all of the people who match your request, so you can then finger the address for the person you want.

Other universities with similar directories include Cornell, MIT, and Yale. It's worth a try — the worst that can happen is that it will say `not found`.

SLED Corp.'s Four11 Online User Directory

SLED Corp.'s Four11 Online User Directory is an Internet white pages service you can use to look for someone's e-mail address or home page. Anyone can be listed for free. Four11 will also certify and list your PGP key for a fee. For more on PGP, see Chapter 18.

Please, please Mr. Postman

Sometimes you have a pretty good idea what machine someone uses, but you don't know the name. In that case, you can try writing to the *postmaster*. Every *domain,* the part of the address after @ (the at sign) that can receive Internet mail has the e-mail address `postmaster`, which contacts someone responsible for that machine. So if you're pretty sure that your friend uses `my.bluesuede.org`, you might try asking (politely, of course) `postmaster@my.bluesuede.org` what the address is. (We assume that, for some reason, you can't just call your friend and ask what the e-mail address is.)

Most postmasters are overworked system administrators who don't mind an occasional polite question, but you shouldn't expect any big favors. Also keep in mind that the larger the mail domain, the less likely that the postmaster knows all the users personally. Don't write to `postmaster@ibm.com` to try to find someone's e-mail address at IBM. Fortunately, for people who want to find correspondents in the Blue Zone, IBM has a whois server. See "Whois whatzit" later in this chapter.

Postmaster is also the appropriate place to write when you're having trouble with mail to or from a site. If your messages to someone are coming back with a cryptic error message that suggests the mail system is fouled up, or if you're receiving a flood of mechanically generated junk mail from a deranged automatic mail server, the postmaster at the relevant site is the one to contact.

To try out the service and at least register your address, send e-mail to `info@Four11.com`. Their directory is pretty spotty. When presented with John's name, it found 25 matches, five of which were him, but with Margy's name it found one match, which was someone else.

If you use Microsoft's Internet Mail and News, its address book can connect to Four11 for you so that you can add some of the addresses it finds to your local address book. When creating a message, click on the little address card on the To: line. Then, in the window that appears, click the Find button to get to the Search window. There are three or four search services available, so click one of them (like Four11), enter as much of the person's name as possible into the "Look for" fields, and click Find Now to do the search.

Other directories on the Web

Although Four11 is the best known directory of e-mail addresses, there are lots more. They all have somewhat different lists of people, so if you don't find your correspondent one place, try another.

TIP

Finding people at big companies

Some companies have services that let you look up people's addresses. IBM, for example, has a mail server that lets you look up people's names. Send a message to nic@vnet.ibm.com that contains a line like this: whois Watson, T. You can also use it through their Web site at http://whois.ibm.com.

The service lists any users with e-mail addresses whose names match your request. Although nearly all IBM employees have internal e-mail addresses, only a fraction can receive mail from the outside, and you can see only those addresses. (Makes sense — no point in telling you about mail addresses you can't use.)

Many other companies have a straight-forward addressing system that gives everyone at the company an alias such as Firstname.Lastname. This works at AT&T, so mailing to the address Theodore.Vail@att.com finds someone pretty reliably. This technique also works at Sun Microsystems (sun.com). It's always worth a try because the worst that can happen is that you get your message back as undeliverable. If several people have the same name, you usually get a mechanical response telling you how to figure out which of them you want and what the correct address is.

✔ Internet Address Finder: http://www.iaf.net/

✔ Bigfoot: http://bigfoot.com

✔ Who Where: http://www.whowhere.com

Whois whatzit

Quite a long time ago (at least, a long time ago in the *network* frame of mind — 15 or 20 years), some of the network managers began keeping directories of network people. This time, of course, was when Men were Men and Internet connections were UNIX. The shell command that lets you look up people in these directories is called *whois*. Some systems have a whois command, so in principle you can type this line: whois Smith, and it should contact the whois database and tell you about all the people named Smith.

In practice, however, whois isn't quite that simple. For one thing, around the end of 1992, the main system that keeps the Internet whois database moved, and some whois commands still haven't been updated to reflect that move. The old standard server now holds only the names of people who work for the Department of Defense.

Fortunately, you can tell the whois program to use a particular server, as in `whois -h whois.internic.net Smith` because the civilian Internet service is now at `whois.internic.net`. The `-h` stands for *host,* as in the host where the server is located. But keep in mind that it still lists only network managers and administrative contacts. Here at Dummies Central, for example, `whois` will find John, because he's the network manager, and Margy, who manages some name domains. But you won't find Carol, who, instead of being a network manager, has a life.

For systems that don't have the whois command but do have other Internet services, you can use one of these Web pages instead:

```
http://rs.internic.net/cgi-bin/whois
http://www.intellinet.com/CoolTools/Whois/
```

Chapter 15

Attaching Your Refrigerator to Your E-Mail Message and Other Technical Stuff

. . . .

In This Chapter

▶ Details that you might eventually have to know

. . . .

*I*n this chapter, we cover a grab-bag of relatively technical topics related to e-mail. We suggest you skim or skip this the first time through the book and come back here when a technical question bothers you. It may also be useful in stubborn cases of insomnia.

What's a Demon Doing in My Computer?

No, wait, there's no need to call an exorcist. A *demon* or *dæmon* (spelled that way because on some early computers, file names were limited to six letters and they didn't want to waste any) is just a special kind of computer program. Most non-dæmon programs run when somebody wants to do something — for example, when you want to edit some text, you run a text editor. A dæmon, on the other hand, lurks in the background waiting for something to do, and does it, usually silently and without human intervention. It may sound a little creepy, but in fact it's quite useful and benign. Dæmons aren't entirely independent of people because someone has to arrange for them to start running in the first place, but they quite often run for weeks or months without human intervention.

The e-mail angle is that almost all e-mail is actually processed and delivered by dæmons. When you compose a mail message, the program you use is known as a *mail user agent* (MUA). The mail agent doesn't actually try to deliver the message itself. Rather, it hands your message to a *mail transfer agent* (MTA) to do the actual delivery. MTAs are invariably dæmons, working in the background to process the mail. If a message is destined for a user on the same computer, the MTA delivers the mail directly. If not, it communicates over the Net to another MTA on the destination computer to deliver the mail there.

This division of labor is, for the most part, a good idea. Delivering the message may take a while (what if the other computer isn't on the Net right now, or the connection is really slow?), and most users have better things to do than to hang around and wait for delivery to finish. Also, most systems have several different MUAs. On our system, for example, different users prefer Pine, Elm, and several versions of Eudora, but because they all use the same MTA, they all exchange mail without trouble.

Normally, all of the MTA stuff happens without you having to worry about it, but two situations involving your MTA will grab your attention:

✔ When you send mail to an invalid address

✔ When the MTA is broken

Tales from the dæmon

When you send a mail message, your mail program (that is, your MUA) can make only the most general checks that the addresses you specify are valid. Once you've written your message, valid or not, your MUA hands it to the MTA for delivery.

If the address isn't valid, you'll get back a message like this:

```
From: <MAILER-DAEMON@ntw.org>
Subject: mail failed, returning to sender
Date: 2 Nov 1997 15:57:06 -0500
Message-ID: <mOtiSXZ-001TKpC@shamu.ntw.org>
Reference: <mOtiSXY-001TKoC@shamu.ntw.org>

|— Message log follows: —|
 no valid recipients were found for this message
|— Failed addresses follow: —|
 <elvis@ntw.org> ... unknown user
|— Message text follows: —|
Message-Id: <2.2.16.19960202205659.0e1f49cc@shamu.ntw.org>
Date: Fri, 02 Nov 1997 15:56:59 -0500
```

```
To: elvis@ntw.org
From: John Lennon <mryoko@ntw.org>
Subject: Yo, King!

Anyone home?


Regards,
John
```

The dæmon deep in your mail system wakes up and writes you back to complain about the invalid address. For addresses on the local system, you'll generally hear back in a few seconds. But for addresses destined for remote systems, hours or sometimes days can pass before the error message comes back.

In a perfect world, error messages would be in a standardized format so that, for example, your mail program could check and see if the address is in your address book and offer to delete it. But no, that would be too easy. No widely used standard exists for mailed error messages, so although most of them look pretty much like the one above, enough variation occurs that even experienced human users can't always figure out what the problem was.

It's dead, Jim

Now and then the mail dæmon (that is, the MTA) in your system might just stop working. (This problem has occurred once or twice when our system manager made a tiny little change that turned out not to be quite as tiny as he thought. Oops.) The most common symptom is that all mail delivery stops, but sometimes you get all mail, whether addresses are valid or otherwise, returned to you.

The most common MTAs are called `sendmail` and `smail`. If you start getting error messages saying something like `sendmail: not found`, contact your system manager immediately.

Considering the nature of the problem, this situation is one of the few times when a phone call is definitely preferable to e-mail.

More about Headers

Back in Chapter 3, we talk about mail headers, the stuff at the front of the message that describes who a message is to and from, what it's about, and so forth. Well, lots more headers are out there besides the ones we listed. Here's a typical message with *all* the headers:

```
From jqpublic Tue Nov  4 22:58:43 1997
Return-Path: <jqpublic@sample.org>
Received: from babbitt.sample.org by ivan.ntw.org with smtp
    (Smail3.1.29.1 #11) id m0thTgx-001TOJC; Tue, 04 Nov 97
         22:58 EST
Message-ID: <310EE8B4.4A74@sample.org>
Date: Tue,  4 Nov 1997 22:57:40 -0500
X-UIDL: 823060777.001
From: John Q Public <jqpublic@sample.org>
Organization: The Sample Organization
X-Mailer: Mozilla 3.01 (Win16; I)
MIME-Version: 1.0
Content-Type: text/plain; charset="us-ascii"
To: email@dummies.com
Subject: book report
Status: RO

... actual contents of the message here ...
```

So what are all those headers? Table 15-1 shows a rundown of the ones we didn't discuss in Chapter 3.

Table 15-1	**Headers**
Header	*Meaning*
From	A "From" line as the first line of the message with no colon is a "UNIX mailbox separator." It shows when the mail was put in your mailbox and who appears to have delivered it.
Return-Path:	The address from which the message was sent. This needn't be the same as the "From:" address if the message was sent through a gateway system or via a mailing list.
Received:	Each time a message is processed by a mail transfer agent (MTA, discussed in "What's a Demon Doing in My Computer?" in this chapter) the MTA adds a "Received:" line. The contents are utterly technoid, but they are very useful to mail experts who are trying to figure out how a message went astray or from whence a mystery message came.

Header	Meaning
Organization:	The name of the author's organization (optional).
Status:	The status of the message in the mailbox. *R* means you've read it, and *O* means it's old but unread. (It was in the mailbox the last time you ran your mail program.) Unlike all the other header lines, this line is created and updated by the *receiver's* mail program.

Mail programs are allowed to add any old non-standard headers they want, so long as they put X- in front of them. Table 15-2 shows what typical non-standard headers include.

Table 15-2	Non-Standard Headers
Header	**Meaning**
X-UIDL:	Unique identifier, used by POP mail programs such as Eudora to figure out which messages they've already downloaded.
X-Mailer:	The name of the program used to create the message. In the example previous, "Mozilla" is the developers' code name for Netscape they evidently never bothered to remove.

What's the Difference between an E-Mail Address and a URL?

This is an e-mail address:

```
email2@dummies.net
```

And this is a uniform resource locator (URL):

```
http://net.dummies.net/books/toc-email2.html
```

What's the difference? You use them for entirely different things. You send mail to an e-mail address — the normal thing to do with one is to type it on the To: line in your mail program.

A URL, on the other hand, is the name of a "page" of information in the World Wide Web. You use it to tell your Web browser, Netscape, Internet Explorer, or Lynx, for example, what page to retrieve. URLs and e-mail addresses are not interchangeable, and you have to use the right kind of program to handle each. This task is made somewhat easier if you use a multi-purpose program like Netscape that handles both Web pages and mail. In Netscape, you select File⇨New Mail Message to start sending mail, but you use File⇨Open Location to tell it to go to a URL.

E-mail addresses are generally shorter and always contain an at-sign (@). URLs start with a code, usually `http:`, followed by the host name of a computer and the name of the page on that computer.

In the interest of maximized confusion, a special kind of URL is actually an e-mail address. It looks like this: `mailto:email2@dummies.net`.

This kind of URL tells the Web browser to open a mail window (or sometimes, to start up a separate mail program) and start a message to that address. These URLs aren't very useful for humans because going to the mail window directly is easier, but they sometimes appear in other Web pages to make sending mail to the owner of the page easier.

IP Addresses

We've told you, dozens of times by now, that computers on the Internet have multipart names like `chico.iecc.com`. Well, we were simplifying a little bit. They do have names, but they also have numbers, similar to phone numbers. These numbers are used by the underlying Internet Protocol, which moves data from one place to another on the Internet, so they're called IP addresses.

An IP address is written as four numbers separated by dots, like this: 205.238.207.92. Quite a lot can be said about the structure of IP addresses, none of which will be said here because it's not all that interesting. (See *MORE Internet For Dummies,* 3rd Edition, if you like.)

You can send Internet e-mail to IP addresses, an option that is useful now and then when some piece of the name system goes West. You put the IP address in square brackets, like this: `email@[205.238.207.92]`.

You might think that every name on the Net corresponds to one IP address, but that's not true. (It's not like every name in the phone book corresponds to a single phone number, either.) Many computers on the Internet have more than one IP address, if they're connected to more than one network. Some computers, particularly those used for internal network functions, have an IP address but no name at all. And some names correspond to more than one computer. For example, delphi.com corresponds to five different IP addresses on five different computers.

Fortunately, if a computer has more than one IP address, you can use any of them, and if a name corresponds to more than one address on more than one computer, you can still use whichever one you want because all of the computers are invariably set up to do the same thing.

Some names don't correspond to any IP addresses at all, including some major ones like aol.com. Those are called *mail exchange* or *MX* names. If a system has an MX name, some other computer has arranged to receive mail for it. In AOL's case, eight computers named a.mx.aol.com through h.mx.aol.com stand ready to receive AOL's mail. Unless your mail system's configuration is messed up, a situation that happens occasionally, mail to and from MX names works exactly the same as mail to regular names, so you don't have to worry about it.

I'm So Attached to You

Internet mail for many years only officially handled text, not pictures, word-processor documents, or any other kind of file. The relatively new MIME standard now provides an official way to send non-text material, but as you might suspect, people were sending files around for years before MIME came along, using non-standard hackery.

MIME

As we mentioned in Chapter 3, you can recognize a MIME message by the MIME headers at the beginning of the message, which look something like this:

```
Mime-Version: 1.0
Content-Type: multipart/mixed; boundary=
"======================_823336045==_"
```

If you have a modern mail program like Eudora, Pine, or Netscape, your mail program automatically recognizes a MIME message and reconstitutes the file contained in it. Some of the cleverer ones even figure out what kind of file it is and run an appropriate program to display it for you.

Unfortunately, some older mail programs don't handle MIME, in which case you're out of luck. This problem occurs frequently with local mail systems attached to the Internet through a gateway system. On one LAN (that's *Local Area Network*, if you care) system we deal with, we've been asking them to get MIME working for two years, and they haven't been able to do it yet.

If your mail system is MIME-impaired, you can still usually use one of the other older informal attachment schemes that we describe next.

Uuencode

Back in ancient days (like about 1979) a mail system named UUCP worked over dial-up modems. It didn't handle attached files, so a couple of students whipped up a pair of programs called uuencode and uudecode that let them disguise files as text for the purpose of sending them as UUCP mail. These days, UUCP is nearing the end of its useful life (and not a moment too soon), but uuencoding lives on.

A uuencoded file appears in a message bracketed by begin and end lines. The name of the file appears after the begin (you can ignore the three-digit number between them).

```
begin 600 efdb202.bmp
MODT-!'$""#"""#"#8$""#"#""H""30(",'!"'!"@
"""",!""""'
M""""""""%4"'J""_P""E"!5)
0"JB4"/\E""2"'
M54@"*I("#_2""&T"%5M"J;0"_VT"'"2
"!5D@"JI("/^2""
... lots more illegible glop here ...
'
end
```

Better mail programs such as Eudora automatically recognize uuencoded files and extract their contents. Even if your mail program doesn't understand uuencoded files, on most systems, you can use a decoding program, such as uudecode on UNIX systems and Wincode on Windows systems, to extract the encoded file. Ask your system manager which, if any, of them are available.

BinHex

Macintosh programmers invented their own equivalent of uuencoding, called *BinHex*. It's most popular on Macs, although it works on any kind of computer. BinHex-ed files start with this surprisingly understandable message:

```
(This file must be converted with BinHex 4.0)
```

(We've never seen a version of BinHex other than 4.0.) Once again, Eudora and a few other mail programs automatically extract BinHex-ed files. Lacking automatic extraction, separate un-BinHexers are widely available on Macs and less so on other systems.

So how should I send my files?

The answer depends on the capabilities both of your mail system and of those of the mail system used by the people with whom you correspond. MIME has been available for several years and is quite widely accepted, so in most cases you should just be able to send MIME messages and expect success. (AOL, for example, supports MIME completely.)

If you find that your correspondents' systems can't deal with MIME, your next best bet is BinHex if they're using Macs and uuencoded if they're using anything else.

Mutant Mail

For the first thirty years that e-mail existed, you could be pretty sure that if you sent a text message to someone, the message would arrive in his or her mailbox as a text message. Unfortunately, in the great computer industry tradition of never, ever, leaving well enough alone, in 1996 Microsoft invented a new, incompatible form of *enriched* mail that lets you add fancy formatting to your mail, and Netscape, never one to let the Redmond Monolith outmaneuver them, added their own almost-but-not-quite-compatible enriched mail in Netscape 4.0.

Unfortunately, if you send enriched mail to any of the 90 percent of mail users that don't understand that kind of enrichment, your mail arrives filled with so many format codes as to be utterly indecipherable. For example, you think you wrote:

Hi, Mom.

I had a *very* interesting day in school, which I'll tell you about in my next message. Gotta run.

Love,
Chelsea

But what Mom gets is:

```
<html><head></head><BODY bgcolor=3D"#FFFFFF"><p><font
          size=3D2 =
color=3D"#000000" face=3D"Arial">Hi, Mom.<br><br>I had a
          <i>very =
</i>interesting day in school, which I'll tell you about in
          my next =
message.  Gotta run.<br><br>Love,<br>Chelsea<br><br></
          p>
</font></body></html>
```

So don't send formatted or enriched mail unless you are 110-percent sure your correspondent is using a mail program that can handle it.

Graphics Formats

Perhaps you felt that having three different but similar ways to send attached files was too many. Little did you suspect how simple your life was.

"How many different ways can you store a picture in a computer?" you might ask. Dozens, maybe hundreds, that's how many. On a Windows machine, you may have run into BMP, PCX, DIB, GIF, JPG, TGA, and other files, all of which contain various kinds of pictures. If for some reason you want more details on this convoluted state of affairs, you probably won't be surprised to hear that we suggest *Graphic File Formats,* 2nd Edition, by David Kay and John Levine (Windcrest) and *Programming for Graphics Files in C and C++* (Wiley), which John wrote by himself.

Fortunately, two picture formats are much more popular than the rest: GIF and JPEG. Lengthy, er, free and frank discussions have occurred on the Net concerning the relative merits of the two formats. Because John is an Official Graphics Format Expert (by virtue of having persuaded two otherwise reputable publishers to publish his books on the topic) here are his opinions:

JPEG

JPEG, named after the Joint Photographic Experts Group that designed it, is a format specifically intended to store digitized photographs.

- Best format for scanned photographs
- Handles "true color" better
- Files are usually smaller than GIF
- Doesn't handle large areas of solid color or sharp edges well
- Slower to decode than GIF

GIF

GIF, a format designed by CompuServe, comes in two slightly different versions, GIF87 and GIF89. Fortunately, the two versions are similar enough that all the GIF-handling programs we know can deal equally well with both.

- Best format for computer-drawn cartoons and icons
- Handles solid color areas well
- Faster to decode

GIF's designers used a compression technique that turned out, after many years, to be patented by Unisys, and in 1995, Unisys started demanding patent royalties. In response, an industry group came up with a replacement for GIF called PNG (Portable Network Graphics), which is patent-free and solves a few other minor GIF deficiencies. GIF is being replaced by PNG, but they'll co-exist for several years.

Everything else

The next most popular format is TIFF (Tagged Image File Format), popular with fax programs and graphic design programs. TIFF can in principle be converted easily to other formats such as GIF, but TIFF is fantastically complex with dozens of internal options, so it's dismayingly common to find that a TIFF file written by one program can't be read by another.

Other formats are popular on particular computers, such as BMP and PCX on Windows and PICT on Macs. If you know you're sending a file to someone with the same kind of computer you have, you can just send the file. If not, you should probably convert it to GIF or JPEG to up the chances that your recipient can read it.

Lights! Action! Multimedia

Multimedia in theory means any sort of file or presentation that combines more than one kind of computer output (sound and smell-o-vision, for example), but in practice it means movies. The two most common multimedia formats are Quicktime and MPEG.

Quicktime

Quicktime is a format designed by Apple and handled quite nicely by Macintoshes because the support is built right into the Mac's system software. Apple also has Quicktime software available for Windows, but it's much less popular.

MPEG

MPEG, the Motion Pictures Experts Group, was down the hall from the JPEG group and built on their work. (That's practically unprecedented in the history of standardization.) MPEG is more popular on Windows and other non-Mac systems.

Firewalls

Let's say you work for a company with an internal network, and you want to hook that network to the Internet. That's technically straightforward, involving a *gateway* or *router* computer that passes traffic back and forth between the internal network and the outside. But the Internet has a certain number of, shall we say, *undisciplined* users who delight in trying to break into computers where they don't belong. If your internal network has 1,000 computers, you'd have to make sure that the security setup on each and every one of those thousand computers was correct, and in practice, you never will. What's a network manager to do?

The answer is a *firewall* computer. Rather than passing any old network traffic between the inside and the outside, a firewall strictly limits what can pass. So long as the security on the firewall is set up correctly, the entire internal network is protected. Firewalls frequently act as *proxy servers*, a fancy term meaning a computer that provides a service to the internal network that the proxy in turn has received from the outside (checking to make sure there's no security breach in the process).

Firewalls tend not to make much difference to e-mail users because even if mail has to be forwarded via a firewall or a proxy server, the addressing and delivery work the same as they always do. But if you use any other network service such as the World Wide Web, you'll have to do extra setup steps so that your program uses the proxy server. In Netscape, for example, you see a Proxy tab on the Options⇨Network Preferences window.

Protocols

Rules agreed upon and used in particular kinds of communications are known as *protocols*. E-mail and the computer networks that make it work depend on numerous protocols that control how data flow around the network. This section contains a quick roundup of some of the most important protocols used for e-mail.

Most of these protocols are defined by so-called Request For Comment (RFC) documents available on the Internet. (Despite their names, we're about 15 years too late to comment on most of them.) See Chapter 19 for advice on retrieving files, including RFCs, by mail.

POP

POP (Post Office Protocol) version 3 is what programs like Netscape and Eudora use to download mail from a central server to the computer on your desk. It's defined by RFC 1725.

SMTP

SMTP (Simple Mail Transfer Protocol) is used to transfer messages from one system on the Internet to another. It's defined by RFC 821.

The difference between SMTP and POP is that SMTP is used to pass mail from system to system until it's delivered to the recipient's mailbox, and POP is used by an individual user to retrieve mail that's been delivered to his or her mailbox.

X.400

A competitor to SMTP, defined by the International Telecommunications Union (ITU). Much more complex than SMTP and much less widely used. We tell you all about X.400 addressing in Chapter 4.

X.500

A "white pages" service defined by the ITU to make it possible to look up peoples' e-mail addresses. Alleged to be coming soon but not widely used yet.

DNS

The Domain Name System, which keeps track of the names of the millions of computers on the Internet, like `dummies.net`. Defined by RFCs 1034, 1035, 1101, and 1348. (It's pretty complicated.)

TCP/IP

Transmission Control Protocol (TCP) and Internet Protocol (IP), which together define the way that data are actually sent from one computer to another on the Internet. IP is defined by RFC 791 and TCP by RFC 793. SMTP and DNS use TCP/IP to make the actual connections from one computer to another.

Chapter 16
Mailing List Fever

Pen Pals Galore

So you've heard that gazillions of people are out there just ready to send you mail. How do you find them and how can they find you? Well, since you probably don't really want to correspond with all of them, we suggest you start by thinking about what interests you. You may have gone your whole life without ever finding someone who shares your interest in shitake mushrooms, tantric yoga, and Alfonso Sastre. Now's your chance.

The Internet is chock-full, and getting chock-fuller every second, of people with shared interests using electronic mail mailing lists to create a running conversation. E-mail mailing lists are a source for both information and entertainment, and with over twelve thousand of them out there, one is bound to appeal to your interests or tickle your fancy.

How a mailing list works is simple. The list has its own special e-mail address, and anything that you send to that address is sent to all the people on the list. Because some of the people on the list, in turn, may respond to your messages, the result is a running conversation.

Different lists have different styles, tones, and senses of focus. Some are relatively formal, hewing closely to the official topic of the list. Others tend to go flying off into outer space, figuratively and literally. You have to read them for a while to be able to tell which list works which way.

Some mailing lists generate hundreds of messages per day or more. Don't get carried away and join ten mailing lists in one sitting. Join them one or two at a time and see how it goes.

Sign Me Up!

The way you get on or off a mailing list is simple: You send a mail message.

The message you send to get on and off a mailing list goes to a special *administrative address*, not the address where you send messages to distribute to the members of the list. Sending a "put me on the list" or "take me off the list" message to the entire group is one of the big no-nos of mailing lists. Figuring out the right way to do these things is a bit complex, but that's what *we're* here for. Read on.

Two general schools of mailing-list management exist: *manual* and *automatic*. Manual management is the low-tech way: Your message is read by a human being who updates an address file to put you on or take you off the list. The advantage of manual management is that you get personal service; the disadvantage is that the list maintainer may not get around to handling your request for quite a while if more pressing business (such as his or her real job) intervenes.

These days, having lists maintained automatically is more common. Such lists only need human attention when things get fouled up. Automatic lists are managed by computer programs known as list managers. LISTSERV, Majordomo, and Listproc are the most common names you'll see, and they each get their own sections later in this chapter.

A widely observed convention regarding list and maintainer addresses exists for the manual lists. Suppose that you want to join a list for fans of Chester Alan Arthur (the 21st president of the United States), and the list's name is `arthur-lovers@dummies.net`. The manager's address is almost certainly `arthur-lovers-request@dummies.net`. In other words, just add `-request` to the list's address to get the manager's address. Because the list is maintained by hand, your request to be added or dropped doesn't have to take any particular form, as long as it's polite. `Please add me to the arthur-lovers list` does quite well. When you decide that you have had all the Arthur you can stand, another message saying `Please remove me from the arthur-lovers list` does equally well.

Messages to `-request` addresses are read and handled by human beings who sometimes eat, sleep, and work regular jobs as well as maintain mailing lists. Therefore, they don't necessarily read your request the moment it arrives. Being added to or removed from a list can take a day or so, and after you ask to be removed, you usually get a few more messages before they remove you. Be patient. And *don't* send cranky follow-ups — they just cheese off the list maintainer.

Yeah, Now What Do I Do?

Here's a handy tip: After you subscribe to a list, don't send any messages until you read it for a week. Trust us — the list has been getting along without your insights since it began, and it can get along without them for one more week.

This method gives you a chance to learn the sorts of topics that people really discuss, the tone of the list, and other helpful hints about behavior on this particular list. Reading the list for a week also gives you a fair idea about which topics people are tired of. The classic newcomer gaffe is to subscribe to a list and immediately send a message asking a dumb question that isn't really germane to the topic and that was beaten to death three days earlier. Bide your time, and don't let this faux pas happen to you. (As a small exception to this rule, a few lists ask new members to send a message introducing themselves. Check the introductory message you get when you join a list to see if an intro is expected.)

Make sure that you read all the information the list has sent you before you start asking questions. Look for the *FAQs* — the list of frequently asked questions (and their answers) — that people have thoughtfully provided so that when a newcomer like you joins up, they don't have to answer the same question for the fifty-gazillionth time.

When you *are* ready to post something to the group, read and reread what you've written thoroughly. You are what you type. Make sure that you're saying what you think you're saying, keep the message civil, and observe the conventions of the group. We talk more about sending messages to the list later in this chapter.

Automagic Mailing List Service: LISTSERV

Once upon a time, the crowd at BITNET network (a network of large computers, now mostly merged into the Internet) developed lots and lots of mailing lists as a convenient to stay in touch. Because maintaining all those mailing lists was (and still is) a great deal of work, they came up with a program called *LISTSERV* to manage the mailing lists.

LISTSERV is a little klunky to use, but has the great advantage of being able to easily handle enormous mailing lists that contain thousands of members — something that makes most regular Internet mail programs choke.

Enlisting with LISTSERV

You put yourself on and off a LISTSERV mailing list by sending mail to LISTSERV@*some.machine.or.other*, where *some.machine.or.other* is the name of the particular machine on which the mailing list lives. Because they're computer programs, LISTSERV list managers are pretty simpleminded, so you have to speak to them clearly and distinctly.

Suppose that you want to join a list called SNUFLE-L (LISTSERV mailing lists often end with -L), that lives at bluesuede.org. To join, send to LISTSERV@bluesuede.org a message that contains this line:

```
SUB SNUFLE-L Roger Sherman
```

You don't have to add a subject line or anything else to this message. SUB is short for subscribe, SNUFLE-L is the name of the list, and anything after that is supposed to be your real name. (You can put whatever you want there, but keep in mind that the name you use shows up in the return address of anything you send to the list.) Shortly afterward, you should get two messages back:

✔ A chatty, machine-generated welcoming message, telling you that you've joined the list, along with a description of some commands you can use to fiddle with your mailing-list membership. Sometimes this message includes a request to confirm that you got this message. Follow the instructions by replying to this message with the single word *OK* in the body of the message. This helps lists ensure that they aren't mailing into the void. If you don't provide this confirmation, you don't get on the list.

✔ An incredibly boring message, telling you that the IBM mainframe ran a program to handle your request and reporting the exact number of milliseconds of computer time and number of disk operations the request took. (It is sobering to think that somewhere there are people who find these facts interesting.)

If you get a confirmation message from a list you never asked to join, someone's playing games. Just ignore the message and you won't hear from that list again.

Keep the chatty, informative message that tells you about all the commands you can use when dealing with the list. For one thing, this message tells you how to get *off* the mailing list if you choose to. We have a folder called *Mailing Lists* in our mail program, in which we store the welcome messages from all the mailing lists we join.

To send a message to a list (after you subscribe), mail to the list name at the same machine — in this case, SNUFLE-L@bluesuede.org. Be sure to provide a descriptive subject for the multitudes who will benefit from your pearls of wisdom. Within a matter of minutes, people from all over the world will read your message.

To get off a list, you again write to *LISTSERV@some.machine.or.other*, this time sending

```
SIGNOFF SNUFLE-L
```

or whatever the list's name is. You don't have to give your name again because after you're off the list, LISTSERV has no more interest in you and completely forgets that you ever existed.

Some lists are more difficult to get on and off than others are. Usually you ask to get on a list, and you're on the list. In some cases, however, the list isn't open to all comers, and the human list owner screens requests to join the list, in which case you may get some messages from the list owner to discuss your request to join.

To contact the actual human being who runs a particular list, the mail address is OWNER- followed by the list name (OWNER-SNUFLE-L, for example). The owner can do all sorts of things to lists that mere mortals can't do. In particular, the owner can fix screwed-up names on the list or add a name that for some reason the automatic method doesn't handle.

Telling LISTSERV how to behave

The people who maintain the LISTSERV program have added so many bells and whistles to it that it would take an entire book to describe them all, and, frankly, they're not that interesting. But here are some of the things LISTSERV can do. For each of them, you send a message to LISTSERV@some.machine.or.other to talk to the LISTSERV program. You can send several commands in the same message if you want to do two or three tricks at one time.

✔ **Temporarily stop mail:** Sometimes you're going to be away for a week or two and you don't want to get a bunch of mailing-list mail in the meantime. But because you're planning to come back, you don't want to take yourself off the list, either. This feature is especially useful for restricted lists where you had to get approved by the list owner to join.

To stop mail temporarily from the SNUFLE-L mailing list, send `SET SNUFLE-L NOMAIL` and the list stops sending you messages. To turn the mail back on, send this message: `SET SNUFLE-L MAIL`

Turning off your mailing lists temporarily when you go on vacation or won't be reading your mail for some other reason is a good idea. Be aware that some mailing list programs send a confirmation message, asking if you really want to stop mail. So if you send out your `NOMAIL` messages, turn out the lights, and hop in the car, you may be unpleasantly surprised when you get back to find your mailbox has overflowed and you did not get important mail. Moral: Don't wait until the last minute to `NOMAIL`.

✔ **Get messages as a digest:** If you're getting a large number of messages from a list and would rather get them all at one time as a daily digest, send this message: `SET SNUFLE-L DIGEST`

Not all lists can be digested, but the indigestible ones let you know and don't take offense.

✔ **Find out who's on a list:** To find out who subscribes to a list, send this message: `REVIEW SNUFLE-L`

Some lists can be reviewed only by people on the list, and others not at all. Some lists are enormous, so be prepared to get back an enormous message listing thousands of subscribers.

✔ **Get files:** Most LISTSERV servers have a library of files available, usually documents contributed by the mailing-list members. To find out which files are available, send this command: `INDEX`

To have LISTSERV send you a particular file by e-mail, send the message `GET`*fname* where *fname* is the name of a file from the INDEX command. On IBM systems, files have two-part names separated by a space (for example, `GET SNUFLE-L MEMO`).

✔ **Get LISTSERV to do other things:** Lots of other commands lurk in LISTSERV, most of which apply only to people on IBM mainframes. If you are one of these people or if you're just nosy, send a message containing this line: `HELP`. You'll receive a helpful response that lists other commands.

Major Major Domo Domo

Another widely used mailing-list manager is Brent Chapman's *Majordomo*. Majordomo started out as a LISTSERV wannabe for workstations but has evolved into a system that works quite well. Because of its wannabe origins, Majordomo commands are almost, but (pretend to be surprised now) not quite, the same as their LISTSERV equivalents.

The mailing address for Majordomo commands, as you might expect, is majordomo@*some.machine.or.other*. Majordomo lists tend to have long and expressive names. One of our favorites is called explosive-cargo, a very funny weekly column written by a guy in Boston who also writes for a computer magazine. To subscribe, because the list is maintained on host world.std.com, send this message to Majordomo@world.std.com:

```
subscribe explosive-cargo
```

Unlike with LISTSERV, you *don't* put your real name in the subscribe command.

To unsubscribe

```
unsubscribe explosive-cargo
```

As with LISTSERV, lists that use the most recent versions of Majordomo can require confirmation before you subscribe to a list. If a list does require confirmation, you'll get a message asking if it was really you who subscribed. Create a reply to that message and follow the instructions in the message, usually to put a word like yes or OK in the first line of the reply.

Once you subscribe, you can send a message to everyone on the mailing list by addressing it to listname@some.machine.or.other. (You can't post messages to explosive-cargo because it's an *announcements-only list:* — that is, only the guy in Boston who runs the list is allowed to post messages.)

Not to be outdone by LISTSERV, Majordomo has its own set of not particularly useful commands (as with LISTSERV, you can send in a single message as many of these as you want):

- ✔ Majordomo also can keep files related to its lists. To find the names of the files for a particular list, enter index *name-of-list.*

- ✔ To tell Majordomo to send you one of the files by e-mail, enter get name-of-list *name-of-file.*

- ✔ To find out the rest of the goofy things Majordomo can do, enter help.

- ✔ If you need to contact the human manager of a Majordomo system because you can't get off a list you want to leave or otherwise have an insoluble problem, send a polite message to owner-majordomo@ hostname. Remember that humans eat, sleep, and have real jobs, so getting an answer may take a day or two.

It's Not a Crock, It's Listproc

Listproc is not as widely used as LISTSERV and Majordomo, but Listproc is increasing in popularity because it is easier to install than LISTSERV, cheaper, and almost as powerful. (When we say "cheaper" here, we mean for the people who have to acquire the list maintenance software. For the subscriber, all list-managing software is the same. Sometimes people charge for subscriptions, but that's not the kind of cost we're talking about here.)

To subscribe to a Listproc mailing list, you send the message `subscribe listname yourname` to `listproc@some-computer`. For example, to subscribe to the `chickens` mailing list on `dummies.net`, you send the message `subscribe chickens George Washington` to `listproc@dummies.net` (assuming that you were named after the same person that the first president of the U.S. was named after).

To get off the mailing list, send the message `signoff` listname to the same address. You don't have to provide your name — the Listproc program should already know it!

Once you subscribe to the list, you can send messages to everyone on the list by addressing e-mail to *listname@some-computer* — for example, `chickens@dummies.net`.

To find out other things that Listproc can do, send the message `help` to `listproc@whatever`, where *whatever* is the name of the computer where the Listproc mailing list lives.

LISTSERV, Listproc, and Majordomo: They could have made them the same, but n-o-o-o-o

Because LISTSERV, Listproc, and Majordomo work sort of in the same way, even experienced mailing-list mavens get their commands confused. Following are the important differences:

✔ The address for LISTSERV is `LISTSERV@hostname`, the address for Majordomo is `majordomo@hostname`, and the address for Listproc is `listproc@hostname`.

✔ To subscribe to a LISTSERV or Listproc list, send `subscribe` followed by the list name followed by your real name. To subscribe to a Majordomo list, just send `subscribe` and the list name.

Sending Messages to Mailing Lists

Some lists encourage new subscribers to send in a message introducing themselves and saying briefly what their interests are. Others don't. So don't send anything until you have something to say.

After you watch the flow of messages on a list for a while, what we're talking about will become obvious.

Mailing list protocol

Some mailing lists have rules about who is allowed to send messages, meaning that just because you're on the list doesn't automatically mean that any messages you send will appear on the list. Some lists are *moderated:* Any message you send in gets sent to a human *moderator,* who decides what goes to the list and what doesn't. This policy may sound sort of fascist, but in practice the arrangement makes a list about 50 times more interesting than it would be otherwise because a good moderator can filter out the boring and irrelevant messages and keep the list on track. Indeed, the people who complain the loudest about moderator censorship are usually the ones whose messages most deserve to be filtered out.

If your message to a moderated list doesn't appear, and you really don't know why, post a polite inquiry to the same list.

Another rule that sometimes causes trouble is that many lists allow messages to be sent only from people whose addresses appear on the list. This rule becomes a pain if your mailing address changes. Suppose that you get a well-organized, new mail administrator and that your official e-mail address changes from `jj@shamu.pol.bluesuede.org` to `John.Jay@ bluesuede.org`, although your old address still works. You may find that some lists begin *bouncing* your messages (sending them back to you rather than to the list) because they don't understand that `John.Jay@bluesuede.org`, the name under which you now send messages, is the same as `jj@shamu.pol. bluesuede.org`, the name under which you originally subscribed to the list. Worse, LISTSERV doesn't let you take yourself off the list for the same reason. To resolve this mess, you have to write to the human list owners of any lists in which this problem arises and ask them to fix the problem by hand.

Bouncing messages

Computer accounts are created and deleted often enough and mail addresses change often enough that, at any given moment, a large list always contains some addresses that are no longer valid. So if you send a message to the list, your message is forwarded to these invalid addresses, and a return message reporting the bad addresses is generated for each of them. Normally, mailing-list managers (both human and computer) try to deflect the error messages so that they go to the list owner, who can do something about them, rather than go to you. But as often as not, a persistently dumb mail system sends one of these failure messages directly to you. Just delete the message and forget about it because you can't do a thing about it.

Mailing list etiquette

The list of e-mail etiquette rules listed in Chapter 4 applies even more to messages sent to mailing lists because *far* more people will read the message you send. Here are some other rules you should follow:

✔ Be sure that your message is appropriate for the list.

✔ Don't send a message saying that another message is inappropriate. The sender probably knows and doesn't care. Even worse, the responses to the responses only create a flood of messages that waste everyone's time and give the sender even more publicity. Silence is the best answer.

✔ Read the entire preceding thread to make sure that your point hasn't been raised already.

✔ Edit down any quoted material in your message to the bare minimum needed to establish the context of your reply.

✔ Don't cross-post to multiple lists.

✔ Watch out for *trolls*. These are messages calculated to provoke a storm of replies. Not every stupid comment needs a response.

✔ Save your message overnight and reread the message the next day before sending it off to the list.

Urrp! Computers digest messages!

Some mailing lists are *digested*. No, they're not dripping with digital gastric juices; they're digested more in the sense of *Reader's Digest*. All the messages over a particular period (usually a day or two) are gathered into one big message with a table of contents added at the front. Many people find this method more convenient than getting messages separately because you can easily look at all the messages on the topic at one time. (For the picky reader — the *Reader's Digest* also abridges articles. Most mailing list digests don't.)

Some mail programs give you the option of dividing digests back into the individual messages so that you can see them one at a time, yet still grouped together. This option is sometimes known as *undigestifying,* or *exploding,* a digest. (First it's digested, and then it explodes, sort of like a burrito.) Check the specifics of your particular mail program to see if the program has an option for digest-exploding.

Often you respond to an interesting message from a list by clicking your e-mail program's Reply button. But does your reply go *just* to the person who sent the original message, or does your reply go to the *entire list?* The answer depends mainly on how the list owner set up the software that handles the list. Fortunately, you're in charge. When you start to create a reply, your mail program shows you the address to which you're replying. Look to see if your mail is going to the group or to an individual. If you don't like the address being used, change it. Check the To and Cc fields to make sure that you're sending your message where you want it to go.

While you're fixing the recipient's address, you may also want to change the Subject line. After a few rounds of replies to replies to replies, the topic of discussion often wanders away from the original topic, and changing the subject to better describe what is really under discussion is a nice gesture.

Some Neat Mailing Lists

A large number of lists reside on the Internet — so many, in fact, that entire *books* have been written that just enumerate all the *lists*.

Stephanie da Silva maintains and updates a large directory of publicly available mailing lists monthly. This directory is the most complete list of lists we know. She posts her lists to the USENET group news.lists. The list is also available at http://www.neosoft.com/internet/paml.

There are several good directories of mailing lists on the World Wide Web:

- ✔ http://www.tile.net
- ✔ http://www.liszt.com
- ✔ http://catalog.com/vivian/interest-group-search.html

To get you started, here are a bunch of lists we find interesting and short descriptions of what they are:

Ghostletters

Join lively two-, three- or even all-way conversations between a host of historical and fictional characters! You choose a persona from fiction, history, or of your own making, and you may soon find yourself discussing any number of topics with personalities from literature, your nation's past, animals, Hollywood celebrities, mythical creatures, or unique and unusual members of your own community. Only one person is permitted to take on any individual persona, so confirmation is required.

To subscribe, send the following message: subscribe GHOSTLETTERS *yourcharactersname* to listserv@listserv.aol.com.

For example: subscribe GHOSTLETTERS King David

Internet TourBus

A virtual tour of cyberspace that comes out every week or so. It's entertaining even if you do not have full Internet access. Their motto is "Why Surf When You Can Ride the Bus?"

To subscribe, send the message Send SUBSCRIBE TOURBUS *yourfirstname yourlastname*to LISTSERV@LISTSERV.AOL.COM.

PBS Previews

The weekly online newsletter of the U.S. Public Broadcasting Service.

To subscribe, send the message sub web-update to www@pbs.org.

E-Zines

This Internet Web site has a long list of electronic magazines or *e-zines* that are delivered via e-mail. You can subscribe to most of them using only e-mail as well.

```
http://propagandist.com/tkemzl/
```

Dilbert Newsletter

A sporadic newsletter written by Scott Adams, author of the most authoritative source of information on the computer industry, the comic strip *Dilbert*.

To subscribe, send a message with the subject line:

```
newsletter
```

and the message body

```
subscribe Dilbert_News yourfirstname yourlastname
```

to listserv@listserv.unitedmedia.com

Pen pals

Finally, we did promise you pen pals at the beginning of this chapter. Here is a Web site where you can register and be matched up with a pen pal somewhere else in the world — just for general chatting and whatnot.

Unfortunately, you need Internet access and a Web browser to use this site. But once you have your e-pal's address, you can correspond using only e-mail.

```
http://www.comenius.com/keypal/index.html
```

More, More, More Mailing Lists

Thousands of mailing lists exist. Keeping score is difficult. In the "Part of Tens" later in this book, we give you some more to try.

You can find out if a LISTSERV list has "XYZ" in its name or title by sending the following message to any LISTSERV server: LIST GLOBAL/XYZ

The LISTSERV server sends you e-mail with all the matches. If you leave out the /XYZ, you will get back a message containing all known LISTSERV mailing lists. That's one loooooong list.

Starting Your Own Mailing List

You can start a simple manual list with nothing more than an e-mail program that supports distribution lists. When a message comes in, you just forward the message to the distribution list. That's all there is to it; you have a mailing list!

Before you start a new list, check to see if a list that meets your needs already exists.

You will soon tire of administering your list manually. Many local Internet providers offer mailing list support, sometimes for a small fee. Many universities also maintain mailing lists. If someone in your group has a university affiliation, he or she may be able to have a list maintained there.

To add your list to Stephanie da Silva's compilation, send a request to arielle@tarongo.com. Include the following information:

- The listname
- The contact (request) address
- The list address
- A brief description of your list, following the format of other entries in da Silva's database

Chapter 17

E-Mail Security

*W*e are nice people. We're sure that you, having the discernment to buy this book, are a nice person. We bet that most of your friends are nice people, too. Nice people just don't read mail that is not intended for them.

Not everyone has such scruples. Some people are just nosy busybodies. Others believe what they are doing is *sooo* important that they *need* to read your e-mail — as, for example, in the following situations:

✔ Your employers may believe that they have a right to know what the company's computers are being used for, so they monitor everyone's e-mail. Depending on where you work, they may actually have a legal right to do this.

✔ The United States government, which only wants to protect you from terrorists, drug dealers, and child pornographers, believes so strongly that its agents must read your mail that it has pressured e-mail software suppliers not to provide security features unless they permit the government to access your data.

✔ Other governments, which just want to help their local corporations keep up on the competition, are using their intelligence agencies, built up during the Cold War, to monitor commercial communications.

Many people, ourselves included, find that the general lack of security for e-mail is a real threat to personal privacy. We would like all mail users to have the option of sending their e-mail messages in a coded form that no one but the intended recipient can read — a process called *encryption*.

Phil Zimmermann, an Internet folk hero who invented a popular encryption program called PGP (Pretty Good Privacy) — which we discuss in the following chapter — offers the following neat analogy to emphasize e-mail users' need for encryption:

> Perhaps you think your e-mail is legitimate enough that encryption is unwarranted. If you really are a law-abiding citizen with nothing to hide, why don't you always send your paper mail on postcards? . . . Are you trying to hide something? You must be a subversive or a drug dealer if you hide your mail inside envelopes. Or maybe a paranoid nut. Do law-abiding citizens have any need to encrypt their e-mail?

A major reason for the lack of Internet and e-mail security has been the United States government's strong opposition to the widespread commercial availability of secure computer systems. For much of this century, the U.S. intelligence community has used intercepted communications as a major source of intelligence on foreign and domestic activities considered hostile and does not want to give up that strategic advantage.

Other governments like to eavesdrop, too, of course, but the United States is the world's largest source of computer software, and our government uses its laws to limit the export of secure computer systems. U.S. computer manufacturers avoid export hassles by keeping their products cryptographically inoffensive. As a result, the components on which the Internet is built are full of security holes.

The U.S. Government is now pushing a technology called Government Access to Keys (GAK), which will allow software companies to include strong encryption in their products as long as they build in a way for the government to access your data — without your knowledge — if it gets a court order. This proposal is like requiring you to deposit an extra set of front door keys with your local police department in case they ever get a warrant to search your house.

When e-mail was a toy for computer geeks, its lack of privacy may not have mattered. With e-mail poised to become a nearly universal means of communication in the 21st century, privacy matters now. No perfect solutions to this problem are out there yet, but the following sections described some of the best options you have for now.

How Can Anyone Even See My Mail?

You may wonder how all those supposed snoops out there can get their dirty hands on your e-mail. Unfortunately, accessing e-mail messages is not that hard to do. As your e-mail message makes its way to its destination,

Should I give out my credit card number over e-mail?

Two different views on this practice prevail.

One camp says that many other ways are available for crooks to steal credit card numbers, so why worry about sending yours over the Net? Crooks can fish discarded paper receipts out of dumpsters much more easily than they can intercept e-mail messages. And, at least in the United States, consumers' liability in case of fraud is limited to $50 per credit card, as long as problems are reported promptly.

The other camp counters that computer use enables fraud to occur on a much more massive scale than we have seen in the past. The best technology available, therefore, should be used to make cyberspace as safe as it can be, and everyone should insist on secure links before using e-mail or the Internet for credit card and other financial transactions.

that message passes through many different computers. In most of these computers, your message is stored for only the briefest moment while the computer decides what to do with it. Someone who knows what he or she is doing and has access to the inner software sanctum of these wayside computers, however, can install a special program called a *packet sniffer*. This program can intercept all the messages that pass through that computer or, if so instructed, can nose out only those messages with *your* name in the address.

In fact, e-mail is especially vulnerable to snooping. Electronic eavesdroppers can program computers to filter, sort, and file away intercepted messages. Wiretapping a phone call is a much more labor-intensive task — a human ultimately must listen to each conversation.

Unless you encrypt your e-mail, anyone who intercepts your message can read it as easily as you can. These days, nothing is safe without precautions.

Encryption

So what is this encryption stuff, anyway? If you ever got a secret decoder ring as a prize in a candy box or worked a cryptoquote puzzle in the newspaper, you have an idea of how encryption works.

Roughly speaking, each letter in your message is replaced by a different letter based on some predetermined rule. The secret decoder ring, for example, may replace all *A*s with *C*s, all *B*s with *D*s, and so on. The person on the other end reverses the process to read the message.

Encryptors used for e-mail, however, employ much more complicated rules. Exactly how these rules work is determined by a special string of *bits* — ones and zeros — in the computer. This string is called a *key*. If you and the person with whom you're corresponding both have the same key, you can communicate with one another. If you keep your shared key secret from everyone else, no one but the two of you can read your mail. Those nasty folks using the sniffer to try to read your e-mail see only nonsense, such as the following:

```
I9UOKi724BTVqbTlcc+VfolfWv/szrYO+KrUNEnq1hyAVkJRpbhY4
yU1aCMKL4C/QCXA3OTZRhYM1yJi24csvEZwaMkAKRcRk5QwcPRAAR
```

People who work with codes call these scrambled nonsense letters *ciphertext*. The original message is called *plaintext*. The set of rules used for scrambling the letters is called the *encryption algorithm* or just the *cipher*.

My key is bigger than your key

For the most part, you don't need to know how encryptors work. One fact about an encryptor, however, does affect you: how many bits are in the keys it uses. If an encryptor is well designed, the only way you can crack a message encrypted by it is to try all the possible keys until you find the right one. If the encryptor's key length is long enough — 128 bits is sufficient — trying all the keys that may exist is physically impossible. If the key length is shorter, security depends on how big the cracker's computer is and how short your key is. Key length is a major factor that the U.S. government considers in deciding whether a company may export software that uses encryption.

Table 17-1 lists key length, products that use keys of that size, and how strong each key is in terms of its security.

Table 17-1	Key Lengths	
Size	*Where Used*	*How Strong*
128 bits	PGP, Netscape Navigator (U.S. version)	Secure for the foreseeable future
80 bits	Clipper, Tessara	Secure for the next twenty years at least
64 bit	Lotus Notes, Domestic version	Secure against all but the most powerful opponent
56 bits	DES	Can be broken with moderate resources
40 bits	Export versions of Netscape Navigator	Can be broken with a few fast PCs

The keys to the kingdom — public key cryptography

You may be thinking, I keep losing the keys to my car. How am I going to keep track of all the e-mail keys I need to talk to my friends? I need a key for each person I want to talk to. That can be a *lot* of keys. And how do I have a private conversation with someone I've never met? Keeping all those keys secret isn't easy, either.

Some people think they have a solution to this messy key-management problem — one called *public key cryptography*.

Invented in the mid-1970s, public key cryptography simplifies encrypted communication. Public key cryptography gives you two keys, one that you keep secret (your *private* or secret key) and another that you can give to everyone (your *public* key). Here's how the system works:

1. **For two people (say, John and Tonia) to communicate by using encrypted e-mail, each must first have the other's public key in the computer.**
2. **John encodes messages to Tonia by using Tonia's public key.**
3. **Tonia decodes John's messages by using her secret key.**
4. **Tonia encodes her reply to John by using John's public key.**
5. **John decodes Tonia's reply by using his secret key.**

You use public keys to encode messages; you use secret keys to decode them. The only secret key you ever need is your own. You should *never* give anyone else your secret key.

If you are curious to see what a public key looks like, here is a printout of Arnold's public key:

```
—BEGIN PGP PUBLIC KEY BLOCK—
Version: 2.6.2

mQCPAy9MyROAAAEEANejhFb64tLhD1xa/
kOmLHRPuXNW2vVvjaOluCX1Ntcu7EWA
K8PnmWqruEOWflkBA42g6iwta9B/Bm8JOYfkk6T7CrnAeBN/
IuepQa4uJXXk7AqO
whO3vF8TzPk6STIJAPTQ9CWQ+6MHnwmDk9RzDwxtnS8dMKGXiWtruC2sMYShABEB
AAGOKOFybm9sZCBHLiBSZW1uaG9sZCA8cmVpbmhvbGRAd29ybGQuc3RkLmNvbT6J
AJUDBRAwwLyzkGCWpQlZ7KkBARKaBADCggEzWe2tLvHn9/
QkSfPnTMJhXiSDzz6V
```

(continued)

(continued)

```
K2Xwzyo/TElV632ZNQ6yQ9IMRObQAs95LNwwd4iGPoeZ30CqNvqaGkU
4fJjz6gW9
v/szgwOfINa9lsRtfOJWvKyBiq9J9JC/q9mA6T7mmhDsoWXJZ6/
h49AeNF2KCszE
LyybOtAgAokAlQMFEC925FzVMiHPX201uQEBxCMD/
33cCtdo6yGPWdCddZlx+aBh
tTrat81WwYc2QfIdSphryVeP5nK95YOmsR+94ESgKEzpJQGIYJsK8ZLsu7AaQrYE
CNHkQhe6EkW/
Oy4t4X36Yx3qufwKmP4jc5WCliT6o4T+RpCidbrGm3mw9loWJexV
UBp4apxK/
rRPaZX7AgoriQCVAwUQLOzKK2truC2sMYShAQELTAQAyOAbV87SYPAJ
tzm3iJwBkcxDoBE/
VOdY29H9ZgKSGnebVSySqKpeo5rJq+XFr1sDZ7cZyYac0paR
FcCFE7sAZoy7bLTMBu6KbhX5YndWqRL+uT8xkNscugPi609RTo7lroMeA847TuQ7
fl9tYFB25HpDWeKh+CR2Gh3mf4LnvCc=
=M7fR
——END PGP PUBLIC KEY BLOCK——
```

Ugly, huh? Fortunately, programs such as PGP enable you to keep all your friends' public keys in a special file called a *keyring* so that you never need to look at this stuff. In addition, a number of key servers exist around the world — many accessible by using only e-mail — where you can look for a friend's public key and list your own.

Despite many promises, the only popular programs that use public key cryptography to protect e-mail are PGP and Lotus Notes. You can now purchase a PGP plug-in for Eudora that gives Eudora mail the protection of PGP encryption. Web browsers, such as Netscape and Internet Explorer, use public key cryptography to protect online transactions, like credit card purchases. Secure e-mail features are coming soon, they say.

Sign on the Dotted Line

Public key cryptography can be used for more than just keeping information secret; it can also be used to sign your e-mail messages by adding an electronic signature that cannot be forged — at least in theory. The same technique that creates the electronic signature can tell you whether a signed document that you receive is complete and unaltered. This signature- and message-verification process is called *authentication*.

How do they do that?

Here's how authentication works: The electronic version of your document is passed through something called a *hashing function,* a little computer program that produces a string of bits that depend on all the information in the documents with some cryptographic magic thrown in. This technique keeps bad guys from altering a document in such a way that its hash value remains unchanged — for example, in an attempt to change the sale price in a contract.

The hash bits are then encrypted with the signer's secret key, and the resulting signature field is transmitted along with the document. The recipient can then hash the received document, decrypt the signature field using the signer's public key, and compare the two; if both hashes match, the recipient can be sure that the sender actually sent it. The recipient can also be sure that the document received is exactly what was sent.

Gimme that key

This theory assumes that the sender's private key has not been stolen. The sender must protect the private key at all times. Suppose that the sender was a bit sloppy one time. How do you prove that the key was not compromised? Fortunately, United States law, as we understand it (lawyers we ain't), takes a broad view as to what constitutes a valid signature, so electronic signatures are likely to remain widely accepted in commercial practice. And several states have passed, or are considering, new laws that explicitly recognize electronic signatures.

The recipient also needs some way to get a valid copy of the sender's public key. This problem is not unique to digital signatures; managing keys is the biggest problem in all forms of practical cryptography.

One solution is to use *certificate agents* who, for a fee, issue keys to the general public that were signed by the agent. You get your signed key in the form of an electronic file called a *certificate*. If you send a copy of your public key certificate to someone else, they can verify it if they have the agent's public key. Web browsers already come with the public keys of several certificate agents built in.

One company that sells key certificates is VeriSign, Inc., 2593 Coast Avenue, Mountain View, CA 94043. You can get more information about VeriSign by sending e-mail to info@verisign.com or by visiting the company's Web site at http://www.verisign.com.

VeriSign likes to call the key certificates "Internet Driver Licenses." They offer these licenses at the following three levels:

- ✔ **CLASS 1:** Low level of assurance; only uniqueness of the owner's name is verified, with no proof of identity. Sometimes offered free with other software, a Class 1 certificate normally costs $6 per year.

- ✔ **CLASS 2:** Next level of assurance. Owner identity is checked using consumer databases, but without requiring the person's physical presence. Cost is $12 per year.

- ✔ **CLASS 3:** A higher level of assurance; additional verification and physical appearance before an agent such as a notary public is required. Cost is $24 per year.

Some observers have criticized certificate agents as being unwieldy and potentially dangerous. The PGP people use a different method, known as *a web of trust.* You sign your friends' PGP keys; they sign yours; their friends sign *their* keys; and so on. Eventually, enough of these signature chains exist that you can find someone you know who has signed the key of someone else who has signed the key of the stranger with whom you need to establish signature trust. This concept somewhat resembles the letters of introduction of olden days.

How secure is public key cryptography?

Subject to the following several big *ifs,* public key cryptography is quite secure:

- ✔ If the program you use is carefully written. Only careful scrutiny by cryptographic experts over an extended time, however, can determine just how carefully such a program is written. In the fall of 1995, for example, errors in the encryption code then used by Netscape enabled two graduate students, Ian Goldberg and David Wagner, to discover ways to break Netscape's code. Fortunately, those errors have now been fixed, and we hope this kind of public review catches other errors quickly.

- ✔ If your key is long enough. (See the following section.)

- ✔ If no breakthroughs occur in the mathematical knowledge needed to crack public keys. (Progress to date has been slow but steady.)

- ✔ If you use it correctly and can ensure security for the computers that encrypt and decrypt your messages.

Are you sure you want an electronic signature?

Years ago, while we were visiting Japan, our hosts gave us a *chop:* a carved wooden stamp with our name translated into Japanese kanji characters. They offered to take us to an office in Tokyo where we could register our chop. For a few yen, we could get a nicely calligraphed certificate that we could frame. The only problem was that the chop would then become "official," and anyone who stole it could sign our name in a legally binding way. We declined.

An electronic signature is much like a chop, with one big difference: You are likely to notice if your chop is stolen; on the other hand, your private key and its enabling pass phrase can be copied off your computer in several ways, and you may never learn about the theft until it is too late.

Try a simple experiment. With a pen, write "*E-Mail For Dummies* Private-Key Awareness Test" on a blank 3.5-inch diskette. Now try for a week to keep the diskette under your total personal control. Keep it in your pocket during the day; put it under your pillow at night; don't forget to take it into the shower with you. If you do need to put it down, make sure that you hide it well or lock it up. At the end of the week, think about who could possibly have had access to it while you weren't watching. Then ask yourself, "Do I want to add to my life a physical object that requires this kind of attention as long as I live?"

Some public-key schemes encrypt the private key by using a *pass phrase*. This pass phrase makes theft more difficult, but not so difficult that you can be careless with your key disk. So think carefully before issuing a public electronic signature. Unless you really need one, you may want to wait until better technology is available — for example, secure PCMCIA key cards. If you can't resist or if your work requires you to have an electronic signature, be prepared to protect it as one of your most important possessions.

Although public key technology is strong now, you cannot rely on the current technology to keep your messages secret forever.

How big should my public key be?

If you use PGP for encryption, you are asked in the beginning how big you want your public key to be. We recommend that you select the 1,024-bit option.

Some products limit you to 512 bits because of United States export restrictions. Is this big enough? Not if you are worried about someone with the resources of a large government or major corporation behind them reading your mail.

Your public key is formed by multiplying together two *prime numbers* — numbers that cannot be divided evenly by any other number. The numbers 3, 5, 13, and 127, for example, are prime numbers, but 4, 15, and 49 are not. Your secret key is the *pair of prime numbers,* each typically 75 to 150 digits long, that your program uses in making up the public key.

Public key cryptography works because mathematicians have a difficult time determining the two primes that produce the public key if the key is big enough. If, for example, we ask you for the product of 1,823 times 2,617, you can probably figure out the answer, 4,770,791, even without a calculator. If, on the other hand, we ask you to find the two numbers that you need to multiply together to get 51,978,374,799,051, you are almost certain to have a hard time calculating the answer without a computer. And the bigger products used in public key cryptography are *very* hard to crack even *with* a computer.

As for what's big enough . . .

- ✔ RSA Data Security, Inc., the company that owns the patents on this type of public key cryptography, recommends that your public key be at least this long for varying lengths of security:

    - For short-term security, 768 bits.

    - For medium-term security, 1,024 bits.

    - For long-term security, 2,048 bits.

- ✔ Any 512-bit key, the largest the United States currently allows in software for export, can be broken, albeit with considerable effort.

- ✔ Most PGP users choose at least 1,024-bit keys.

How smart are smart cards for storing my key?

Smart cards look like credit cards, but they have a microchip inside that contains your secret key. When you insert your smart card into a reader slot and enter the correct password or personal identification number (pin), the microchip performs encryption and authentication tasks, but your secret key never leaves the tamper-resistant package.

Smart cards are a much safer way to store your key. Many do not provide a way to back up you secret key, so *losing* your smart card is a dumb thing to do.

Avoid Talking about Religion or Politics Except . . .

Avoiding discussions of religion or politics is considered a good policy in polite society. Unfortunately, the politics of e-mail security may well affect what kinds of encryption products you can get and how private your e-mail may be in the future. Law enforcement agencies around the world are appalled at widespread public use of encryption and are trying their best to control it. The following controls, for example, are among those employed in the United States and elsewhere:

✔ Export of strong cryptographic software is illegal in the United States.

✔ The United States is pressuring software manufacturers to adopt encryption standards that include requiring a way for the government to have access to your secret keys.

✔ Great Britian and the European Union are considering restrictions on cryptography that requires government to have access to your keys.

✔ France and Russia have banned cryptography outright.

✔ Many other countries are considering restrictions on cryptography.

What are key escrow and GAK?

Key escrow is a new class of encryption technologies in which a master key that can read all your messages is split into two pieces and the pieces are stored for safekeeping with two different *escrow agents* — special organizations that promise not to give out your key information without proper authorization. This type of technology appeals primarily to the following types of individuals:

✔ Those who run large organizations and who fear an employee may abscond with the keys needed to decode vital data.

✔ Representatives of law enforcement and intelligence agencies who need to read the messages of people considered a threat to society.

The United States government's first attempt to push key escrow, the Clipper chip, never caught on. Clipper was an attempt to get everyone to use special encryption hardware, developed by the National Security Agency, that had built-in key escrow. The U.S. government is proposing a new regulation called *Government Access to Keys (GAK)*. Software vendors can now get approval to export stronger encryption if they agree to add, within two years, features that let the government have your key under court order. These GAK features will automatically send copies of your keys to approved private-sector key escrow agents.

The European Union is working on a GAK regulation of its own. Some people consider GAK to be a reasonable compromise that may finally allow encryption technology to see widespread use. Civil liberties groups and many people on the Internet, however, are horrified by the idea of GAK, likening it to the police demanding a key to your home to keep in case they ever need to search it. The government access to keys battle is far from over. Stay tuned.

Why are there domestic and international versions of software?

Using encryption within the United States is not illegal — at least not yet. What *is* illegal is exporting encryption software from the United States without a license. The U.S. State Department grants export licenses only to encryption software that is relatively weak. Usually, this means that the maximum key sizes allowed are 40 bits for conventional encryption and 512 bits for RSA encryption. This also means that software vendors who want to sell any product in the United States with credible strength must make two versions, one for sale and use in North America and one for overseas sales. U.S. vendors can export products with 56-bit keys if they agree to incorporate government access to keys within two years.

Both 40-bit session keys and 512-bit RSA keys can be broken by an organization with enough computers. In a recent contest, a 40-bit key was broken by students in under three hours. The International Security version of Netscape Navigator (which may be exported) uses 128-bit session keys, but it reveals all but 40 bits of the session key in the message header, making it easy to break. The U.S. security version supports full 128-bit keys without compromise. You can find out which version you are using by selecting About Netscape.

PGP also comes in domestic and international versions, but in its case, the two versions are necessary because of patent problems, not allowable key sizes. Both versions use 128-bit session keys and allow RSA keys up to 2,047 bits in length. Both are equally strong. The United States government does not approve of the export of PGP, and, for a while, was considering prosecuting Phil Zimmermann when someone (not Phil) did export it.

What can happen if I don't use encryption?

A stolen customer list could cost you sales. A leaked positive HIV test could ruin a person's life. An investigative reporter's field notes on a drug cartel could get the reporter killed. The more severe the consequences of data compromise, the more carefully the data needs to be protected.

What about anonymous remailers?

Several sites on the Internet offer anonymous remailing services. If you are unwilling to reveal your true identity when sending mail or posting news, you can send your message to one of these sites. The sites strip off all identifying information in your message's header and then repost the message with a randomly assigned pseudonym. Some sites enable recipients to use that same pseudonym in replying to you.

How safe are these services? Here's what one wrote about its service:

> Short of having everyone run a public-key crypto system such as PGP, there is no way to protect users from malicious administrators. You have to trust my personal integrity. Worse, you have to trust the administrators on every mail-routing machine on the way, as the message only becomes anonymous once it reaches my machine. Malicious sysadmins and crackers could spy on SMTP mail channels, sendmail queues, and mail logs. But as there are more than 3,000 messages being anonymized every day, you have to be pretty perverted to scan everything.

Let's get real. Electronic intelligence services are omnivorous. They specialize in collecting information that can be used years later. They keep warehouses full of tapes of intercepted traffic, in the hope that some snippet will come in handy someday. With so many messages from people letting their electronic hair down, remailers are a juicy target. You can bet that more than one foreign security agency must be collecting all the e-mail going to and coming from every remailer that it can tap, including the mail before it becomes anonymous. One good lead to someone who can be blackmailed 10 years from now would be worth the effort. Sorry, but that's the world we live in.

In some cases, the law requires you to protect information. A publicly traded company, for example, had better not allow any outsider to see its quarterly financial results before these results are made public. A psychiatrist may be liable for failing to protect clients' treatment records. Europe has especially strict data-privacy laws. In the United Kingdom, for example, the Data Protection Act of 1984 provides penalties for anyone who stores personal information on any computer and fails to take reasonable measures to prevent disclosure of that information.

If you have government-classified information to communicate, the National Security Agency or your local equivalent tells you what to do about it. You had better listen to them — not to us.

What constitutes a good login password?

A password should contain enough randomness to be secure but still needs to be easy enough to remember. Here are some suggestions:

- An unrelated pair of words selected at random from a dictionary, preferably separated by a special character or number (for example, `hotbed%esquire`).

- A pronounceable string of nonsense syllables at least eight characters long (such as `roshantewa`). Some computers can generate such passwords for you. See `http://world.std.com/~reinhold/passgen.html` for a Java applet that does this.

- A random license-plate number you see on the highway. (But *don't* use your own license-plate number!)

Top Ten E-Mail Security Tips

Here are ten tips on how to better protect your e-mail.

- Always use randomly selected keys, passwords, and pass phrases. Never use single dictionary words or your favorite literary quotes.

- Never perform encryption, decryption, or key generation on a multiuser computer or a computer connected to a network.

- Don't connect your sensitive internal network to the Internet without a firewall.

- The best way to perform encryption, decryption, or key generation is on a battery-powered laptop with no cables plugged in.

- Diskettes, tapes, and hard disks that contain sensitive information are very difficult to erase completely.

- Spend ten times more money, time, and effort on physical security than you do on encryption.

- Take security seriously, day in and day out. Don't be careless and don't be cute.

- Don't print sensitive e-mail messages on remote laser printers.

- Remember that copies of your e-mail probably exist on backup tapes at both the sender's and the receiver's computers.

- Be careful not to violate United States export laws if you live in the United States (or if you are a U.S. citizen who plans on coming home).

Chapter 18
Pretty Good Privacy (PGP)

● ●

In This Chapter

▶ Getting a copy of PGP

▶ Creating a good secret pass phrase

▶ Making your public and secret keys

▶ Encrypting and decrypting messages

▶ Signing messages

● ●

*P*GP, which stands for *Pretty Good Privacy*, is a freeware encryption program with a very loyal following. The program was first written by Phil Zimmermann and released over the Internet in 1991. Phil has recently started his own company, PGP Inc., to sell PGP-based products. Here are some things you should know about PGP:

✔ The free version of PGP is still available over the Internet, but only for noncommercial use.

✔ Commercial versions of PGP are available from PGP Inc. at `http://www.pgp.com`.

✔ The free version of PGP is harder to use than a lot of software you might be familiar with, like Eudora, but PGP Inc. now sells a more user-friendly version called PGPMail 4.5.

✔ PGP enables you to make your own public and secret key pairs.

✔ PGP public keys are distributed and certified via an informal network called "The Web of Trust," which is kind of like the letters of introduction popular in the pre-electronic era.

✔ Most experts consider PGP very secure if used correctly.

✔ For three years, Philip Zimmermann, the developer of PGP, was threatened with federal prosecution in the United States for alleged involvement with exporting PGP. The investigation was finally dropped in January 1996.

In this chapter, we describe how to use the basic command line version of free PGP that runs on a PC under MS-DOS, in a DOS window under Microsoft Windows 3.1 and Windows 95, and on UNIX. We also describe how to use MacPGP2.6.2, which runs on almost any Macintosh computer.

A variety of freeware and shareware PGP add-on programs are available on the Internet that attempt to make PGP easier to use. PGPMail 4.5 also fixes many usability problems, but it is not free, it cannot be sold outside North America, and is only availabe for Windows 95 and Windows NT at this time. While the actual commands differ, much of what we say in this chapter about the Macintosh version of PGP will help you use these programs as well.

Getting Ready to Use PGP

Setting up PGP is more complicated than setting up most application programs. Before you can start using PGP, you must take the following steps:

1. **Get a current version of PGP that works on your computer.**

2. **Unpack and install PGP on your computer.**

3. **Make up a good secret pass phrase.**

4. **Create your own public and private keys.**

5. **Validate your public key.**

6. **Give copies of public key to your friends.**

7. **Get copies of your friends' public keys.**

Each of these steps takes some effort to get right. Make yourself comfortable and we'll go through them one at a time.

Encryption technology is beset by legal issues, both in the United States and in many — if not most — other countries. We believe that you have a legal right to use PGP in the United States, but we are not lawyers and cannot give legal advice. We suggest that you consult a lawyer if you have legal questions. But be aware that lawyers who are knowledgeable in this field are few and far between.

For more on the politics of PGP visit Francis Litterio's Cryptography, PGP, and Your Privacy page:

```
http://world.std.com/~franl/crypto.html
```

Getting a current version of PGP that works on your computer

How you can legally obtain a copy of PGP and which version to get depends on who and where you are. Before you blame the complexity of what you are about to read on the Byzantine minds of the developers of PGP, realize that this system is probably the best they could come up with, given U.S. export laws and the maze of patents and copyrights that apply to PGP. After all, until recently, PGP was considered to be in the same category as anti-aircraft missiles.

You are a U.S. citizen currently living in the United States

If you are a U.S. citizen or permanent resident and live in the United States right now, you have the following three choices for obtaining PGP:

- Buy the commercial version of PGP from PGP Inc., 2121 S. El Camino Real, Suite 902, San Mateo, CA 94403. Call them at 1-888-747-3011 or 602-944-0773.

- Get a copy from a friend who has PGP. As far as we can determine, this is perfectly legal if your friend knows that you are a U.S. citizen. You may want to get a copy of the Immigration and Naturalization Service's Form I-9 to find out what the INS considers valid proof of citizenship.

- Download a copy of the PGP program over the Internet. This option is the one most people use. In the rest of this section, we tell you how to do this.

Sites that distribute PGP take special precautions to verify that you live in the United States and agree to obey U.S. export restrictions. These sites also ask you to acknowledge a license from RSA Data Security, Inc., which holds many of the patents on Public Key Cryptography used in PGP.

The primary North American distribution site for PGP is the Massachusetts Institute of Technology (MIT) in Cambridge, MA. If you have Netscape Navigator or another World Wide Web browser, perhaps the easiest way to get PGP is to go to the MIT PGP Web page at the following location:

```
http://web.mit.edu/network/pgp.html
```

You are asked if you are a citizen or permanent resident of the United States. If you say "yes," if MIT can figure out from your Internet address that you are in the United States, and if you started at the right time, you can download PGP or MacPGP without much fuss. You are asked to answer the following four questions:

```
1. Are you a citizen or national of the United
States or a person who has been lawfully admitted
for permanent residence in the United States?

2. Do you agree not to export PGP 2.6.2, or
RSAREF to the extent incorporated therein, in
violation of the export control laws of the United
States of America as implemented by the United
States Department of State Office of Defense Trade
Controls?

3. Do you agree to the terms and conditions of
the RSAREF license (in /pub/PGP/rsalicen.txt)?

4. Will you use PGP 2.6.2 solely for noncommercial
purposes?
```

If you said "yes" to all the above, if MIT can figure out from your Internet address that you are in the United States, and if you started at the right time, you can download PGP or MacPGP without much fuss.

Yes, that's right, we said "started at the right time." To make sure that you can get PGP only by going through the listed procedure, MIT changes the name of the directory where the PGP software is kept every 30 minutes. The name changes at the hour and on the half-hour. If you don't get everything you need before the name change, you have to start over. So a good idea is to begin this little treasure hunt just after the hour (say, between 3 and 3:10 p.m.) or just after the half-hour (say, between 3:30 and 3:40 p.m.) to give yourself as much time as possible to download the program. The PGP files generally download in under 12 minutes on a good day.

If you don't have Web access but do have both telnet and FTP access, you can telnet to `net-dist.mit.edu` and login as `getpgp`. You are asked the same questions. If you pass the test, you are then given the magic name for the PGP distribution directory that is valid at that moment.

You then have until the end of the half-hour-pumpkin-time to FTP on over to `net-dist.mit.edu`, login as `anonymous`, enter your e-mail address as the password, `cd` to the magic directory name you were given and `get` the right files. Pheew.

If you only have e-mail, you can try using the FTP-via-e-mail methods described in Chapter 19, but you may have difficulty negotiating the anti-export features at most PGP repositories.

If you live in Canada

The method for Internet PGP distribution to Canada is a little bit different. If you're using a Web browser, go to MIT's Canada page at the following address:

```
http://web.mit.edu/network/pgp-form-canada.html
```

You are asked a set of questions oriented to Canadian residents. From there on, the procedure is the same as for the U.S. residents, as described in the preceding section.

If you live outside North America

People living outside of the U.S. and Canada in countries that permit PGP use can obtain PGP over the Internet pretty much without restriction. The primary international distribution site is at the following address:

```
http://www.ifi.uio.no/pgp
```

You can also get PGP by using FTP from numerous other FTP sites, including the following sites:

```
ftp://ftp.ox.ac.uk/pub/crypto/pgp
ftp://ftp.nl.net/pub/crypto/pgp
ftp://ftp.funet.fi/pub/crypt
```

If you plan on using the international version for commercial purposes, you need to get an end-user license for the IDEA encryption technology that PGP uses. Prices start at $15 per user for up to 50 users. For information, send e-mail to IDEA@ascom.ch or check its Web page at http://www.ascom.ch/ systec. The PGP Inc. version for commercial use in North America includes the required IDEA license.

Why shouldn't North American users download PGP2.6.2i from an international site? Well, a big fuss arose over PGP's use of patented RSA technology. The deal that settled everyone down requires that things be set up the way they are. If you use the international version in North America, you risk the ire of RSADSI for violating their patents.

Which version of PGP should I get?

If you live in North America and own a Macintosh with a 68020, 68030 or 68040 processor or a PowerMac, get MacPGP2.6.2. If you own an older, 68000-based Macintosh, get MacPGP2.6.

If you have an IBM PC or compatible, get PGP2.6.2 for DOS.

If you live outside North America, get one of the international versions. They have similar names but end in an *i* — for example, PGP2.6.3i.

For a more complete and up-to-date list of download locations and available versions, see the "Where To Get The Pretty Good Privacy Program (PGP) FAQ" at the following address:

```
http://world.std.com/~franl/pgp/where-to-get-pgp.html
```

If you use Microsoft Windows, you can buy PGPMail 4.5 or you can get one of a number of free or shareware Windows front ends to PGP. You still need PGP2.6.2 for DOS, but you can access the program by using the Windows front end to provide a graphical interface.

The most popular Windows front ends are available for free or as shareware over the Internet. They include the following programs, among many:

- **AEgis Shell.** The developer, AEgis Research, says that the shell works with Windows 3.1, Windows 95, and Windows NT.
- **PGP Winfront.** Developed by Ugali International Corp.
- **Private Idaho.** This utility for PGP and anonymous remailing for Windows e-mail software was written by Joel McNamara. Private Idaho enables you to send and receive encrypted e-mail in standard Internet format.

You can find links to all these front ends and more at the following Web page:

```
http://www.primenet.com/~shauert/pgpwins.htm
```

or Francis Litterio's PGP page:

```
http://world.std.com/~franl/pgp
```

Unpacking and installing PGP on your computer

PGP is distributed in compressed format. The DOS version is usually transmitted in Zip format. You need a program such as WINZIP or pkunzip to extract the file. The Macintosh version is supplied as self-extracting archives in BinHex format.

PGP is shipped "double-wrapped" so that it can be signed. For example, after you first extract the contents of the Macintosh version in the MacPGP2.6.2 Binhex file you download, you see a .sea file. This file is a self-extracting archive. You need only to double-click its icon to open this file.

The extraction process creates a folder called *MacPGP2.6.2-Installation Folder.* Inside this folder is *another* self-extracting archive called *MacPGP2.6.2-130v1-inner* and a file called *MacPGP2.6.2-130v1-inner.asc*, which contains a PGP signature for the second self-extracting archive. You can go ahead and double-click the "inner" file icon to extract PGP, but don't throw out the "inner" archive if you want to do things right and check its signature later.

Similarly, after you unzip the DOS version of PGP, PGP262.ZIP, you see two files: *PGP262I.ZIP* and *PGP262I.ASC.* The PGP262I.ASC file contains the signature for PGP262I.ZIP. You needn't worry about this yet. Just unzip PGP262I.ZIP for now.

The PGP262I.ZIP file that appears after you unzip the PGP distribution is the "inner" zip file that is signed. This file has nothing to do with PGP262i, the international version of PGP we told you about earlier in this chapter. (Sorry. We didn't set things up this way.)

Making up a good secret pass phrase

Before you make your public and secret keys, you need a *pass phrase.* Because just walking up to a computer and copying someone's secret key file is so easy, the designers of PGP added a feature that stores the secret key in a coded form. To unlock this coded secret key, you must type in the right pass phrase.

Pass phrases, as used in PGP, were invented by Sigmund Porter in 1982. They can be longer than the typical 8- to 10-character password and are used to give added security.

A lot of mumbo-jumbo has been written on how to make up your pass phrase. We have a simple prescription: Just pick five words at random from a dictionary. A password chosen this way provides very good protection for your secret key — better than most PGP users enjoy — and five words is not too much to remember or too long to type in each time you need it.

A pass phrase word list

A dictionary of very short words, designed to simplify picking out random words by using ordinary dice, is available from the Internet at the following Web address:

```
http://net.dummies.net/diceware.wordlist.asc
```

The word list is indexed so that words can be randomly selected by tossing five dice. The list is made up of short English words, abbreviations, and easy-to-remember character strings. The average length of each word is about 4.2 characters. The longest words are 6 characters. The list is based on a longer word list posted to the Internet by Peter Kwangjun Suk.

The following is a short excerpt from this word list:

```
16665     cleft
16666     clerk
21111     cliche
21112     click
21113     cliff
21114     climb
```

Using the list

Each word in the list is preceded by five numbers ranging between 1 and 6, corresponding to the marks on an ordinary die (which is the singular term for *dice*, if you didn't already know). To pick a random word, just shake a die in a glass, throw it five times, write down the five numbers, and then look up the numbers in the word list. If, for example, you rolled the die five times and it came up 2, 1, 1, 1, 3, you look up 21113, and your next pass phrase word is *cliff*. Repeat this process until you have five words. Those five words are your pass phrase.

If you want to work from a printed copy of the word list, open it in your word processor and format it with four columns and 54 lines per page. You get a neat, 36-page printout in which the first two dice throws are constant for each page. This printout makes looking up word values especially easy. Be careful not to mark the printed copy while you are selecting words. Someone might use the marks to guess your pass phrase.

Nineteenth-century security precautions are in order here: Make sure that you are alone. Close the curtains. Write your words on a hard surface, not on a pad. Burn your notes and pulverize the ashes after you memorize your pass phrase. Or eat the paper, if necessary.

The following are some sample pass phrases generated by using this list:

```
le puddly flame hang beside
cohn jewett ewe epic jones
creek 36th broom foggy evade cogent
```

Again, we recommend a five-word pass phrase for use with PGP. If you are lazy, a four-word pass phrase still provides reasonable protection. A six-word pass phrase makes attacks on your pass phrase unfeasible for the foreseeable future.

Pass phrases are case-sensitive, which means that the following two phrases are *not* the same:

Should I write down my pass phrase?

Most authorities say that you should never write down your pass phrase. We don't agree. Most of us just are not that confident of our ability to memorize passwords and phrases, especially those for infrequently used accounts. The risk of someone trying to steal your secret key is theoretical for most of us. The risk of forgetting is all too real.

At best, losing a pass phrase means the hassle of creating a new key pair, revoking the old key, and distributing the new public key. At worst, the loss could result in your inability to read important mail in time to act on it — or even losing valuable data files forever. As a result, even people who know better may choose a short pass phrase that is easy to remember — and equally easy to guess.

If writing down your pass phrase spurs you to pick a stronger pass phrase, we say go ahead and write it down — but keep it in a safe place. What's a safe place? Your wallet; a secret hiding place at home; or, if you have a great many paper files, a random file folder (but *not* one labeled "Pass Phrase"). For high-security situations, a bank safe-deposit box is a good choice. *Never store your pass phrase on or near your computer.*

```
early think vy haul book
Early Think Vy Haul Book
```

Some people encourage you to use weird capitalization in your pass phrase to make it more secure. We think that doing this just makes remembering and accurately typing your pass phrase too hard and is not worth the trouble. Add a sixth word if you are paranoid.

Creating your own public and private (secret) keys

Before you make your keys, you must tell PGP where to put them. (If you have gotten this far, you may have some scatological ideas about this, but just take a deep breath and go on.) PGP stores keys in special files called *keyrings*. Normally, you keep your keyrings on your hard disk with the rest of PGP. If you like, you can keep PGP on your hard disk, but keep your keyrings on a floppy disk stored in a safe place.

Making your keyring

If you use a PC, read the following section. If you use a Mac, jump to the section after this one.

For PC users

If you use a PC version of PGP, copy CONFIG.TXT to the floppy disk along with the keyrings. PGP creates the other files it needs. You also need to set your PGPPATH environment variable so that PGP can find the files it needs. To do so, add the following lines to your AUTOEXEC.BAT file:

```
SET PGPPATH=C:\PGP
SET PATH=C:\PGP;%PATH%
SET TZ=EST5EDT
```

(These lines specify that PGP and the keyrings are on your hard disk.)

Alternatively, add the following lines:

```
SET PGPPATH=A:\
SET PATH=C:\PGP;%PATH%
SET TZ=EST5EDT
```

These lines specify that your keyrings are on your floppy disk A: drive.

The first line in each set of code tells PGP where to find the keyrings and CONFIG.TXT. The second line tells your system where to find PGP. The third line specifies your local time zone; see the file DOC\SETUP.DOC that comes with PGP for a more complete list.

Now reboot your system.

For quick Help at any time, enter **pgp -h** at the DOS prompt.

For Mac users

For MacPGP users, insert the diskette you want to use (if any), choose Options⇨Set Keyring, click the button next to the keyring you want to set, and click Do It. Then select the disk and folder where you want your keyrings located and click Open.

For quick Help at any time, choose Apple⇨Help from the menu bar.

Making your keys

This is the big moment. You are now ready to create your very own public and private PGP key pair.

From a PC, enter the command **pgp -kg** at the DOS prompt.

From a Mac, choose Key⇨Generate Key.

PGP prompts you for the rest of the information it needs. You are asked to enter the following three items of information:

- ✔ Your pass phrase.

- ✔ Your user ID, which is then associated with the key. The preferred form is *Firstname Lastname <email@address>* — for example, `Allen Dulles <oss@dummies.net>`

- ✔ The size of your public key. Most PGP users choose 1,024 bits, which is more than enough for anyone whose computer is not under armed guard 24 hours a day.

Backing up your secret key

Your private or secret key is stored in your secret keyring file. You need to make a backup copy of this file on a floppy disk of its own and keep the disk in a safe place. Better yet, make two backup copies and store them in different locations. If you lose your secret key, *no one* can re-create it for you.

Validating your public key

The first thing you need to do is to sign your public key. Remember way back when we told you that can use PGP to sign documents? Well, you also sign public keys. Signing a public key is a way of saying, "I know the person to whom this key belongs." Signing a public key does not mean that you vouch for the person's integrity — or even like the person. This action means only that you know that the person is who he or she claims to be.

Spinning a Web of Trust

A big problem with all this public key stuff is knowing that a public key really came from the person whose name is on it. Other advocates of public key technology are proposing complex hierarchies in which your key is registered with some big organization that signs your key. The big organization's key is signed by some bigger agency and so on up to some super-dooper master certifying agency, maybe at the UN or something.

The developers of PGP don't like this idea. They believe that having such agencies for signing keys centralizes control of your electronic identity into the hands of big business and big government. (The U.S. Post Office, for example, is thinking of getting into the key certificate business.) So the PGP gang came up with a different, more organic approach called the *Web of Trust*.

The Web of Trust — which has nothing to do with the Internet's World Wide Web, by the way — works by having people sign the keys of people they know. If you have enough signers, and I have enough signers, and all the signers have enough signers, the chances are good that we may have a signer in common. If so, we can be pretty confident that we each are who we say we are. For example, Bill knows Bob who knows Sally. Bill also knows Marko who knows Irena who knows Ofer. So Sally can know who Ofer is. The Web of Trust is a nice concept, and no one can revoke your keys because you didn't pay your parking tickets. We hope that it catches on.

In any case, the first step in the Web of Trust is to sign your *own* key. Signing your own key just proves to the world that your public key comes from someone who has the matching secret key and prevents some of the arcane games that cryptographers spend much of their time worrying about.

To sign your key:

- ✔ From a PC, enter **pgp -ks *yourname*** at the DOS prompt, substituting your actual name for *yourname*.
- ✔ From a Mac, choose Key⇨Certify key and follow the instructions.

Next, you need to copy your public key off your keyring and put it into a little text file of its own that you can give on a floppy disk to someone or paste into an e-mail message. To extract your public key as a text file:

- ✔ From a PC, at the DOS prompt enter **pgp -kxa yourname keyfilename**.

- ✔ From a Mac, choose Key⇨Extract keys and follow the instructions.

Dusting for fingerprints

While you're fussing with your keys, you should extract your *key fingerprint* as well. Suppose that someone who knows you calls you up and says, "Hey ol' buddy, I got this here public key that has your name on it. Is it really yours?" You could sit there on the phone while he reads your public key back to you:

"Small 'M,' capital 'Q,' capital 'C,'' small 'Y,' number '9,' <yawn> . . . ."

A public key can have hundreds of letters in it. Sitting there listening to them is a big drag. To solve this problem, PGP enables you display a *key fingerprint* — a string of characters generated by running a special function on your key. As with human fingerprints, the chance that two PGP users would ever have the same key fingerprints is so small as to be practically nonexistent. Key fingerprints contain only 32 letters and numbers, and the letters are all the same case. Arnold's PGP fingerprint, for example, looks like this:

```
FA C3 82 FB 05 5E 03 1A  34 04 79 EA 9E 76 7B 67
```

and John's looks like this:

```
3A 5B D0 3F D9 A0 6A A4   2D AC 1E 9E A6 36 A3 47
```

If you were checking up on one of these key, you'd need to read only these 32 letters and numbers over the phone, which is only a minor drag.

PGP fanatics put their key fingerprints on their business cards, their stationery, their e-mail signatures, their front doors, the books they write, and so on.

To see your PGP fingerprint:

✔ From a PC, at the DOS prompt type **pgp -kvc** *yourname*.

✔ From a Mac, choose Key⇨Fingerprint Key and then select your key from the list in the dialog box that appears.

Write down your fingerprint in a handy place, such as in your address book, so that you can help someone verify your public key at any time.

Exchanging public keys with your friends

Your friends need your public key to send you coded messages. (When we say *friends*, we really mean anyone with whom you want to communicate in private.) You can safely give your public key to anyone — friend, stranger, or enemy. On the other hand, if someone knocks on your door and says that she is from the phone company, your bank, Dummies Central, or *whatever* and asks to see your secret key, slam the door. Now. Got that?

You can get your public key to someone in the following ways:

✔ **In person.** Just copy the little public key file you made onto a floppy disk and hand it to the person. You can even send the disk by postal mail or express delivery service.

✔ **By e-mail.** Include the file *keyfilename* in a message and e-mail it.

✔ **Use a PGP key server.** We discuss this option in the section "Key servers at your service" later in this chapter.

Adding a key

If a friend gives you his or her public key, you need to add it to your public keyring file. Adding a new key to your public keyring is actually easier than adding a metal key to one of those circle rings, where you have to pry up one end, slip the hole in the key under that half of the circle, and slide the key all the way along until it snaps off the other end.

If you want to add a key you are given that has the filename *newfilename* to your public keyring:

- From a PC, at the DOS prompt enter **pgp -ka newfilename**.
- From a Mac, choose Key⇨Add keys and select *newfilename* from the dialog box.

You are asked if you want to certify this key. Do *not* do so unless you know the person and she personally handed you the key file on disk, or you have verified the key fingerprint over the phone with the person and you recognized her voice.

The PGP distribution should come with a file called `KEYS.ASC`. This file contains the public keys of several PGP honchos. Adding the keys in this file to your public keyring is good practice and you can use the keys to verify that the copy of PGP you have is valid. See the section " Verifying a separate signature" later in this chapter.

To add these big-shots' keys to your keyring:

- From a PC, at the DOS prompt type **pgp -ka keys.asc**.
- From a Mac, choose Key⇨Add keys and then select `keys.asc`.

How do you know that the `KEYS.ASC` file itself hasn't been tampered with?

- From a PC, at the DOS prompt type `pgp -kvc "Philip R. Zimmermann <prz@acm.org>"`.
- From a Mac, choose Key⇨Fingerprint key, select your public keyring in the dialog box, and then select Philip R. Zimmermann from the list.

PGP should reply with the following information:

```
looking for user ID "Philip R. Zimmermann <prz@acm.org>".
Type bits/keyID     Date        User ID
pub  1024/C7A966DD 1993/05/21 Philip R. Zimmermann
            <prz@acm.org>
Key fingerprint =  9E 94 45 13 39 83 5F 70  7B E7 D8 ED C4
            BE 5A A6
1 matching key found.
```

Because the other keys in `KEYS.ASC` are signed by Phil, if the key fingerprint you get matches that in the preceding example, you (and your copy of PGP) are safe.

Well, you're sort of safe. Anyone clever enough to make a doctored version of PGP could have it recognize that you are checking its signature and print out the "all clear" message. You really ought to get PGP from two independent sources and use each to check the other. If you are a gentle, laid-back, trusting sort of soul, this crypto stuff should cure you of that really fast.

Getting your key certified

To get your key certified, first extract a copy of your key:

- ✔ From a PC, at the DOS prompt enter **pgp -kxa yourname yourname.asc**.
- ✔ From a Mac, choose Key⇨Extract keys and follow the instructions given.

Give *yourname.asc* to a friend who has PGP. For that person to add your key to her keyring:

- ✔ From a PC, at the DOS prompt she types **pgp -ka** *yourname.asc*.
- ✔ From a Mac, she chooses Key⇨Add keys and follows the instructions given.

PGP asks if she wants to certify this key. She answers "yes" and enters her personal pass phrase. She now extracts a fresh copy of your key from her keyring:

- ✔ From a PC, at the DOS prompt she types **pgp -kxa** *yourname yourname.asc*.
- ✔ From a Mac, she chooses Key⇨Extract keys.

She then gives the key back to you on a floppy disk.

To add it back into your keyring:

- ✔ From a PC, at the DOS prompt enter: **pgp -ka** *yourname.asc*.
- ✔ From a Mac, choose Key⇨Add keys.

You now have a signature on your key. From now on, anybody who knows your friend, trusts her, and has a copy of her public key knows that your public key is legitimate.

Getting your key certified remotely

Suppose that your friend is a long distance away, but you still want to exchange signatures. Simply send your key to your friend by e-mail. She adds your key to her keyring as before, but she *doesn't* certify it because she has no way to know that the key wasn't tampered with on the way.

Both of you get the key's fingerprint. Remember that a PGP key fingerprint is a string of 32 letters and numbers. (See the section, "Dusting for fingerprints," earlier in this chapter.) Now call your friend on the phone, make sure that you recognize her voice, and read her the 32 letters and numbers in the fingerprint. If the fingerprint matches what she has, she knows that she has a legitimate copy of your key. She can now sign your key, extract it, and e-mail it back to you. You then add it to your public keyring as before.

What a pretty keyring!

To view all the keys in your public keyring:

- ✔ From a PC, at the DOS prompt enter **pgp -kv**.
- ✔ From a Mac, choose Key⇨View Keyring and select your public keyring in the file dialog box.

To view all the keys in your public keyring, along with who has certified each key:

- ✔ From a PC, at the DOS prompt enter **pgp -kvv**.
- ✔ From a Mac, choose Key⇨View Keyring, select your public keyring in the file dialog box, and in the next dialog box that appears, select the Show Signatures Also check box.

Key servers at your service

A number of universities and other organizations around the world operate public PGP *key servers* on a volunteer basis. These key servers enable you to submit your key and look for keys submitted by others. You can submit and search for keys by Internet FTP or by e-mail.

Most of the organizations that run these key servers make no attempt whatsoever to verify the keys. (One exception, however, is Four-eleven, which does ask for some ID and then signs your public key. But Four-eleven also charges a $20 fee to list your public key. Four-eleven is on the Web at http://www.Four11.com, or send e-mail to info@Four11.com.)

Most key servers process requests from you that are sent as e-mail messages. You give the server one command per message. Commands are entered on the *subject* line of your message, as in the following example:

```
To: pgp-public-keys@pgp.mit.edu
From: Arnold Reinhold@world.std.com
Subject: help
```

You only need to send your key to one volunteer server. That server forwards your Add request to the other servers automatically.

To add your key to a key server, for example, or to update your key if it is already there, send a message similar to the following to any server:

```
To: pgp-public-keys@keys.us.pgp.net
From: Arnold Reinhold@world.std.com
Subject: add
—BEGIN PGP PUBLIC KEY BLOCK—
Version: 2.6.2

mQCPAy9MyROAAAEEANejhFb64tLhD1xa/
kOmLHRPuXNW2vVvjaOluCX1Ntcu7EWA
K8PnmWqruEOWflkBA42g6iwta9B/Bm8JOYfkk6T7CrnAeBN/
IuepQa4uJXXk7AqO
whO3vF8TzPk6STIJAPTQ9CWQ+6MHnwmDk9RzDwxtnS8dMKGXiWtruC2sMYShABEB
AAG0KOFybm9sZCBHLiBSZWluaG9sZCA8cmVpbmhvbGRAd29ybGQucc3RkLmNvbT6J
AJUDBRAwwLyzkGCWpQlZ7KkBARKaBADCggEzWe2tLvHn9/
QkSfPnTMJhXiSDzz6VK2Xwzyo/
TElV632ZNQ6yQ9IMRObQAs95LNwwd4iGPoeZ3OCqNvqaGkU4fJjz6gW9
v/szgwOfINa9lsRtfOJWvKyBiq9J9JC/q9mA6T7mmhDsoWXJZ6/
h49AeNF2KCszE
LyybOtAgAokAlQMFEC925FzVMiHPX2OluQEBxCMD/
33cCtdo6yGPWdCddZlx+aBh
tTrat81WwYc2QfIdSphryVeP5nK95YOmsR+94ESgKEzpJQGIYJsK8ZLsu7AaQrYE
CNHkQhe6EkWOy4t4X36Yx3qufwKmP4jc5WCliT6o4T+RpCidbrGm3mw91oWJexV
UBp4apxKrRPaZX7AgoriQCVAwUQLOzKK2truC2sMYShAQELTAQAyOAbV87SYPAJ
tzm3iJwBkcxDoBEVOdY29H9ZgKSGnebVSySqKpeo5rJq+XFr1sDZ7cZyYacOpaR
FcCFE7sAZoy7bLTMBu6KbhX5YndWqRL+uT8xkNscugPi6O9RTo7lroMeA847TuQ7
fl9tYFB25HpDWeKh+CR2Gh3mf4LnvCc=
=M7fR
—END PGP PUBLIC KEY BLOCK—
```

Most key servers accept the commands shown in Table 18-1.

Table 18-1	Server Commands
Command	*Meaning*
ADD	Your PGP public key. (The key to add is the body of the message.)
INDEX *userid*	List of all the PGP keys that match the user ID.
VERBOSE INDEX *userid*	List of matching PGP keys, along with any signatures they may have.
GET *userid*	Get just that one key.
MGET *pattern*	Get all keys that match *pattern*.

What if someone steals your secret key?

If you have reason to believe that your secret key was compromised, the only thing you can do is revoke your public key, create a new pair of PGP keys, and circulate the revocation file containing your new public key as widely as possible. To revoke your public key:

✔ From a PC, at the DOS prompt enter **pgp -kd** *yourkeyid*.

✔ From a Mac, choose Key⇨Disable/ Reenable key.

PGP asks if you really want to do this and then prompts for your pass phrase. You then extract a plain-text copy of your now-revoked key and distribute it widely, just as you did after you first made it. You also need to make a new key pair for yourself, extract the public key, and distribute the new public key at the same time. After you revoke your own key, you cannot re-enable it, despite what the Mac command name implies.

Notice that you need both your secret key and pass phrase to revoke your key. If you lose either of them, you 're stuck. This situation is why we recommend that you make at least two backup copies of your secret key and why we think that writing your pass phrase down and keeping it somewhere safe is okay.

You should normally send e-mail key server requests to the following address:

```
pgp-public-keys@keys.pgp.net
```

Or send them to your national server at one of the following addresses:

```
pgp-public-keys@keys.us.pgp.net
pgp-public-keys@keys.de.pgp.net
pgp-public-keys@keys.nl.pgp.net
pgp-public-keys@keys.no.pgp.net
pgp-public-keys@keys.uk.pgp.net
```

Use `ftp.pgp.net:pub/pgp/` for FTP access to key servers.

Using PGP

This section tells you (at last!) how you actually use PGP to send and receive encoded messages.

Sending George a secret message

We assume that you have George's public key on your keyring. (See the section "Adding a key" earlier in this chapter if you don't.)

Begin by typing your message in a file and saving it as plain text. (We use *textfile* in the following examples as a substitute for whatever name you choose for the file.)

From a PC, at the DOS prompt enter **pgp -esat** *textfile* "George". (**estat** stands for **e**ncrypt, **s**ign, **A**SCII output, files are **t**ext.) Leave out the **s** if you don't want to sign the document you are encrypting. Leave out the **t** if the original file is not an plain-text file.

If you tell PGP that a file is a text file, PGP handles the file's end-of-line characters, which vary from computer to computer, in a way that should work on any computer.

From a Mac, choose File⇨Encrypt/Sign and choose the name of the file you want to encrypt.

PGP prompts you for your pass phrase and then creates the file *textfile.asc*, encrypted and signed by you, suitable for mailing.

Signing a document

You can sign a document as part of the encryption process, or you can sign a document while leaving the body of the document unencrypted. You can even produce a signature file that is independent of the document.

To sign a text file without encrypting it:

- ✔ From a PC, at the DOS prompt enter **pgp -sat** *textfile*.
- ✔ From a Mac, choose File⇨Sign Only and select the text file you want to sign.

PGP asks for your pass phrase and then adds a PGP signature, similar to the one in the following example, to the end of the text file, as follows:

```
—BEGIN PGP SIGNATURE—
Version: 2.6

iQCVAwUBMArBSGtruC2sMYShAQEwEwQAzNIpRm29UXQwpT9AGctbnn/
4GrRibWCt
rgSUJaCYn+fP3NMalYUbEbljd+AbWXACuLSUCagKPEoC2vu6fzpO7h2q6TAFewrn
JAHFLJHIfvhUXKsQF84BbWdvK6u+qaDjJeTlvTrD4L2dUlEAOOtOVa9ntwPmzt+l
dHzeD3JBHFY=
=akuU
—END PGP SIGNATURE—
```

Signing a file separately

Sometimes, you want the signature file to be separate from the signed document. You may, for example, want to protect a binary file from viruses and tampering, the way PGP distributions are protected.

To sign a file separately:

- ✔ From a PC, at the DOS prompt enter **pgp -sba binfile**. (**sba** stands for **s**ign, **b**reak signature from file, **A**SCII output.)

  This creates a new file, named binfile.asc, which is the signature to binfile. Any modifications to binfile makes the signature invalid.

- ✔ From a Mac, choose File⇨Sign Only and then select the file you want to sign — for example, **binfile**. Then mark the Create Separate Signature File check box in the dialog box.

Reading encrypted files and verifying signatures

PGP is pretty clever in reading files. If you open a file in PGP, the program decrypts that file (if encrypted) or verifies the signature (if the file has one). If the file is signed and encrypted, PGP performs both functions.

From a PC, at the DOS prompt enter **pgp *thefilename***.

From a Mac, choose File⇨Open/Decrypt and then select the file you want to open from the file dialog box.

You are asked for your pass phrase if the file is encrypted. You are also asked where to put the output file. The output file is the actual signed document, decrypted if necessary. You can open the output file in any word processor. Most e-mail programs also enable you to open the file.

MacPGP has a handy option that decrypts to MacPGP's display window. This option enables you to view a message without writing an unencrypted version to disk.

A bug was found in older versions of PGP that affects plain-text signatures. The following line is meant to be followed by a *blank* line:

```
—BEGIN PGP SIGNED MESSAGE—
```

A signed document can be tampered with by adding text in front of that blank line.

Always examine the output of PGP when verifying a document signed with versions before 2.6.2. The input may be tampered with, but the output cannot be.

Verifying a separate signature

You verify the signature on a separate file by giving PGP both file names. For example, to check the signature on the copy of PGP you downloaded:

- ✔ From a PC, at the DOS prompt enter **pgp pgp262i.asc pgp262i.zip**.

- ✔ From a Mac, first choose File⇨MacBinarize and then select the file MacPGP2.6.2-130v1-inner. Next, choose File⇨Open/Decrypt and select the signature file in the file dialog box— in this case, MacPGP2.6.2-130v1-inner.asc. PGP then asks you what the signature applies to. Select MacPGP2.6.2-130v1-inner.bin.

PGP should tell you about a good signature from one Jeffrey I. Schiller. PGP also warns you that Jeffrey I. Schiller's signature hasn't been certified by anybody you know. This warning is normal.

Mac users can now drag the MacPGP2.6.2-130v1-inner.bin file into the Trash. We needed the file only to check the signature.

Can the NSA Crack PGP?

This question, regarding the NSA's ability to undo PGP encryption, is a perennial one on Internet newsgroups such as sci.crypt and alt.security.pgp. The NSA, of course, is the United States National Security Agency. NSA is the largest code-breaking outfit in the world, getting a big piece of the United States' $29 billion annual budget for intelligence. The days when the NSA's mere existence was a secret, however, are long gone. The agency has a nice World Wide Web home page at the following address:

```
http://www.nsa.gov:8080
```

The NSA certainly can crack PGP if you use a key length of 512 bits or less. But what if you use the 1,024-bit key size we recommend? The truth is that no one outside the NSA (and very few inside) can say for sure. No techniques that have been published are even remotely close to breaking keys that big. And the 128-bit session keys seem equally impregnable. Our gut feeling is that the NSA cannot crack the codes used in PGP. Is our gut feeling worth much? Probably not.

If the NSA really wants to obtain data encrypted with PGP, can they do so? More often than not, we think, they can. To achieve the level of security PGP is capable of takes discipline. See Chapter 17. Remember, however, that PGP promises only pretty good privacy. Without more attention to security than an average person is likely to stand for, that is all PGP can provide. It's a tough world.

Chapter 19
The Internet by E-Mail

*T*he Internet contains many *mail servers* that provide access to various services. You send an e-mail message to the server telling it what you want, and it sends back a response, which — with any luck — is actually what you asked for. Retrieving information this way isn't as quick as the *native* connection to these services (Netscape for the World Wide Web, for example), but it's a lot better than nothing. A few services that we list are available *only* by e-mail.

Mailing Many Makes of Files

Some servers return files of non-text information, such as programs and digitized images or sounds. The servers use the same file-mailing techniques, MIME and uuencoding, that we discuss in Chapters 3 and 15. If you receive a non-text file from a server, handle the file the same way that you handle an attached file received from anyone else. (See "A picture is worth a million bytes" in Chapter 3 and "I'm So Attached to You" in Chapter 15 for the details.)

FTP by Mail

FTP (file transfer protocol) is the Internet's way of letting you retrieve files from public archives all over the Net. For example, thousands of archives exist with hundreds of thousands, maybe millions, of files ranging from software to pictures to the text of *Alice in Wonderland*.

Mail server tips

✔ Most servers respond quickly (within a few minutes) after you send a request. But some, particularly the FTP-by-mail servers described later in this chapter, are very heavily loaded and can take days to respond. Patience is a virtue.

✔ If your mail program automatically adds a signature to your message, tell it not to do so to your request messages because servers won't understand the signature.

✔ You can usually send multiple requests in a single message. Put each request on a separate line.

✔ Most servers ignore the Subject: line of your message, so requests must be in the body of the message. But to keep life interesting, a few servers *require* that the request be in the Subject: line. Read the descriptions for each server carefully.

Several systems offer FTP by mail. These servers are all very slow, frequently taking several days to respond, but they're a lot better than nothing. The two most widely available services are FTPMAIL and BITFTP.

The most confusing thing about FTP by mail is that two separate computers other than your computer are involved: the one providing the FTP-by-mail service, and the one where the files actually reside. Any FTP-by-mail server can retrieve files available on any FTP server.

Table 19-1 lists the major public servers we know about. If the e-mail address starts with `ftpmail`, it's an FTPMAIL server; if it starts with `bitftp` it's a BITFTP server.

Table 19-1	FTP-by-Mail Servers
E-Mail Address	*Location*
`ftpmail@ftp.ramona.vix.com`	California, United States
`ftpmail@ieunet.ie`	Ireland
`bitftp@plearn.edu.pl`	Poland
`ftpmail@doc.ic.ac.uk`	Britain

FTPMAIL

FTPMAIL is a system that was originally written at Digital Equipment's lab in California and is now available at several sites (see Table 19-1). Use the site closest to you to minimize the load on expensive international network links.

You send FTPMAIL a list of commands that tell who you are, what system you want to retrieve your files from, and what files you want. The commands should include a *reply-to command* (if you're not sure, the return address on your mail gives your correct address) followed by *open* and other commands to specify what to retrieve.

Before trying to retrieve any files from an FTPMAIL server, first send it a one-line message containing

```
help
```

This verifies that the server is still available and gets you a list of the exact commands that the server supports. All of the FTPMAIL servers are more or less the same, but they all have minor differences that can trip up the unwary. The standard FTPMAIL commands are listed in Table 19-2.

Table 19-2	An FTPMAIL Cheat Sheet
Command	*Description*
reply-to *address*	Where to send the response.
open *host user password*	Where to FTP to. The default user is anonymous, and the default password is your e-mail address, usually the correct values to use for public FTP archives. At some sites this is connect rather than open.
cd *directory*	Change directory.
ls *directory*	List directory, short form. Default directory is the current directory.
dir *directory*	List directory, long form. Default directory is the current directory.
get *file*	Retrieve that file and mail it to you.
compress	Compress returned files or directory listings with UNIX compress.
gzip	Compress returned files or directory listings with GNU gzip.
uuencode	Encode binary files using uuencode, the default. (See Chapter 15.)
btoa	Encode non-text files using btoa (an older uuencode-like system).
mime	Encode non-text files using MIME.

(continued)

Table 19-2 *(continued)*

Command	Description
force uuencode	Encode all files using uuencode.
force btoa	Encode all files using btoa.
force mime	Encode all files using MIME.
size *nnn*[K|M]	Set the size pieces in which a large file will be returned. For many mail systems, 64K is a good value. On some servers, this command is `chunksize`.
mode binary	Get subsequent files in binary (nontext) mode. (Default.)
mode ascii	Get subsequent files in ASCII (text) mode.
quit	Ignore any following lines (useful if you can't suppress your signature).

Let's say that you want to retrieve a file called `rfc821.txt` that is in the directory `rfc` on the server `ds.internic.net`. (This is one of the RFC documents we discuss at the end of Chapter 15.) You send a message to one of the FTPMAIL servers containing the following lines:

```
open ds.internic.net
cd pub
get rfc821.txt
quit
```

This says to go to the host `ds.internic.net`, go to the directory `pub`, and return the file `rfc821.txt`. Because this is a text file, it'll be returned as a regular text e-mail message.

You can get a list of files in a directory on a particular server in much the same way. To get a list of all the RFC documents, send this message:

```
open ds.internic.net
ls pub
quit
```

If your computer can handle files compressed by the `gzip` compression utility (most UNIX systems have gzip itself, and the popular Windows shareware WinZip can decode gzip files), you can request to receive the document in a more compact form by sending this message:

```
open ds.internic.net
gzip
mime
cd pub
get rfc821.txt
quit
```

This tells the server to compress the file using gzip and then send it as a MIME attached file. When you receive the response, you un-gzip the received file to recover the original. The gzipped version of the file is considerably smaller than the original, so if you receive mail via a dial-up connection, a gzipped version of a file downloads considerably faster than the plain text. Non-text files in most archives are already stored compressed, so gzipping won't help them any.

BITFTP

BITFTP, another FTP-by-mail system, was originally written for BITNET, an older network mostly containing IBM mainframe computers. BITFTP is now available to any user with Internet mail access. See Table 19-1 for a BITFTP server.

As with FTPMAIL, send a message containing `help` to a server before you retrieve files so that you can verify the availability of the server and find out about its particular commands. The standard BITFTP commands are listed in Table 19-3.

Also, as with FTPMAIL, the message you send should contain commands to specify the host, a USER command to log in, and then other commands to retrieve files, but of course the syntax is slightly different.

Here's the general sketch of what you send to BITFTP:

```
FTP hostname UUENCODE
USER username [password]
... commands ...
QUIT
```

The UUENCODE tells the server to uuencode binary files. (Other options are not pertinent to Internet users.) The most commonly used user name is anonymous, a general name that you can use on systems for which you don't need a personal account or a password.

Table 19-3	A BITFTP Cheat Sheet
Command	*Description*
ACCT *acctinfo*	Sends an ACCT command to the host to specify an account. Useful only in special cases.
ASCII	Retrieves files as text.
BINARY	Retrieves files as non-text.
CD *dir*	Changes to given directory.
DIR	Lists entries in current directory.
EBCDIC	Retrieves files in EBCDIC (used on IBM mainframes).
GET *filename*	Retrieves the specified file.
LS *dir*	Lists files in a directory.
MODE S|B	Retrieves files in Stream or Block mode. (Stream, the default, is almost always what you want.)
PWD	Prints current directory name.
QUIT	Ends session, disregards anything else in the message (useful if you can't suppress your signature).
SYSTEM	Prints the name of the FTP host's operating system.
TYPE A|I|B|E|F	Retrieved files are in ASCII (A), image (I), Kanji Shift JIS (B), EBCDIC (E), or EBCDIC IBM Kanji (F). By far the most common are A for text files and I for non-text files.

For the RFC example in the preceding section, you'd send this:

```
FTP rs.internic.net UUENCODE
CD pub
GET rfc821.txt
QUIT
```

Unlike FTPMAIL, BITFTP doesn't offer compression or any file-attachment scheme other than uuencoding.

What FTP servers are there?

Now that you know how to get files from FTP servers by mail, you have to find out what the FTP servers are. Fortunately, a large list is available from a mail server. To get this list, send a message to `mail-server@rtfm.mit.edu`, and in the message put:

```
send usenet/news.answers/ftp-list/sitelist/part1
send usenet/news.answers/ftp-list/sitelist/part2
send usenet/news.answers/ftp-list/sitelist/part3
... and so on up to ...
send usenet/news.answers/ftp-list/sitelist/part27
```

Each part of the list is 60,000 characters long, so unless you're sure you want a lot of mail in your mailbox, you should start by getting one or two parts of the site list and then get more after the first parts arrive.

The same server has lots and lots of FAQ (frequently asked questions) documents available. To get the one that talks about FTP, send a message containing this line:

```
send usenet/news.answers/ftp-list/faq
```

Archie by Mail

Archie is a service that helps you find servers that contain files available for FTP. You send Archie a request consisting primarily of a filename or a text pattern that specifies an approximate filename, and the server sends back a list of matching names and the FTP hosts where the files are available. Once you know which server has your file, you can use FTP-by-mail to retrieve the actual file.

Many Archie servers exist around the world. Pick a nearby one from Table 19-4.

Table 19-4	Archie Servers
Address	*Country*
archie@archie.unl.edu	United States
archie@archie.ans.net	United States
archie@internic.net	United States

(continued)

Table 19-4 *(continued)*

Address	Country
archie@archie.rutgers.edu	United States
archie@archie.doc.ic.ac.uk	United Kingdom
archie@archie.univie.ac.at	Austria
archie@archie.funet.fi	Finland
archie@archie.th-darmstadt.de	Germany
archie@archie.rediris.es	Spain
archie@archie.luth.se	Sweden
archie@archie.unipi.it	Italy
archie@bunyip.com	Canada
archie@archie.sogang.ac.kr	Korea

Archie servers support all sorts of complicated options, as you can see in Table 19-5, but for most purposes the only command you need is `find`, which is the way you ask the Archie server to search for a filename. For example:

```
find winzip
```

You may want to use a few other commands before you use the `find` command:

- ✔ `set maxhits 50`: Normally, Archie returns a maximum of 100 files that match your request. You can set the number higher or lower. Usually a few dozen hits is more than plenty — how many different places do you need to find copies of the same thing? (You want Archie to find enough places so that at least one of them is in your country, though, to avoid slow international file retrievals.)

- ✔ `compress`: Compress and uuencode the results. If you can handle uuencoded mail (as Eudora can) and can decode UNIX *compress* format archives (using either compress itself or a program like WinZip, which knows about compress), this command can make the returned message smaller and hence faster to download to your PC.

Table 19-5	An Archie Cheat Sheet
Command	*Description*
find *name*	Returns files that match that name.
whatis *name*	Returns entries from the "whatis" descriptive database that match that name.
compress	Compresses and uuencodes the response.
set *options*	Set optional parameters. Plain "set" returns all current settings.
servers	Returns a list of Archie servers.
path *addr*	Returns the response to that address rather than to the return address on the request.
help	Sends a help message.
quit	Disregards anything else in the message.

Gopher by Mail

Gopher is a networked menu system that was a predecessor to the better-known World Wide Web. The Gopher system organizes all of its information into pages that contain menu items. Some items refer to other menus, while some are documents and other kinds of files.

Gophermail returns Gopher pages by e-mail. It is a nicely designed service — you can go from one page to the next easily by responding to the pages sent by the server.

Servers currently include

- gophermail@ncc.go.jp (Japan)
- gopher@pip.shsu.edu (Texas, United States)
- gophermail@eunet.cz (Czech Republic)
- gopher@nig.ac.jp (Japan)

Start by sending an empty message to one of the servers. The server should send you back a copy of its home page, as shown in Figure 19-1. To retrieve any entry from that page, merely mail back the page it sent you with an X in front of each menu item that you want. When the server returns subsequent pages, you can, in turn, send those pages back with Xs in front of the items you want.

```
Mail this file back to gopher with an X before the menu items that you want.
If you don't mark any items, gopher will send all of them.
For best results, remove this message and all e-mail headers above it prior
to returning it to the GopherMail server.
1. Sam Houston State University Information/
2. Current Time and Weather in Huntsville, Texas, USA.
3. Daily Almanac (from UChicago).
4. Economics (SHSU Network Access Initiative Project)/
5. Information by Subject Area/
6. DIU Library Prototype Demonstration Area/
7. Network-based Information and References/
8. Other Gopher and Information Servers in the World/
9. TeX-related Materials/
10. Literate Programming Library/
11. VMS Gopher-related file library/
12. Veronica (search menu items in most of GopherSpace)/
13. Professional Sports Schedules from culine.Colorado.edu/
14. anonymous ftp archives on Niord.SHSU.edu/
15. anonymous ftp archives on ftp.shsu.edu/
16. Texas Legislative Gopher/
17. GopherMail @nd Gopher via Electronic Mail!!
```

Some Gopher items are *search* items. To use a search item, you provide some words in the Subject: line of your message, and the Gopher server looks for items in an index that match your search words.

The most well known Gopher searcher is Veronica, which searches through a large database of Gopher items. But there are many other indexes as well. If you select a search item, remember to put the words to search for in the Subject: line of your reply. (In the absence of search items, the Subject: line is ignored.)

For more details, send a message containing the word `help` to one of the Gophermail servers.

Chapter 20

E-Mail in the Round — Online Chat

In This Chapter

▶ Let's have a chat

▶ Chatting on America Online (AOL)

▶ Chatting on CompuServe's Chat (or CB Simulator)

▶ Chatting on Internet Relay Chat (IRC)

*I*f you like e-mail, and you like instant gratification, online chatting may be just what you're looking for. E-mail is fast, but sometimes you have to wait awhile for the other person to get around to logging in, checking their e-mail, and replying to your message. *Online chat* lets you communicate with another person who is logged in anywhere in the world — instantaneously. Chatting is like talking by typing — sending messages back and forth as fast as your fingers let you. In this chapter, we tell you about chat and how to get the most out of it.

Let's Have a Chat

Remember passing notes in school? You'd write a sentence or two on a slip of paper and pass it to a friend. She'd add a line or two and pass it back. Maybe a third or fourth person would join in. You could carry on a whole conversation during algebra class. Chatting is like that except that you type what you want to say on your computer's keyboard and read the other people's replies on your screen. The other people are in front of their computers at the same time you are. That is what people mean when they say chat is *live* or takes place in *real time*.

If e-mail is like sending a letter, only faster, online chatting is like talking on the telephone, only slower. Most of us can talk faster than we can type, and while you usually see the other person's response immediately, there can be an annoying *lag* when the chat system is busy.

Besides the fact that you use your fingers and eyes instead of your mouth and ears to communicate, chat differs from the telephone in two other major ways:

> ✔ You often chat with more than one person at the same time.

> ✔ You often chat with complete strangers.

The latter is one of chat's biggest attractions — chat is a great way to meet people. You will be amazed at how easy it is to connect emotionally — even with a total stranger — using online chat.

Online chat comes in different flavors — well, different dominions. Where you chat depends on how you access the Internet. If you access the Internet through America Online, you chat with other AOL users. If you access the Internet through CompuServe, you chat with other CompuServe users. If you use any other kind of Internet service provider, you use Internet Relay Chat (IRC) to chat. IRC is a little bit more difficult to set up. (AOL and CompuServe are all set up and ready for you to chat.) There are actually different IRC networks, which don't communicate with each other, but we tell you more about that later in this chapter.

A Rose by Any Other Name

When you're considering plunging into online chatting, there are a few things you should know. Most people select a special name called a *screen name*, *handle,* or *nickname* to use when chatting. This name can, and often does, differ from your login name or e-mail address. Many people pick a name that says something about who they are, where they are, or what interests them. You can have more than one screen name. Here are some examples of screen names you might see:

> ✔ Steve825: 825 might be his birthdate or a number assigned by his provider.

> ✔ LaGal37: A 41-year-old woman from Los Angeles.

> ✔ CatLover3: CatLover1 and CatLover 2 were taken.

> ✔ HotSxyBabe: Most likely a 15-year-old boy.

> ✔ IntrntBkWtr: Highly intelligent and desirable publishing professional.

While your special chat name gives you some privacy online, someone could possibly find out your real identity, particularly if your service provider cooperates. Don't go wild out there.

Ways to chat

Chat systems generally offer two different modes, group conversations and private messages.

Just you and me, babe

You can select an individual to chat with by using their screen name, or someone can initiate a private chat with you. In this case, you see a special message window on your computer. You type what you want to say to the person in a separate box. When you click the Send button, your message appears in the conversation box, along with any responses.

Most systems let you turn off the messaging feature altogether if you do not want to be bothered. You generally cannot block messages from particular individuals, though you can simply choose not to reply.

Across a crowded room

In a group conversation, you see a window on your computer where the ongoing conversation appears. You type what you want to say to the group in a separate box. When you click the Send button, your message appears in the conversation box, along with any responses. You do not have to address each message, and your comments are limited to a sentence or two in each exchange.

Different terms exist for the online areas where group conversations take place. America Online (AOL) calls them *rooms*, while CompuServe and Internet Relay Chat (IRC) call them *channels*.

People in chat groups can be very unruly and even vicious. AOL and CompuServe's chat groups are, at least in theory, tamer because they provide some supervision. If you have children, you should carefully supervise their chat use.

Following the conversation

It takes practice to learn how to follow a group conversation if you want to make any sense of chats. Here is a sample of what you might see (screen names and identifying content have been changed):

```
NCGrl    : I LIVE IN CHAPEL HILL NC
LINDA157 : Well, I guess it's better than nothing
RShenk2720 : don't shout nc chick
Bobger   : hello for a sec
LINDA157 : hello Bobger
```

(continued)

(continued)

```
NCGrl    : im sorry im just really used to writing in caps
Renk2435 : nc chick do you have a gif?
Bobger   : followed soon by a "bye"   (hello linda)
QGal97   : hello room
BZarian3 : Hi QGal.  You're back in the same room.
QGal97   : any single guys out there?
Renk1635 : gal do you have a gif?
QGal97   : no gif and u?
Renk1635 : no
Sail869  : age/sex/location everyone
Renk1635 : what do you look like gal?
QGal97   : so why ask?
BZarian3 : 27/M/CA
QGal97   : 25/f
GoPats3  : Hello everyone!
Renk1735 : want to know what you look like
GAGRL    : 33/f/s,ga
Turtleb654 : 25/f/or
QGal97   : 5'8" dirty blond hair and brown eyes
Bobger   : <—————5' 7"
Badgerdig : 36/m/ca, about to sign off and produce more :)
BillyMD  : I'm short
Vixen5589 : bobger  produce more what?
Bobger   : work stuff, gotta presentation tmw
```

Here are some suggestions for getting used to chat rooms:

✔ There is usually a conversation that is already in progress when you enter a chat room. You cannot see what went on before you entered.

✔ Wait a minute or two for a pageful of exchanges to appear on-screen so you can understand some of the context before you start reading.

✔ Start by following the comments of a single screen name. Then follow the people that person mentions or who reply to that person.

✔ After you can follow one thread, try picking up another. It takes practice to get the hang of it.

✔ Some services, like AOL, let you highlight the messages from one or more screen names. Doing this can make things easier to follow.

✔ You can also indicate screen names to ignore. Messages from these chatters will no longer appear on-screen, though other members' replies to them will appear.

- ✔ Scroll up to see older messages if you have to, but remember that after you have scrolled up, no new messages will appear until you scroll back down.

- ✔ Many of the messages are greetings to familiar names as they join or leave the chat group.

- ✔ A few regulars often dominate the conversation.

- ✔ The real action often takes place in private one-on-one side discussions, which you cannot see.

Online etiquette

Chatting etiquette is not that much different from e-mail etiquette (see Chapter 4), and common sense is your best online guide, but here are some additional chat behavior tips.

- ✔ The first rule of chatting is not to hurt anyone. A real person with real feelings is at the other end of the computer chat connection.

- ✔ The second rule is to be cautious. You really have no idea who that other person is. See "Online chat safety awareness," the next section in this chapter.

- ✔ Read messages for a while to figure out what is happening before sending a message to a chat group. (Reading what's happening in a chat room or mailing list without actually saying anything is known as *lurking.*)

- ✔ Keep your messages short and to the point.

- ✔ Don't insult people and don't use foul language.

- ✔ Create a profile with information about yourself. Most chat systems have provisions for creating profiles that other members can access.

- ✔ You don't have to tell everything about yourself in your profile, but what you do say should be truthful.

- ✔ If you want to talk to someone in private, send that person a message saying hi, who you are, and what you want.

- ✔ If the tone of conversation in one chat room offends you, try another. As in real life, there may be more people out there whom you *don't* want to meet than people whom you *do.*

For more information on the history and art of meeting people online, see Philippe Le Roux's lead chapter, "Virtual Intimacy — Tales from Minitel and More" in *Internet Secrets,* from IDG Books Worldwide, Inc.

Online chat safety awareness

Here are some guidelines for conducting safe and healthy chats.

- ✔ Many people on chat groups lie about their occupation, age, locality, and yes, even gender. Some just think they are being cute, some are exploring their own fantasies, while others are really sick.

- ✔ Be careful about revealing information that allows someone to find you personally — where you live or work or your phone number. This includes last names, phone numbers, mailing address, schools that your kids go to, and so on.

- ✔ Never give out your password to anyone. No one should ever ask you for it. If they do, do not give it out, and let your service provider know about the request. (We were on AOL recently and received a message saying "There's been a serious threat to security and we need your password to help determine the problem." If you ever get a message like that, inform the provider's staff. No legitimate person will ever ask you for your password.)

- ✔ If your chat service offers profiles and a person without a profile wishes to chat with you, be extra cautious.

- ✔ If you are a child, never, ever meet someone without your parents. Do not give out personal information about yourself or any member of your family, even when you are offered some sort of prize for filling out a form.

- ✔ If your children use chat, realize that others may try to meet them. Review these guidelines with your kids before they log on. AOL has some additional guidelines. Go to the keyword **Parental Controls**, click Online Safety Tips, and open Take Five for Safety.

- ✔ Do not hesitate to report anyone who you believe is behaving inappropriately on a value-added service's chat group. On AOL, go to the keyword **TOS** and follow the instructions there. On CompuServe, go to the keyword **FEEDBACK.**

If you choose to meet an online friend in person, use at least the same caution that you would use when meeting someone through a newspaper ad:

- ✔ Don't arrange a meeting until you have talked to a person a number of times, including conversations at length by telephone over the course of days or weeks.

- ✔ Meet in a well-lit public place.

- ✔ Bring a friend along, if you can. If not, at least let someone know what you are doing and agree to call that person at, say, half an hour after the planned meeting time.

✔ Arrange to stay in a hotel if you travel a long distance to meet someone. Don't commit yourself to staying at that person's home.

Chat abbreviations and emoticons

Many chat abbreviations are the same as those used in e-mail (*see* Chapter 4), but, because chat is live, some are unique. Here is a list of chat abbreviations and emoticons:

```
AFK        Away From Keyboard
A/S/L      Age/Sex/Location (response might be 35/f/LA)
BAK        Back At Keyboard
BRB        Be Right Back
BTW        By The Way
GIF        A picture of oneself (see Chapter 15)
GMTA       Great Minds Think Alike
IM         Instant Message
IMHO       In My Humble Opinion
IMNSHO     In My Not So Humble Opinion
LTNS       Long Time No See
LOL        Laughing Out Loud
M4M        men seeking other men
ROTFL      Rolling On The Floor Laughing
TOS        Terms Of Service (AOL's member contract)
TTFN       Ta-Ta For Now!
WAV        a sound file
WB         Welcome Back
WTG        Way To Go!
:D         smile/big grin
:) or :-)  smile
;)         wink
{{{{bob}}}}      a hug for bob
:( or :-(  frown
:'(        crying
O:)        angel
}:>        devil
:P         sticking out tongue
***        kisses
<—    action marker (for example,  <—eating pizza)
```

In addition to the above, chatters sometimes use simple shorthand abbreviations. For example, "If u cn rd ths u r rdy 4 chat."

There's trouble — right here in River City

Some people act very badly online while hiding behind the anonymity that chat provides. You have four good options and one bad option when this happens.

The good options include

- Going to another chat room. Some rooms are just nasty. You needn't hang around.

- Paying no attention to the troublemaker and just conversing with the other folks.

- Making offenders disappear from your screen. On AOL, double-click the jerk's screen name in the room list and then click the Ignore box. On CompuServe, select People⇨Squelch and click the check box next to the slob's name.

- Complaining to the individual's service provider. This is most effective on the value-added services. See "Calling the room/channel police" under the heading for each service described later in this chapter.

The bad option is:

- Responding in kind, which just gives the offender the attention he or she wants and might get *you* kicked off your service.

Chatting on America Online (AOL)

Chat lets AOL users meet and have a conversation with other AOL users. People Connection is one of the most popular features AOL provides. The quality of AOL chat is a major reason why it is the largest value-added service provider. This section describes chatting using America Online 3.0 software.

Getting started chatting

To start chatting, click the People Connection icon in the main Channels screen or go to the keyword **Chat**. You see the People Connection Town Square screen and enter a Lobby room automatically. An actual online conversation appears in the large text window. A smaller window, the People Here window, lists all the people in the room.

If you double-click a screen name from the list in People Here, a window pops up and gives you three options:

- ✔ **Get Info:** Click here to see this member's profile, if it exists.
- ✔ **Message:** Click here to send this member an Instant Message.
- ✔ **Ignore:** Check this box and you will no longer see messages from this member.

You may find what you want in the Lobby room, but we doubt it. To see a list of other rooms you can visit, click the List Rooms icon and select a category in the left-hand window by double-clicking. Then double-click the room you want to visit. AOL takes you to that room, maybe.

AOL puts a limit on how many members can be in any one room, usually about 23 people. Some rooms are very popular and AOL automatically creates additional copies of that room type as earlier rooms of that type fill up. When this happens, you get a message:

```
The room you requested is full. Would you like to go to a
room like it?
```

You may as well click Yes; you don't have much choice anyway.

There's a room for you

You will find the conversation in most rooms pretty thin. Finding one you like takes some effort. Poke around. Look for a room with a narrow charter — locality, hobbies, medical problems, age, or religion, for example — that matches your interests.

AOL groups rooms into categories:

- ✔ **Lobby:** You are automatically in a Lobby room when you go to the People Connection. Many people never leave the Lobby room, so it is not uncommon to be in a room called Lobby 234 — meaning 233 other Lobby rooms were created before this one.
- ✔ **Town Square:** Contains the lobbies and other meeting rooms. The names of Town Square chat rooms vary, but they all feel about the same.
- ✔ **Arts & Entertainment:** Rooms here are organized around pop culture themes, with simulated bars, trivia quizzes, Trekkies, and other fun stuff.

✔ **Life:** You find a variety of lifestyles here, from gays to born-agains to born-again gays.

✔ **News, Sports, Finance:** Money, politics, and jocks are here.

✔ **Places:** Organized by major metropolitan areas in the United States.

✔ **Romance:** You see all the variations on boy meets girl, boy meets boy, girl meets girl — you name it.

✔ **Special Interests:** Meet people interested in certain hobbies, pets, computers, or whatever.

✔ **Country-specific rooms:** For example, Canada, eh!

✔ **Member rooms:** You have to click the Member Room button to see these. Anyone can create a member room by clicking the icon so marked. Many member rooms are locality-specific. A few are serious. Most are silly or kinky.

Not all AOL rooms appear in the List Rooms screen. Some groups have their own chat areas that are not listed here. You can sometimes find them by looking in AOL's Lifestyles and Interests channel. Or just try guessing the keyword.

What's my name?

AOL uses your login name as your screen name unless you make up a special screen name. Many people use a separate screen name on chat to preserve their anonymity. To make a new screen name when you are online:

1. **Choose Members⇨My AOL from the menu.**

2. **Click the Set Up AOL Now button.**

3. **Click the Screen Names button along the left side of the window.**

4. **Click the Set Up Now button in the lower-right corner of the window.**

5. **Double-click Create a Screen Name.**

6. **Type a new screen name. (The one you want may be taken — in fact, all the good names are — so be creative.)**

7. **Click the Create a Screen Name button. AOL checks whether the name you typed is already used by someone else. If it is, you see a message to that effect; click OK and return to Step 6.**

8. **Enter the password to be used for this screen name by typing it twice, once in each box. The password must be different from your main password.**

9. **Click Set Password. AOL makes the screen name and then asks you what this screen name should be allowed to do.**

10. **Click the setting appropriate for the person using this screen name. Choose from General, Teen, or Child. You see a message telling you that your screen name is ready for use.**

11. **Click OK.**

AOL lets you have up to five screen names. The names can be used for other family members, for example, or for your multiple personalities. Some people use one name for business and another for personal contacts. You have to log off your main account and log on under the new name in order to use the new name.

Calling the room police

AOL has rules governing online behavior in their Terms of Service (TOS), which you can see by going to the keyword **TOS**. If things get really bad, you can report a violation from this screen or click the Notify AOL icon in the People Connection screen. Selecting the keyword **GUIDEPAGER** asks an AOL official to visit the room and set things straight.

Whisper in my ear — instant messages

Instant Messages (or IMs) are a way to have a private conversation with a member. IM is used as a verb on AOL. You can send an IM to anyone in a chat room.

To start an IM session, double-click the person's name in a room list and click Message. You can also select Members⇨Send an Instant Message and type in the member's screen name.

When someone sends you an IM, that person's message appears in a small window, and if your computer has sound turned on, you hear a distinctive chime. Respond by clicking Respond and by typing what you want to say in the smaller text box. Then click Send.

Meet me in a private room

Private rooms let you chat with other members a bit more conveniently than sending Instant Messages. Any AOL member can create a private room. To visit one, you have to learn the name of the room. Then click the Private Rooms icon on the People Connection screen, type in that name, and click Go.

The same procedure lets you create your own room if you pick a name that is not in use. Remember: You cannot see a list of private room names — that is what makes them private!

Private rooms have a somewhat sleazy connotation. If you are invited into one you may be approached to have *cybersex*, which is an exchange of intimate messages designed to arouse you. Digital pillow talk may not be your cup of tea, but if you give it a try, remember:

- ✔ Some members lie about anything, especially gender.

- ✔ Occasionally a member will not take no for an answer and may continue to pester you.

- ✔ It's impolite to send an Instant Message to someone who is in a private room.

- ✔ Respect the privacy of the other person or persons in the room.

- ✔ Remember that other people may not respect your privacy. Your conversation can be saved to a file and even shown to others.

Who am I? See my profile!

Your profile tells other members a little about you. Create your profile by going to the keyword **PROFILE** and filling out the form. Leave parts you do not want to answer blank.

Look at another member's profile by double-clicking the person's screen name in the list of people in a room and clicking the Get Info button. You can also select Members⇨Get a Member's Profile and type in a screen name.

Hi there, buddy!

Buddy Lists save you the trouble of searching to see which of your chat friends are online at the moment. After you create a Buddy List, when a buddy logs on, AOL lets you know in a special window. You can then:

- ✔ Find which chat room they are in by clicking the Locate icon.

- ✔ Send them an Instant Message by clicking the IM icon.

- ✔ Invite them to a private room by clicking the Invite icon.

You can make several Buddy Lists, each one for various groups of buddies.

For example, you might have one for business associates and one for people who share your interest in vegetarian Indian cooking. To make a Buddy List:

1. **Select Members➪Buddy Lists. You see your Buddy Lists window, with a list of the Buddy Lists you've already made, if any.**

2. **Click the Create button. You see the Create a Buddy List window.**

3. **Type a name for your new list in the Buddy List Group Name box.**

4. **Type the screen name of a friend you want on this list and click Add Buddy.**

   Repeat this step for each person you want on this list.

5. **Click Save.**

The Buddy Lists screen also lets you edit your Buddy Lists, search the AOL member directory, and set Buddy List Preferences. In Preferences you can ask AOL to:

✔ Play a sound when a buddy signs on or signs off.

✔ Allow or block all members from including you on their Buddy Lists.

✔ Allow or block specific members from including you on their Buddy Lists.

Sound off

You can make sounds come out of other members' computers by typing a message with the name of a special file between asterisks. For example, sending a message containing *goodbye* causes everyone in the chat room to hear the familiar AOL "goodbye" sound.

These special files are called .*wav files* or *sound files.* You can download many sound files from http://www.nwlaser.com/wavs (some of these sound files have adult content). You must put them in the same directory as your AOL program.

Chat sounds are fun occasionally, but every now and then someone in a rooms goes overboard and blasts out your speakers. To turn off the sound feature, select Members➪Preferences, click the Chat icon, and uncheck the Play chat sounds sent by other members or Enable chat room sounds box.

CompuServe Chat (CB Simulator)

CompuServe members can converse with one another using a system called Chat (in CompuServe 3.0) or CB Simulator (in older versions). This section describes how to use Chat with CompuServe 3.0.1 for Windows and CompuServe 3.0 for Macintosh.

CompuServe is a fine online service and CompuServe Chat is a popular feature, but CompuServe Chat is nowhere near as widely used as AOL's Chat.

Chatting on CompuServe

To get started chatting:

1. **Click the Chat icon on the Home Desktop window or go to the keyword** CHAT.

   If you are not already connected to CompuServe, your program dials in and connects. Then you see the CompuServe Chat window with a list of chat categories: General, Adult, and others.

2. **Double-click the category you want. General Chat Areas is a good place to start. If you see another list of types of chats, click General Chat again.**

   CompuServe may need to download a program to your computer at this point — this happens automagically if needed, but you have to wait a minute while it happens.

3. **If you haven't chatted before, CompuServe asks you for your nickname or handle (see "Pick a nickname" in the next section). Type a nickname — your first name, initials, or a fanciful name — and click OK.**

   You see the Chat Desktop, with buttons to read announcements, chat, learn more about chatting, and leave the chat area.

4. **To get started, click the Chat button.**

   You see a window listing *chat rooms*. Each chat room has a title, like Breakfast Club or Teens Only. You also see how many members are present in each room.

   Note: On older versions of CompuServe, you see a window with a few dozen numbered boxes, each representing a chat room, also called a *channel.* Click a number to see its title and how many members are on that channel. These channels in the older CompuServe versions are the same as the rooms you find in CompuServe 3.0 — with the same people in them.

5. **Double-click a room to join it. You see a window showing the conversation as it unfolds, along with a box at the bottom of the window for you to type your messages in.**

6. **If you want to know who is in the chat room with you, click the <u>W</u>ho's Here button to see a window that lists the nickname of each member in the room along with his or her CompuServe member ID.**

   The Who's Here window also contains buttons that let you talk to a selected user or see the person's profile.

7. **To make a comment, type it in the box at the bottom of the Chat window and press Enter or click the Send button.**

Pick a nickname

CompuServe uses your numeric login ID as your Chat (CB Simulator) name unless you choose a special alphanumeric name called a *nickname* or *handle*. Most members use a nickname on Chat. In CompuServe 3.0.1 for Windows, choose <u>A</u>ccess⇨<u>P</u>references from the menu and click the Chat tab along the top of the window. In CompuServe 3.0 for Macintosh, choose File⇨Preferences from the menu and click the Chat button. Then type the name you want to use in the Nickname box and click OK.

What's on Channel 2?

A key step in chatting on CompuServe is finding a suitable chat room (or channel). The good news — and the bad news — is that there are fewer choices on CompuServe than on AOL.

Welcome Newcomers (Channel 2) is reserved for new folks, and it's a good place to ask questions. Also, a Chat Helper can assist you during the evening (North American time).

For the most part, channel names are just suggestive. The character of a channel depends on who is there at the moment.

Calling the channel police

CompuServe has rules governing online behavior in the Member Agreement, which you can see by going to the keyword **RULES**. If things get really bad, you can report a violation by going to the keyword **FEEDBACK** and sending CompuServe a message.

Chatting in private

Private chats let you converse with other users in a place that others cannot access.

Any CompuServe user can invite other members to a private chat by clicking the <u>W</u>ho's Here button, clicking the name of the person he or she wants to chat with, and clicking <u>P</u>rivate Chat. If this happens to you, you see a Private Chat Invitation window and hear a "You're invited!" sound. Accept or decline the invitation.

If you do not want to receive chat invitations from a particular member, select that member's name in the Who's Here window and click Private Chat. Then, in the Private Chat window, click the Prohibit button. You can block invitation messages from that member for this session only, or until you remove the prohibition.

Who am I? See my profile!

Tells other members a little about yourself by creating a profile. Go to the keyword **CBPROFILES**, double-click Enter/Change Your Profile, and fill out the form.

Look at another member's profile by clicking the <u>W</u>ho's Here button, clicking the person's name, and clicking <u>M</u>ember Profile.

For some reason we can't figure out, CompuServe profiles do not have a space for gender. Maybe they figure people who will put up with a numerical name are above the temptations of the flesh. We suggest you mention your gender and the gender you prefer meeting, if that's germane, under Interests.

Internet Relay Chat (IRC)

Internet Relay Chat (IRC) is the Internet's chat service. IRC is available from most Internet providers. You can even participate in IRC through most value-added providers, though IRC is completely separate from the value-added provider's own chat services.

If you have a SLIP or PPP account or you use America Online or CompuServe, you need an *IRC client program.* An IRC client (or just *IRC program*) is another Internet program, like your Web browser or e-mail program, and freeware and shareware programs are available for you to download from the Net. If you use Windows, use a Winsock-compatible program; if you use a Mac, use a MacTCP-compatible program. Two of the best shareware IRC programs are included on our CD-ROM. They are:

- ✔ **mIRC** for Windows
- ✔ **Ircle** for Macintosh

Note that Ircle's Help file is accessed by selecting Help from the Apple menu.

If you do not have a CD-ROM reader, you can also find these IRC programs, along with others, at the shareware Web sites such as `http://www.tucows.com` or at `http://www.mirc.co.uk` (mIRC) and `http://ircle.bridge.net` (Ircle).

For more detailed information on setting these programs up, see `http://www.neosoft.com/~biscuits/setup.html` (mIRC) or `http://deckard.mc.duke.edu/~jyl/ircle_setup.html` (Ircle).

Check with your Internet provider for any additional information you might need to use IRC. If you have a direct link to the Internet, ask your system administrator if the link supports IRC.

The two main ways of using IRC are through the following:

- ✔ *Channels,* which are like an ongoing conference call with a bunch of people. After you join a channel, you can read what people are saying on-screen and then add your own comments just by typing them and pressing Enter.
- ✔ *Direct connection,* which is a private conversation.

Starting up IRC

1. **Connect to the Internet and run your IRC program.**
2. **Connect to an IRC server.**
3. **Join a channel.**

You're ready to chat!

If you are on a value-added service, follow its instructions for connecting to the Internet. If you are using a UNIX shell Internet provider that offers IRC, type **ircii** or **irc** at the UNIX prompt.

A server at your service

To use IRC, you use your IRC program to connect to an *IRC server* — that is, an Internet host computer that serves as a switchboard for IRC conversations. Dozens of IRC servers are available, but many are full most of the time and may refuse your connection. You may have to try several servers, or the same one dozens of times, before you can connect. A list of servers is included in the IRC client programs on the CD-ROM included with this book.

When choosing a server, pick one that is geographically close to you, to minimize response lag, and is on the network you want. See "Networks of servers" later in this chapter.

To connect to a server:

> ✔ In mIRC, select File➪Setup, or press Alt+E to display the mIRC Setup window, and then click the IRC Servers tab. When you start mIRC, it gives this command for you automatically, so you see the mIRC Setup window right away. Double-click a server on the list to attempt to connect to it.

> ✔ In Ircle, select File➪Preferences➪Startup. Select a server and then select File➪Save Preferences.

At peak times the servers can be very busy. If at first you don't connect, try, try again.

Networks of servers

IRC servers are organized into networks. Servers within each network talk to each other. But servers on one IRC network don't connect to servers on other networks. Someone on EFnet can't talk to someone on Undernet, for example.

The three biggest networks are:

> ✔ **EFnet**, the original and biggest network of servers, with the most users. It has a help page at http://www.irchelp.org.

> ✔ **Undernet**, the second-largest network. See its Web page at http://www.undernet.org.

> ✔ **DALNet**, the third-largest network. See its Web page at http://www.dal.net.

Most people on IRC eventually develop a preference for one network.

Usually it's the one where their friends hang out.

Lots of smaller IRC networks exist. Here are some, with the addresses of Web pages that have more information about them:

- **NewNet** (http://www.newnet.org)
- **X-world** (http://www.x-world.org)
- **Kidsworld** (http://www.kidsworld.org)
- **AnotherNet** (http://www.another.org)
- **StarLink** (http://www.starlink.org)
- **GalaxyNet** (http://www.galaxynet.org)

Telling IRC what to do

You control what is happening during your chat session by typing IRC commands. All IRC commands start with the slash character (/). You can type IRC commands in upper- or lowercase or a mixture — IRC doesn't care.

If anyone ever tells you to type commands that you don't understand into IRC, *don't do it. Ever.* You can unwittingly give away control of your IRC program and even your computer account to another person that way. (No, we're not going to tell you the commands!)

The most important command for you to know is

```
/quit
```

which gets you out of IRC. The second most important command is

```
/help
```

which gives you an online summary of the various IRC commands. Here are a few of the most useful IRC commands:

- /admin server displays information about a server.
- /away tells IRC that you will be away for a while. You don't need to leave such a message; but if you do, it is displayed to anyone who wants to talk to you.
- /clear clears your screen.

✔ /join joins a channel. See "A channel called #hottub?" later in this chapter.

✔ /leave leaves a channel.

✔ /me sends a message that describes what you are doing. If Arnold types /me bangs head on table, other users see *Arnold bangs head on table.

✔ /time displays the date and time in case you can't take your eyes off the screen even for a moment.

✔ /topic whatwearetalkingabout sets the topic message for the current channel.

✔ /who channel lists all the people on *channel*. If you type /who *, you see displayed the names of the people on the channel you are on.

Remember: Everything you type while in IRC goes directly out to the Internet, except lines that start with a slash.

If you use mIRC or Ircle, you can achieve most of the same effects controlled by IRC commands by choosing from the menu bar or clicking icons on the toolbar. But these IRC commands work, too, and some IRC programs don't have menu bar or toolbar equivalents.

A channel called #hottub?

The most popular way to use IRC is through *channels*. Most channels have names that start with the # character. Channel names are not case-sensitive. Numbered channels also exist (when you type a channel number, don't use the # character).

There are thousands of IRC channels. You can find an annotated list of some of the best by visiting http://www.funet.fi/~irc/channels.html. Each channel listed there has its own linked home page that tells a lot more about what that channel offers.

Good channels to know about include

✔ **#irchelp:** A place to ask questions about IRC.

✔ **#newbies:** All of your IRC questions answered.

✔ **#21plus:** and **#30plus:** Age-appropriate meeting places.

✔ **#41plus:** A more mature channel (many on it are younger).

> ✔ **#teens:** For teenagers — chill and chat.
>
> ✔ **#hottub:** A rougher meeting place.
>
> ✔ **#macintosh:** Mac users meet here.
>
> ✔ **#windows95:** Windows users meet here.
>
> ✔ **#chat:** A friendly chat channel.
>
> ✔ **#mirc:** A help channel for mIRC users.

Also, try # followed by the name of a country or major city.

How do I join a channel?

You join a channel by typing the following:

```
/join #channelname
```

For example, to join the #dummies channel, type **/join #dummies** and press Enter. Don't forget the / before the command or the # before the channel name.

In mIRC, you can click the Channels Folder button on the toolbar and then double-click one of the channels listed.

In Ircle, select Command⇨Join from the menu.

After you join a channel, everything you type that doesn't start with a slash (/) appears on the screen of everyone in that channel after you press Enter. The text of your messages is preceded by your nickname.

How do I leave a channel

You leave a channel by typing the following:

```
/leave
```

In mIRC you can leave a channel by closing the window for that channel.

In Ircle, select Command⇨Part from the menu.

The Lag's a drag and a split's the pits

Two phenomena — the *lag* and *netsplits* — are the bane of an IRCer's existence. Lag is the delay between when you type a message and when it appears on other people's screens. Lags really foul up conversations. Sometimes one group of people in a channel are lagged while another group is not, and the first group's messages appear after delays of several minutes. You can check on the amount of time a message takes to get from you to another person and back again by typing the command /ping *nickname*.

A netsplit breaks the connection between IRC servers — the network of connected IRC servers gets split into two smaller networks. A netsplit looks like a whole bunch of people suddenly leaving your channel, then reappearing en masse sometime later. All the people who are connected to the IRC servers in one half can chat among themselves but can't communicate with the people connected to the IRC servers in the other half of the network. Eventually (after minutes or hours) the two networks reconnect and the netsplit is over.

What channels are out there?

To see available channels in mIRC, click the List Channels button on the toolbar. If you are looking for a particular channel name, type the text you are looking for in the Match text box. If you want to see channels with at least several people in them (rather than the hundreds of channels with one bored, lonely, or lascivious person waiting), type a number in the min box. Then click Get List. The list of channels can be very long, so displaying the list may take a few minutes. If you want to see the channels listed in your Channels folder (the list of channels you visit frequently), click the Channels Folder button instead.

In any IRC program, you can find out all the public and private channels by typing the following command:

```
/list
```

In Ircle, select Command⇨List from the menu.

Before typing **/list**, type the following:

```
/set hold_mode on
```

This phrase keeps the names from flying by so fast on-screen that you can't read them. Don't forget to type `/set hold_mode off` after you finish reading the list.

You can also limit the number of channels listed by typing the following:

```
/list -min 8
```

Only channels with at least eight people on them are listed when you type this phrase.

`Pub` means a public channel. You may see `Prv`, which means a private channel. The @ sign indicates a channel operator (*chanop*), who is in charge of managing the goings-on of the channel.

Make a name for yourself

Everyone using IRC needs a *nickname*. This name can be the same as the user name in your e-mail address, although most people pick a different name. To choose a nickname, type the following:

```
/NICK thenameyouwant
```

Nicknames can be up to nine characters long.

Unlike e-mail addresses, nicknames can change from day to day. Whoever claims a nickname first on an IRC server gets to keep it as long as he or she is logged in. Nicknames are good only for a single session on IRC. If you chatted with someone named ElvisPres yesterday and then run into some-one named ElvisPres today, there's no guarantee that it's the same person.

If you use Ircle or mIRC, you can tell it your preferred nickname so it doesn't ask you each time you run it:

- ✔ In Ircle, select File➪Preferences➪Startup. Enter your name and then select File➪Save Preferences.
- ✔ In mIRC, select File➪Setup or press Alt+E and click the IRC Servers tab. mIRC lets you specify an alternate nickname as well.

To find out more about the person behind a nickname, type the following:

```
/whois nickname
```

The two main ways to learn someone's nickname are to see it on a channel or to have another user reveal it to you.

Where is C3PO when you need him?

Most of what you see on IRC was typed in by a human being. But some remarks come from computer programs called *robots* or just *bots*. Bots participate like a person, though they often seem pretty dumb. Some bots are inoffensive and do such things as hold a channel open and send a cheery welcome message to anyone who joins. Other bots are really obnoxious and send large numbers of annoying messages to people the bot's creator doesn't like.

Remember the spaceport bar scene in *Star Wars* where the robots R2D2 and C3PO choose to leave after the bartender says, "We don't serve their kind in here?" Well, bots really are unwelcome in many IRC channels. No discrimination suits have been filed yet, as far as we know.

Meet me in private

To send a message to someone whose nickname you know, type the following:

```
/msg nickname whatyouwanttosay
```

This method, however, becomes tiresome for more than one or two lines of text. You can instead start a longer conversation by typing the following:

```
/query nickname
```

Now, whenever you type something that doesn't start with /, it appears on *nickname*'s screen, preceded by your nickname, immediately after you press Enter. (Well, usually. See the sidebar "The Lag's a drag and the split's the pits" earlier in this chapter.)

Your "private" conversation can go through many IRC servers, often in different countries, and the operators of any of these servers can log all your messages.

A more private way to chat is via DCC — Direct Client Connections. You don't have to be in the same channel as the person you want to talk to; you just have to know the person's nickname. You type

```
/dcc chat shirley
```

(assuming that you want to talk to Shirley). When someone tries to start a DCC chat with you, mIRC asks if you want to chat with the other person. If you click Yes, mIRC opens a window for the discussion. Your DCC chat window is just like a mini-channel with only two people in it.

You can also use DCC commands to send files to other people. For example, you could send a picture of yourself to a person you have just met. However, if someone offers to send you a file, consider declining unless you know the person. Unsolicited files can be unbelievably rude and disgusting.

A channel of your very own

Each channel has its own channel operator, or *chanop,* who can control, to some extent, what happens on that channel. You can start your own channel and become its chanop by typing the following:

```
/join #unusedchannelname
```

As with nicknames, whoever asks for a channel name first gets it. You can keep the name for as long as you are logged on as the chanop. You can let other people be chanops for your channel, but make sure that they are people you can trust. A channel exists as long as anyone is in it; when the last person leaves, the channel winks out of existence.

Each IRC channel (and each IRC server) has an *operator* or *chanop,* someone with particular authority to give special commands. The first person on a channel is automatically the channel's *operator,* but the operator can anoint other users as operators, too. In the list of nicknames in a channel, operators' nicknames are preceded by an at-sign (@).

As chanop you get to use special commands. The main one is /kick, which kicks someone off your channel, at least for the three seconds until he rejoins the channel. Kicking someone off is a thrill, but a rather small one, sort of like finding a penny on the sidewalk. People usually get kicked out of channels for being rude, or by sending so many garbage messages that they make the channel unusable.

Server operators manage entire servers and can kick unruly users entirely off a server, permanently.

Knock three times and tell them John sent you

The following three types of channels are available in IRC:

  ✔ **Public:** Everyone can see them, and everyone can join.

  ✔ **Private:** Everyone can see them, but you can join them only by invitation.

  ✔ **Secret:** These do not show up in the /list command, and you can join them only by invitation.

If you are on a private or secret channel, you can invite someone else to join by typing the following:

```
/invite nickname
```

If you get an invitation from someone on a private or secret channel and want to join, just type the following:

```
/join -invite
```

Calling the channel police

Compared with AOL and CompuServe, IRC is a lawless frontier. Few rules, if any, exist. If things get really bad, you can try to find out the offender's e-mail address by using the `/whois` command — say it's `badmother@jclt.com`. You can then send an e-mail complaint to `postmaster` at the same host name, in this case `postmaster@jclt.com`. Don't expect too much help, however.

How can I learn more about IRC?

You can discover much more about IRC from the `#irchelp` and `#newbies` channels, from the mIRC and Ircle home pages listed earlier, and from these sources:

- ✔ The official IRC Home Page in Finland (where IRC was invented) at `http://www.funet.fi/~irc`
- ✔ The New IRC user's page at `http://www.neosoft.com/~biscuits/niu.html`
- ✔ The Usenet newsgroup: `alt.irc`
- ✔ Cliff "Edge" Wagner's IRC Web page at `http://shoga.wwa.com/~edge/irc.html`
- ✔ The IRC FAQ at `rtfm.mit.edu`

Part VI
What to Do
with E-Mail

In this part . . .

Here's our "Big Picture" section. How does e-mail fit into the rest of our lives at work and at home? You may be surprised, so read on.

Chapter 21
Putting E-Mail to Work

. . . .

. . . .

*W*e found that when we put our collective heads together, we have a lot to say about using e-mail at work. Roughly speaking, it falls into two broad categories — how to use e-mail to improve your way of doing business, and practical tips for successful e-mail use in your office.

Using E-Mail and the Internet to Better Your Business

Philippe Le Roux, a founder of the Canadian Internet and the online services consulting company VDL2, has been working with the Internet and online services for more than 15 years. VDL2's Internet and online services clients include TV5 international television; Via Rail, Canada's passenger rail company, for whom VDL2 created an interactive Web site; the Montreal Stock Exchange; as well as companies in Europe and in North and South America. In a personal interview with us, Philippe shared his insight and expertise. The material in this section is taken from that interview and from discussions we've had subsequently.

Reaching the world through e-mail

We know you've heard all about surfing the Net, Web sites, and home pages, but the Web (where the surfing happens) is not the best place for you to start if you're new to doing business on the Net. Philippe recommends that you begin with *e-mail*. If you haven't thought about the implications of using e-mail for your business, now's the time to begin. E-mail predates the World Wide Web by more than twenty years, is the only tool used by everyone on the Net, and is a fundamental learning ground for understanding Net culture and potential.

E-mail opens an important new way of communicating within and without an organization. Inside a company, e-mail becomes a powerful tool for company communication and project management. Outside the company, e-mail can help you improve your customer support, support your field offices, get help from experts, and even find new customers.

Preparing employees for the world of e-mail

To get the most out of e-mail for your organization, you need to train your users, not just in the how-to's of your particular e-mail program, but also in the kinds of uses and capabilities inherent in e-mail. You need to teach them *netiquette* — how to behave on the Net. Show them things that they might not stumble across by themselves. Buy them a copy of this book.

Working with E-Mail: Changing the Way We Work

People who use e-mail find that the very technology itself changes how they work. E-mail communication is highly structured, compared to a phone call, for example — yet very versatile and easy to use, compared to traditional forms of written communication.

For example, e-mail provides a written point of departure. You present your issues and questions in text that becomes an easy reference point for further discussion. Every e-mail system has a Reply feature that enables the responder to include the original message in the text of the new message, setting off the original text from the new with special characters. Using the Reply feature to structure their response, people generally respond to e-mail point by point. You can clarify misunderstandings rapidly without typing a lot of separate memos and without countless rounds of telephone tag. Often, many rounds of e-mail happen in short order — a matter of minutes — as opposed to the hours, days, or weeks that traditional media can require.

Improved project management

E-mail facilitates group communications and heightens accountability for projects involving many people. The larger the project, the more you need e-mail. The larger the company, the more you need e-mail. Most projects affect more than just the core people involved.

For example, a new product under development might involve marketing, development, documentation, testing, manufacturing, and shipping. All these different departments need to be aware of what's happening, though they probably don't need to get involved with the daily comings and goings of the project. They don't need to be at the meetings, but they do need to know what happened.

A schedule slip, for example, might throw previously allocated resources into contention. This problem happens all the time. But what mechanisms do you have in place for communicating what's happening? How is everyone who really needs to know going to find out? Well, experienced e-mail managers will tell you that one solution is to set up different mailing lists: mailing lists for the developers, mailing lists for the business team members, and mailing lists that include all the groups.

Mailing lists aid group communications. You don't have to think about whom you should send a message to. When you use the appropriate mailing list address, all the appropriate people automatically find out. When a person joins or leaves the team, you change the alias, but the workings of the group continue unaltered.

Even in small companies where people are working on the same project together, using e-mail to communicate makes a lot of sense. For one thing, you cut down on the number of interruptions. For another, people often have time to gather information before they get back to you. And you've created a written log, something very useful for everyone. People are less likely to forget what you asked about — they have your request right there to check.

Virtual meetings

E-mail can eliminate a lot of meetings. For example, if you have a problem to solve, instead of trying to get everyone in the room at the same time, try addressing the problem in e-mail. Include the same people and make sure they're copied on all the ongoing correspondence. As you discuss the problem in e-mail, you may find you've saved yourself a lot of time. People can respond at a convenient time, and the "meeting" tends to stay more on target. Unless they're on vacation, people usually respond to their mail within a day. (If your request is long and involved, or your recipient gets a few hundred messages a day, cut her some slack.) Finding a time when everyone could be in the same room at the same time could take a week. By then you could have solved your problem using e-mail.

E-mail timing

E-mail is often delivered in a matter of minutes, if not seconds. Depending on whether the person on the other end is connected and reading her mail, a dialog can happen as quickly as people can send messages. Even if the response is not instantaneous, people generally respond to short e-mail messages quickly. If you send a lengthy message requiring a lengthy response, expect it to take a while. Generally speaking, however, you can expect a much more rapid turnaround in e-mail correspondence than you can from other traditional media. Communication among several parties is much easier because you don't need to schedule everyone for a conference call. Even if you do need a conference call, you're probably better off sending the scheduling request and the call's agenda through e-mail.

Because people read e-mail in their own time, using e-mail to communicate project information saves time in meetings and lessens the need to interrupt someone with phone or office chatting. We don't think e-mail replaces actually talking to people; we just know that it's difficult to get a lot of work done with constant interruptions, and e-mail can go a long way toward reducing interruptions.

Corporate communication

E-mail is probably *the* cheapest way to communicate, and absolutely the cheapest way to reach a lot of people around the world. E-mail often reaches its destination in a matter of seconds, and it costs no more to send it to Hong Kong, Lima, or New York City than to an office down the hall. Furthermore, when language is a barrier, reading e-mail in a foreign language is generally easier than understanding subtleties over the phone. (You can even forward the e-mail to someone else to translate.)

Because e-mail is almost free, it costs no more to send a message to 245 people than it does to one. It costs less to send an electronic newsletter around the world than it does to create a paper newsletter for a department. David Letterman's electronic newsletter is sent to 27,000 people each month for only a few cents. The cost of reaching a large audience is dramatically reduced. Not only do you pay no postage, but you also save money on materials, presentation, and printing.

Mailing lists are text-based, so for the time being, you can't wow your fans with graphics. This restriction means that content becomes extremely important. Unless you have something to say, don't bother. People can easily press Delete before they read your mail. Make sure you aren't cluttering mailboxes with garbage.

When you compare the cost of e-mail with the cost of any other kind of express mail delivery, or even the cost of overseas phone calls, you begin to grasp the impact it can have. Compare the cost of shipping software overseas by FedEx to the cost of sending it by e-mail. Suddenly, having good communications with foreign offices and customers doesn't cost a lot.

It pays to collaborate

Suddenly collaborative work is easy, too. People can quickly and cheaply share files, pictures, even video and sound. We know — we've been creating whole books using e-mail for years. Our book *Internet Secrets* involved fifty different contributors e-mailing in their contributions from the U.K., Canada, Texas, and Poland, among other places.

Whether your collaborator is across the hall or in China no longer matters. Because actual word-processing documents can be sent, everyone can easily stay current with changes others make (though you do need to pay attention and decide on procedures for version control so that you don't create diverging strands from the same source). Independent research groups around the world can share a common database, as genetics researchers do.

C.Y.E.

Using e-mail, people begin to communicate easily with all levels of an organization, enabling information to flow much more freely. Many environments find this liberating; others find it terrifying. However, environments that encourage a free flow of information (excluding information that involves confidential material) have found that better communication fosters better employee morale, and in turn, greater creativity and productivity. We warn you, however, that old political games die hard; they don't suddenly disappear with the appearance of e-mail. Remember the old adage "Information is power." E-mail can shift fields of power in an organization and threaten egos that were built by withholding information. If you're in the kind of place where you need to watch your back, you need to watch your e-mail, too.

New customers in the mail

Sure, you can easily envision sending e-mail to your existing customers. Well, maybe not easily, but once you try it for a while, it'll seem perfectly natural. But how about finding new customers with e-mail? We aren't talking about sending out junk e-mail advertisements as a lame imitation of direct mail marketing. We're talking about going to new sources to find out who's looking for your product or service. Those new sources are automatic mailing lists. Mailing lists exist on almost every topic you can imagine (and many more you haven't imagined — trust us). Tens of thousands of mailing lists exist.

Find mailing lists of interest to you and subscribe. Don't limit yourself to lists you think pertain to your business. Check out all the lists that interest you. But add only a few at a time, because some lists are so prolific that you'll be drowning in e-mail faster than you can say unsubscribe. Chapter 16 tells you all about mailing lists — how to subscribe and unsubscribe. As you find lists to your liking and you become comfortable, you can begin to participate actively in the groups, offering your particular expertise.

In the mailing lists, real interactions can lead to real business. You can respond to people privately — you don't always have to respond to the group. You'll probably find people actually looking for what you have to offer. Complete international deals have been formed and cemented using nothing but e-mail. Snail mail was used for invoicing, and electronic funds transfers were used for payment.

Be careful not to advertise, explicitly or implicitly. If you're a travel agent and subscribe to the Travel-L mailing list, for example, don't try to publish fares or specials to the list. And tacking ads onto your signature is considered inappropriate. Make sure your signature is short, sweet, and professional — don't think you can get away with a long trailer and pretend you're just a skywriter drifting by. You'll get booted off the list.

Getting help from the outside

Another good reason to read mailing lists is to find people who know about what you want to know. You can often query an expert in your field if you know his or her e-mail address. If your request isn't inordinate, you'll probably get a response in a timely fashion. Most people don't mind an occasional, reasonable request for help. We get them all the time. As long as people aren't asking us to do their homework for them, we generally try to help. But, in turn, learn one important motto: *Give back to the Net.* When someone queries you, be generous in your response. Try to keep the Net a cordial, responsive environment.

E-mail doesn't replace the need for phone, fax, video-conferencing, and letters, but it does have its strengths, and it can change how you do business. It won't eliminate meetings, but it can make them much more productive if you take the time to circulate an agenda via e-mail, and agree to take some discussions offline. Well, maybe you'll even handle them online — with e-mail.

E-Mail at the Office

We here at Dummies Central have some expertise all our own. We're among those who have been using e-mail since it was two days old, we've already been responsible for six other books that at least mention e-mail and at least thirteen more that cover it in depth, and we like to hear ourselves talk. Here's what we'd like to add:

E-mail and the corporate culture

If your office doesn't have e-mail yet, you are probably in the minority. If e-mail has made your organization palpably more efficient and a better place to work, you may be in the minority, too. In a lot of work places, e-mail is just another office tool, like electric pencil sharpeners. Everyone finds that e-mail is a great way to communicate with remote field offices, or to send out those company memoranda that everybody circular-files anyway. But it can be much, much more.

The success of e-mail in an organization depends a lot on the organization's corporate culture. A friend of ours works for a large corporation that installed Lotus Notes, a premier groupware product that combines e-mail with user-friendly databases to promote efficient information sharing in organizations. The problem is that workers at our friend's company don't share information freely. That is part of their corporate culture. Employees are not even permitted to read their own job descriptions. Information is power. Can you guess how much people at this company are using Notes?

Many managers and consultants claim expertise in changing corporate cultures, but it is a task few are ever able to accomplish. E-mail itself can be useful in this endeavor, but never underestimate the resistance that office bureaucrats can put up.

Making e-mail fly

Here are a few tips on what is needed for e-mail to really have an impact in your place of work:

Make e-mail universal

A huge difference exists between 85 percent of employees being on e-mail and 100 percent being on e-mail. Getting to 100 percent might require public e-mail terminals so the people who don't sit at desks can check their mail, or it might even require printing out messages for those who can't get to a terminal. But once everyone knows they can reach *anyone* in the company, from the day they start work, e-mail will become the preferred way to communicate.

Get folks to check their e-mail daily

Getting everyone to check their e-mail at least once a day is vital for e-mail to succeed. Employees will do this naturally once e-mail takes off in your organization. Until then, make sure information is put out frequently enough to encourage daily checking. It might even be worthwhile to have an online contest or a recipe of the week. Anything's fair to get people to check their e-mail.

Another idea is to post a good company story every few days. This can be a thank-you letter from a customer, an employee suggestion that worked out, or a problem that was successfully fixed.

Yes, you can try to force participation by diktat: "Effective immediately, all Nimbus employees must check their e-mail twice a day." After a few weeks of "No new messages," this rule will be forgotten along with any number of "Effective immediately" pronouncements.

The boss has to use it

Giving the boss an e-mail address is not enough. Employees have to know that their supervisor will *read* their mail on a regular basis. They also have to believe that their boss understands how to use e-mail properly. In one *Dilbert* cartoon, the pointy-haired boss hands his secretary a piece of paper and says, "Send this by e-mail. Fax it, too, in case he doesn't check his e-mail. And mail the original so he has a clean copy." As usual, Scott Adams is on target.

As for messages that jump over boxes in the organization chart, tolerance will vary from company to company. Those that have an "open door" policy, at least on paper, should welcome an open e-mail policy. Remember the story in Chapter 1 about the head of a semiconductor plant who sent e-mail to all his subordinates, asking, "What are we doing that is keeping you from doing your job to the best of your ability?"

That's an order, soldier!

An official of the U.S. Department of Defense recently expressed concern about the effect of e-mail on the military command structure. Rigid hierarchies tend to flatten when people in different parts of the organization can freely exchange messages. An informal network springs up that cuts across the organization chart. Managers demand copies of every e-mail and jump into the online discussions for fear of being left out. "When a superior participates in everyday minutiae," the official said, "subordinates become accustomed to negotiating with or even challenging the superior on technical issues they know. Soon they begin to second-guess him on larger issues."

We think outcomes like this are for the best — even in the Army — but change can be painful. Talking these issues out and making management's expectations clear ahead of time can prevent a lot turmoil.

We do not recommend that you send e-mail over your boss's head in most companies. You would do better spending the time working on your résumé.

Encourage business partners to use e-mail

If you are big enough to have leverage with your suppliers, require them all to have e-mail. If you are a small operation, at least ask potential vendors if they use e-mail. Eventually they'll get the message. E-mail can reduce errors from misunderstood phone calls and illegible faxes.

Some years ago, Arnold was working at a manufacturing company. One day, while walking through the stockroom, he noticed a shelf with a dozen copies of an unusual software documentation set that cost $900 a set. He knew that a particular customer had put in a special order for *one* set of those books, but couldn't imagine why so many had been purchased. After he relentlessly questioned the inventory control people, they finally produced a copy of the original purchase requisition. The multipart form must have slipped askew a bit, because a clerk's initials, "JS," appeared in the adjacent order quantity box on this copy — and someone had read "JS" as "15."

Your customers can be enticed to get online by your providing e-mail access to the people in your company they want to reach. A particularly valuable use of e-mail is online customer service. Most people are fed up with waiting forever for 800 (or worse, 900) numbers to answer. Your customers will love you if you provide an e-mail address for customer service and can achieve a fast — under two hours — response time.

Make finding people easy

A good, up-to-date e-mail address directory must be available, preferably online. It should list people by name and by function. It should also include useful e-mail addresses external to your company, such as the key business partners, the online help desks for the software packages your company uses, the local public library, and so on. Make sure your employees know that this is a confidential company resource, and make sure it's not available outside your company.

Allow personal use

Employees should be allowed reasonable personal use of e-mail. Many companies have a "no personal use" policy for their e-mail. This is counter-productive and is as likely to be respected as similar policies on personal telephone use. Often a fine line exists between personal and professional, in any case. The friend I call today to find out if she can go to the movies is the same person I'll call next week to help me with a tricky problem at work. Companies that try to regulate this level of behavior are usually cutting off their noses to spite their faces.

Reasonable personal e-mail use is a fringe benefit that is highly valued by employees and costs employers almost nothing. Remember, most systems have no per-message charge for e-mail. Allowing personal use also encourages employees to check their e-mail regularly, thus helping e-mail succeed as a corporate tool.

What is unreasonable use? We think companies can fairly prohibit usage that violates the law, reveals confidential company information, supports an employee's side business or political activities, or requires more than a few minutes of time during normal working hours.

Today, many employees are part of the "sandwich generation" — responsible for small children and infirm parents. To the extent that e-mail lets them handle their personal responsibilities more efficiently, it will improve productivity and reduce absenteeism.

Arrange for remote access

Being able to read e-mail at work is not enough. On any given day in most companies, at least one key person is on the road. They need their e-mail. A worker with a sick kid can still get a lot done at home via e-mail. While you're at it, make sure you have an e-mail address on the Internet that reads info@yourcompanyname.com. And have a mailbot (a program that automatically sends a response) all set up to answer.

Respect employee privacy

Monitoring employees' e-mail may be legal in some places, but we do not think it is ethical anywhere. If you *do* choose to snoop in the company e-mail system, at least let your employees know that is your policy.

Building teams

Every few years a new hot management buzzword comes along. Right now it's *team building*. The notion that a group of workers dedicated to a single goal can get a lot done is hardly new, however. Whether you think teams are hype or hope, e-mail can do a lot to make a small group more effective. The first step, of course, is to make sure that all team members have an e-mail account and know one another's addresses. The next step is a team mailing list. Encourage team members to copy fellow members on all important mail. Make replying promptly to other team members' mail a team value. Make sure each team member has a common set of computer applications. Make sure that they all know how to attach and read all the kinds of documents they need to use.

Dealing with incompatible programs

E-mail works great when you are sending simple text messages. When you try to send anything more complex, such as a word-processing document or a picture, problems can arise. That likelihood that problems will arise is directly proportional to the importance of the document.

Actually, there's a simple explanation for this commonly observed phenomenon. Every personal computer made today has an *anxiety sensor* in its keyboard that measures how hard you are typing and how often you have to backspace. When the detected anxiety level is high enough, a signal is sent to your mailer using USP, the user stress protocol, and nothing can go through.

A different explanation, popular with techies, points out that today we have

- ✔ Five major operating systems — Windows, Mac OS, MS-DOS, OS/2, and UNIX

- ✔ Variants within them — Windows 95 versus Windows 3.1 versus Windows NT, Berkeley UNIX versus System V versus Linux

- ✔ Dozens of different types of applications — word processors, spreadsheets, graphics, page layout, browsers, and so on

- ✔ Different brands with different file formats within each application category — Word, WordPerfect, and WordPro in word processors, for example
- ✔ Different versions within each brand — Word 7, Word 6, Word 5
- ✔ Different encoding schemes used by mailers — MIME, uuencode, BinHex
- ✔ Different compression programs — zip, gzip, StuffIt, compress

Think of this list as a giant combination lock. You can easily understand why sending a spreadsheet across the hall is sometimes hard, let alone sending one around the world, if you don't use the same combination as your recipient.

Here are a couple of ways to avoid these headaches:

Agree on a lingua franca

Make up a list for your organization of the preferred format for sending files in each category, including compression and mailer transfer format.

The Macintosh-versus-PC religious debate used to be a big source of file transfer conflict. It is no longer any excuse. Mac software is available that can read just about any file format available for the PC. And all Macs sold in the past five years can read, write, and format PC disks.

Rehearse

Think about what types of documents you will need on a regular basis and try sending sample documents of each type to your colleagues before crunch time. Keep written notes about what worked.

Send a test file with all combinations

If you are having trouble sending an important document to someone with a different mailer program, make up a short sample file in that format — for example, the first page of your document. Then send it out a number of times using all the different encoding formats your mailer can muster. One of them may work.

Don't forget sneaker net

Putting a document on a disk and carrying it to another computer is sometimes called *sneaker net*. It usually works. Also, if you are struggling with an important transmission some afternoon, be aware of the deadline for your overnight delivery service's pickup. Once a disk with your files on it is in the hands of FedEx, UPS, Airborne, or DHL, your keyboard knows that the jig is up, and mysteriously, your next transmission works. If not, at least the recipient will get the disk the next morning.

When all else fails, remember that plain text always works

Well, almost always. Some mailers have trouble with messages longer than 20,000 to 30,000 characters. Also, the characters used to designate the end of a line vary from one operating system to another. Still, plain text is your best bet in a pinch.

When making a disk for sneaker net, always save the file you want to send in several formats. Include text or ASCII as one of those formats.

The legal status of e-mail signatures

Is a signature on a piece of e-mail legally valid? We are not lawyers, but as we understand things in the United States, the law takes a pretty broad view of what constitutes a valid signature. If someone has a piece of e-mail that appears to be signed by you, you will likely have to prove you did not send it. This applies equally to ordinary e-mail and e-mail that has been signed using public key cryptography (see Chapter 17) — though the American Bar Association has developed a draft guideline giving special recognition to cryptographic digital signatures, and several states have recently passed or are considering laws based on those guidelines. (Web users can look at `http://www.state.ut.us/ccjj/digsig/default.htm`.)

E-Mail on the Road

More and more workers are taking their computers with them when they travel. A major reason these road warriors lug their seven-pound laptops, spare batteries, charger, and modem down endless airport corridors is to be able to stay in touch.

Large companies often have local network access numbers in the various cities and countries where they do business. If you don't work for one of these e-mail–savvy firms, you may want to consider finding an e-mail provider that offers local access service in the places you are likely to visit, or that has an 800 number you can use when you're out of town. At Dummies Central, we find having our own 800 number worthwhile for e-mail pickup, even though only one person travels much.

Getting your mail when you are in a foreign country can involve more than finding a local service provider. You may not find a jack in your hotel room that will take your modem cable. Modem standards can vary in different countries as well. One possibility is to visit a cybercafé. These trendy establishments serve Internet with their coffee. If you haven't been to one, imagine a hippy-dippy coffee shop with Internet terminals at every table. Cybercafés are in many major cities. You pay for terminal use by the hour. Because many Internet service providers allow telnet access, you may be able to walk in, rent a terminal, and use telnet to check your e-mail (see *MORE Internet For Dummies,* 3rd Edition, Chapter 11, for information on how to use telnet). Most cybercafés have network-knowledgeable wait staff that can help you figure it all out, even in English. You can even transfer files to your laptop using sneaker net.

We were able to use this method of getting e-mail on a trip to Paris. A cybercafé called Cyberia (`cyberia@easynet.fr`) is in the center of Paris at the Pompidou Center. It was easy and fun. The biggest problem was typing with a French keyboard, which is just different enough to cause lots of typos. If you check it out, be sure to switch the terminal to English mode if that's what your fingers are used to typing.

If you do access your e-mail service provider account from overseas, we recommend that you change your password when you get home. Also, variations in world keyboards make it a good idea to avoid special characters in e-mail account passwords. You may have a hard time finding the character key you need in time to log in.

French-born Philippe Le Roux serves on the national board of the Information Technology Watching Network and is the North American correspondent for Planete Internet. *His article "Virtual Intimacy" can be found in* Internet Secrets *(IDG Books Worldwide, Inc.). You can send e-mail to him at* `leroux@dummies.com.`

Chapter 22
E-Mail in Our Lives

E-mail is already a way of life for a lot of us — some of us can't imagine a day without it. We've actually gone several days without it, but we have to be someplace exotic to make its absence worth our while. You may take a long time before showing signs of addiction, but once you connect with someone you love using e-mail, you'll start to understand what the hoopla is all about.

E-Mail at Home

Electronic mail can help around the house in many ways. Sure, it's a way to get messages when you are not home or don't want to answer the phone. Big deal, an answering machine can do that, too. E-mail can do a lot more for your life.

Keeping in touch with the family mailing list

In our highly mobile society, family members tend to be scattered around the globe. E-mail is a great way to stay in touch. Remember the movie where a guy is having an anxiety attack in Bloomingdale's and his brother asks if anyone has a Valium — and a dozen people offer him some? Well, bring up e-mail at the next family gathering. We'll bet you'll be surprised who has it. Get an e-mail address from everyone in the room who has one. After you get home, send a message to all the people on the list, just saying "Hi!" and asking for any other addresses. Even better, build a family mailing list. Chapter 16 shows you simple ways to do this.

Some of us have seen our family grow as a direct result of e-mail. A long-lost cousin of Carol's found her on the Travel-L mailing list and sent e-mail to see if they were related. And her cousin-the-doctor in Texas helped her via e-mail when her dad was sick last year. Her brother's online at work in Vermont, and now she's finding Baroudis all over the place. It's amazing what a little e-mail can do.

Kids at college

E-mail is a particularly good way to communicate with your offspring who are away at college. Nowadays, almost all colleges give computer accounts with e-mail to their students (considering the price of tuition, it's not a lot to ask). The savings in collect phone calls alone can pay for your e-mail account.

Even more important, e-mail lets you stay in touch with your favorite college students without crowding their space. They can read your mail when they want and respond when they want. This takes some of the angst and guilt away and saves them the embarrassment of talking to you in front of their roommates.

The younger generation has adopted e-mail as their own. With e-mail, you're meeting them on their own turf. It lets them keep their feeling of independence. After all, letting them learn to be on their own is why you took out that second mortgage, isn't it?

E-Mail for Kids

If you have pre-college-age children or are planning to have children, a wide variety of kid-related resources out there can be reached by e-mail.

E-mail can put the whole world at a kid's fingertips. She can make friends anywhere, practice her French or Spanish or Portuguese or Russian or Japanese, search databases for a term paper, and even let political leaders know what a future voter thinks.

The Internet for young children

We have to say up front that we are strong advocates of allowing children to be children, and we believe that children are better teachers than computers are. Neither John nor Carol let their kids watch TV. Now that you know our predisposition, maybe you can guess what we're going to say next: We are not in favor of sticking a young child in front of a screen. How young is young? We feel that younger than age 7 is young. Many educators feel that unstructured computer time under age 11 is inappropriate. We recommend that children get as much human attention as possible, and we believe that computers make lousy babysitters. At young ages, children benefit more from playing with trees, balls, clay, crayons, paint, mud, monkey bars, bicycles, and other kids.

Schools are actively debating e-mail and Internet access for their students. Teachers and parents go round and round, and ignorance seems to prevail. Find out as much as you can and get involved. The more you know, the more you can advocate for appropriate access.

A wonderful book called *The Internet For Teachers,* by David Clark (IDG Books Worldwide, Inc.), can help you understand all that can be gained from e-mail and the Internet, and it can arm you with the information you'll need to face hordes of cynics, including school administrators, teachers, and other parents. The book focuses on the Internet from an educator's perspective, including why the Internet is important, how to use it, and where to find education-specific resources. Though it's aimed at teachers, it's a great find for parents.

What about all that bad stuff I've been hearing?

Parents, educators, and free-speech advocates alike agree that nothing substitutes for parental guidance when it comes to the subject of e-mail and Internet access. Just as we parents want our children to read good books and see quality films, we also want them to find the *good* stuff on the Internet. If you take the time to learn with your children, you have the opportunity to share the experience and to impart critical values and a sense of discrimination that your children need in all areas of their lives.

Remember that the good stuff on the Net far outweighs the bad. Sexually explicit material does exist, but it's a minor percentage of all that's out there. You have to make some effort to get it, and, more and more frequently, you have to *pay* to get to most of it.

Perhaps highest on the list of parents' concerns about e-mail access for children is the question of their kids corresponding with unsavory adults and older kids. We say *perhaps* because parents who have taken the time to learn about access issues understand that the threat is not so great as some would have us believe and that, with reasonable attention, this concern can become a non-issue.

Children can develop inappropriate associations in many places, particularly as they grow older and become more independent. Developing a relationship with your child based on trust, openness, and a willingness to listen is your best long-term defense against these risks. Your child talks to e-mail friends from your home where you can better exercise gentle supervision. Your child's use of e-mail can be a valuable avenue to developing the skills that will protect him or her in the future.

Mailing lists for kids and parents

Mailing lists are a great source of fun, education, and help for kids and parents alike. Chapter 16 tells you how to subscribe to mailing lists. In the rest of this chapter, we provide just the list name and its description. Many more lists are available where these come from, so if none of them strikes your fancy, don't despair.

kidmedia

This mailing list is a professional-level discussion group for people interested in children's media (television, radio, print, and data). To subscribe, send mail to `kidmedia-request@airwaves.chi.il.us` for individual articles, or to `kidmedia-d-request@airwaves.chi.il.us` for daily digests. On the subject line, enter SUBSCRIBE, UNSUBSCRIBE, or HELP (to receive the charter and info file).

kidsphere

The `kidsphere` list was established in 1989 to stimulate the development of an international computer network for use by children and their teachers. Send subscription requests to `kidsphere-request@vms.cis.pitt.edu`.

kid

On this list, children post messages to other children. Send subscription requests to `kids-request@vms.cis.pitt.edu`.

dinosaur

For subscription requests to this low-volume list about dinosaurs, send a message to `listproc@lepomis.psych.upenn.edu` in the following format:

```
SUBSCRIBE DINOSAUR <yourname>
```

pen pals

This list provides a forum in which children correspond electronically with each other. The list is not moderated, but it is monitored for content. Send subscription requests to `pen-pals-request@mainstream.com`.

y-rights

This group, open to everyone, discusses the rights of kids and teens. Send an e-mail message to `LISTSERV@sjuvm.bitnet`. In the text of the message, include one of these lines:

- ✔ To subscribe to the list: `SUB Y-RIGHTS` *firstname lastname* (substitute your own first and last name)
- ✔ To receive the daily digest of the list: `SET Y-RIGHTS DIGEST` *firstname lastname*
- ✔ To receive the list of previous discussions: `GET Y-RIGHTS FILELIST` *firstname lastname*

kid cafes

Kid cafes are mailing lists that exist for kids aged 10 to 15 to have conversations with other kids — kids in general and kids in specific. Kids can find "keypals" with similar interests and exchange messages with them.

Several different kid cafes are available, depending on whether one is joining as an individual or part of a school class. The kid cafes listed in Table 22-1 are all LISTSERV lists managed at `LISTSERV@vm1.nodak.edu`. See Chapter 16 for details on how to subscribe.

Table 22-1	Kid Cafes
Name of list	**Description**
KIDCAFE-INDIVIDUAL	For individual participants looking for keypals
KIDCAFE-SCHOOL	For classroom groups looking for keypals
KIDCAFE-TOPICS	Open discussion of any appropriate topic
KIDCAFE-QUERY	Asking questions of other kidcafe participants

Lists for parents of kids with problems

One of the most profound and heartening human experiences available on the Internet has to do with the help that total strangers freely offer one another. The incredible bonds that form among people sharing their experiences, struggles, strengths, and hopes redefine what it means to reach out and touch someone. We encourage everyone who has a concern to look for people who share that concern. Our experience of participating in mailing lists and newsgroups related to our own problems compels us to enthusiastically encourage you to check things out online. You can do so with complete anonymity. You can watch and learn for a long time, or you can jump into the fray and ask for help.

We caution you that everyone who gives advice is not a medical expert. You have to involve your own practitioners in your process. Many people have found enormous help, however, from people who have gone down similar paths before them. For many of us, it has made all the difference in the world.

We list in this chapter a few of the available online mailing lists and discussion groups. Almost certainly you'll find a mailing list or group specific to your needs, regardless of whether we list it here, and new groups are added every day. If you're using a commercial provider such as America Online, Prodigy, or CompuServe, your provider has special forums that may interest you as well.

In Chapter 16, we describe how to use e-mail mailing lists. If you find something of interest in the rest of this chapter, you'll have a reason to learn how to do it.

Notice that some lists are *talk* lists, which feature free-flow discussion; some lists have very focused discussions; and some lists are almost purely academic. You can't always tell from the name. If it looks interesting, subscribe and see what sort of discussion is going on there. You can always unsubscribe if you don't like it. Table 22-2 provides the names of several parents' lists.

Table 22-2	Self-Help Mailing Lists for Parents	
Resource Name	*Description*	*To Contact*
add-parents	Support and information for parents of children with attention deficit/ hyperactivity disorder	Send e-mail to `add-parents-request@mv.mv.com`
our-kids	Support for parents and others regarding care, diagnosis, and therapy for young children with developmental delays	Send the e-mail message *subscribe our-kids* to `majordomo@tbag.osc.edu`

Resource Name	Description	To Contact
behavior	Support for behavioral and emotional disorders in children	Send the message *subscribe behavior* to `listserv @astuvm.inre.asu.edu`
deafkids	Support for deaf children	Send the message *subscribe deafkids* to `listserv @juvm.stjohns.edu`
cshcn-l	Support for children with special health care needs	Send the message *subscribe cshcn-l* to `listserv @nervm.nerdc.ufl.edu`
dadvocat	Support for dads of children with disabilities	Send the message *subscribe dadvocat* to `listserv @ukcc.uky.edu`
ddline	Children's disability list	Send the message *subscribe ddline* to `listserv @uicvm.uic.edu`
ds-c-imp	Overview of childhood impairment issues	Send the message *subscribe ds-c-imp* to `listserv @list.nih.gov`
ds-c-sb1	Support for spina bifida	Send the message *subscribe ds-c-sb1* to `listserv @list.nih.gov`
ds-c-00	Discussion of major childhood measures issues	Send the message *suscribe ds-c-00* to `listserv @list.nih.gov`

More mailing lists for kids

Table 22-3 includes some other kid-oriented lists you and your family might enjoy.

Table 22-3	Mailing Lists for and about Kids	
Resource Name	**Description**	**To Contact**
kidlit-l	A list about children's and youth literature	Send the message *subscribe kidlit-l* to `listserv@bingvmb .cc.binghamton.edu`
kids-act	"What can I do now?"	Send the message *subscribe kids-act* to `listserv@vml .nodak.edu`

(continued)

Table 22-3 *(continued)*

Resource Name	Description	To Contact
kidzmail	Kids exploring issues and interests electronically	Send the message *subscribe kidzmail* to `listserv@asuvm .inre.asu.edu`
childlit	Children's literature: criticism and theory	Send the message *subscribe childlit* to `listserv@rutvm1 .rutgers.edu`
childri-l	Discussion of UN convention on the rights of children	Send the message *subscribe childri-l* to `listserv@nic .surfnet.nl`
ecenet-l	Early childhood education and young children (0 to 8 years old)	Send the message *subscribe ecenet-l* to `listserv@vmd. cso.uiuc.edu`
eceol-l	Early childhood education	Send the message *subscribe eceol-l* to `listserv@maine .maine.edu`
father-l	Importance of fathers in children's lives	Send the message *subscribe father-l* to `listserv@vm1 .spcs.umn.edu`

Ze E-Mail for ze Lovers

Whether you're looking for love or you have already found it, e-mail can add a little spice to your life. For an in-depth treatise on the affair, we highly recommend the article "Virtual Intimacy" by Philippe Le Roux in *Internet Secrets* (IDG Books Worldwide, Inc.). Meanwhile, we've rounded up the tips from two experienced e-mail lovers, Dionysos and Chica, who have each fallen in love many times in virtual worlds.

✔ If you have a love in your life, ask him, her, or it for an e-mail address. E-mail is a wonderful way to share sweet words. Discovering loving messages in your inbox is always a nice surprise and can help you through a hard day at the office. And sometimes talking about things in e-mail is easier than talking face-to-face, as long as it's not the only way you communicate.

✔ If you want to meet someone, find mailing lists that interest you. Don't go to the singles ads. Look for someone who shares your passions.

✔ When you haven't heard from that special someone in several days, suspect the technology first. E-mail is seductively reliable. You begin to count on its being there, and then all of a sudden, it's not. But more often than not, what has suddenly gone wrong in an e-mail relationship is that mail isn't getting through or someone's connection is down.

✔ Likewise, if your friend seems to be ignoring something you said, or is saying things that seem odd to you or out of context, suspect missing messages. It may happen once in two hundred times, but messages do get lost, or get out of sync, or get delayed (sometimes for days) in some black hole on the Net.

✔ Be slow to anger, quick to forgive. Remember, you can't see the person's face, can't hear his or her tone of voice. Before you take offense, try reading a message over several times. Look for what might have been a typo that could alter the meaning. Try to read it as ironic, sarcastic, or funny before you take it seriously.

✔ Read your own messages carefully — hard to do in fits of passion, we understand, but you're probably not polysyllabic then, anyway. In ordinary conversation, be careful what you type.

✔ If you start to fall for somebody over the Net, get his phone number. Call and talk to him even if for just a few minutes. Often this telephone call will break any serious illusions you have or help you with another level of trust. Besides, one day when you suddenly can't get to your e-mail, it'll be too late to ask for the number. Then what will you do?

✔ Be aware of what you type. Be especially careful of addresses. Make sure the mail you send is going where you intend it to, and understand the consequences for you if someone else were to read it by mistake. For example, if you send your e-mail from work, how would you feel about your boss or coworkers seeing it?

✔ Know that e-mail lands several places in its route. If you compose your mail on your personal computer and you download all your mail to your personal computer, you minimize the chance of someone else reading your mail, but you don't eliminate it. If you leave messages on your computer at work or on your account at your service provider, people (system administrators, for example) can read your mail; and often your entire disk is backed up, your mail included.

✔ Have a good time. E-mail has sparked many wonderful romances, even marriages.

✔ Take care of yourself. The electronic dating is virtual. Discovering somebody by his words is very exciting and interesting. We're all looking for a way to discover people without being influenced by the appearance, the look, and all this artificial stuff. But we humans have developed ways of reading people using a lot of tools and signals (like feelings), and the electronic talks make us miss those tools. Virtual intimacy can be false in two ways: Because the correspondent is lying or because you're lying to yourself, just exaggerating the good feelings you have reading the messages from the other part. Virtual intimacy can make you discover intensity in yourself you never suspected, but can make you live some high deceptions.

✔ If you don't meet your life's partner by e-mail, we're sure you'll discover a lot of interesting people with whom you can form very special friendships.

E-Mail for People with Disabilities

Electronic mail can be a both a boon and a bane for people with disabilities. It is a boon for disabled people who can type at a keyboard and read a CRT screen. It gives those people access to a whole new world of computer networking. For those who cannot read a screen or use a keyboard, it can seem one more barrier to integrating with an increasingly networked world. But adaptive technologies exist that can help make electronic communication a plus in their lives too.

E-mail and the hearing impaired

For people who are deaf or hard of hearing but can use a computer, e-mail is a natural aid. It gives them direct access to a mainstream communications tool.

A few problems make e-mail not quite natural for the deaf:

✔ Expense. Many deaf persons simply cannot afford a computer and e-mail access.

✔ Lack of integration with TTY, the primary means of telecommunication for the deaf and hard of hearing. We explain what TTY is all about in the next section.

✔ Language problems. English is a second language for many deaf people. Their primary language (at least in the United States) is ASL, American Sign Language. Many hearing people believe that ASL is just English expressed as hand movements. Nope. ASL has a unique grammar and vocabulary and is no more like English than French is. Many deaf people write impeccable English, just as many French people do. However, for others, communicating in written English is not that easy.

If you are communicating with a deaf person via e-mail or TTY, show the same patience and courtesy as you would when speaking to a guest from a non-English-speaking country.

TTY versus e-mail

The deaf are no strangers to digital communication. In a way they invented it. Back in the 1960s, when older generations of Teletype machines were being replaced with newer models, a deaf engineer named Robert Weitbrecht had the bright idea of making the surplus machines usable for the deaf. Over time, the Teletype gave the deaf the same ability to communicate over distance that the telephone offers hearing people. Today in North America, most deaf people, many hard of hearing people, and many of their friends use desktop TTY terminals, also known as TDD (Telecommunication Device for the Deaf).

These boxes, about the size of a large hardcover book, contain a keyboard and a display capable of showing one line of text (or more, depending on price). TTY boxes are used for live communication over conventional telephone circuits. A TTY user dials the phone number of the TTY-equipped person with whom he or she wants to chat. When the person answers, whatever is typed on one TTY terminal shows up on the other terminal's display.

TTY users use several abbreviations to control the conversation:

- ✔ GA stands for "go ahead" and means "I'm done typing. It's your turn."
- ✔ GA SK means "I'm ready to hang up unless you have something else to say.
- ✔ SK or SKSK stands for "stop keying" and means "I'm hanging up now."

It is also considered polite to identify yourself at the beginning of a TTY conversation:

```
"THIS IS ARNOLD REINHOLD GA" or "JOHN LEVINE HERE GA"
```

There are no headers because TTY provides live conversations.

TTY is based on very old technology — it operates at 45 bps, glacial compared to the 33,600-bps speed of a modern computer modem. But 45 bps does allow you to type about 70 words a minute, fast enough for most typists. TTY also uses the old Baudot teletype code, the grandmother of ASCII. Baudot has only uppercase letters and requires you to shift to a figures case when you want to type numbers and special characters and then shift back to letters case. Europeans use another communication standard called EDT (European Deaf Teletypewriter), which is not compatible with TTY.

TTY has one big advantage over computer modems: It is not very sensitive to disruptions on the phone line. Computer modems, on the other hand, are very sensitive to such disruptions. Sometimes, when the exhilaration of writing computer books gets to be too much, we go downstairs for a break and realize we forgot to log out from our Internet service provider. When we do, we need only pick up an extension phone for a moment to be sure our modem connection will be broken. By contrast, you cannot break a TTY connection except by hanging up the phone.

Can I use my modem to chat with a friend on TTY?

Basically the answer is no. Unfortunately, almost all computer modems are incapable of talking TTY. Why? For many years, modem manufacturers gave lack of standards as an excuse for not incorporating TTY compatibility. Finally, in 1995, the International Telecommunications Union approved a TTY compatibility mode standard for computer modems, called V.18. Now modem manufacturers are balking at including V.18 capability, claiming the market is too small.

If you want to talk to TTY users — and the Americans with Disabilities Act (ADA) says you must be able to if you are a business in the United States — you have several choices at the moment:

- ✔ A smaller modem vendor, NXi Communications, Inc., of Salt Lake City, Utah, offers a 19,200-bps FAX modem with a TTY mode. It is a bit pricey, but it works. You can contact them via e-mail at nxi@nxicom.com or call 801-466-1258 voice, 801-466-0453 TTY.

- ✔ Buy a TTY modem. These look like a regular computer modem but only support TTY and perhaps 300-bps ASCII.

- ✔ Buy a regular TTY terminal. This is a cop-out, but it is guaranteed to work.

Here are a couple more options that might not pass ADA muster but can let you communicate with a TTY user:

- ✔ Some TTY terminals have an ASCII mode that operates at 300 bps, the lowest speed most computer modems can handle. You can set up a connection with one of these TTY terminals using a terminal emulator program on your computer. Set your computer to 300 baud, N, 8, 1, VT100.

- ✔ You can call a relay service, a service that has human operators who speak on one line and transcribe the conversation to a TTY terminal on the other line. Many states in the U.S. have free relay services for local calls. They are usually listed in the front of your phone book.

AT&T offers a long-distance relay service at regular long-distance rates. You can contact AT&T at 800-855-2881 voice, 800-855-3880 TTY.

✔ There are plans to make 511 and 711 standard numbers for accessing deaf relay services.

E-mail and the vision-impaired

For people who have difficulty reading a computer display or who simply cannot do so, e-mail may seem a step backward. Most vision-impaired people would be happier just talking on the telephone. Electronic messaging is as unnatural for them as it is natural for the deaf. But there are technologies that help vision-impaired people read their messages. And e-mail does offer some benefits, particularly at work. To the extent that corporate communications flow on e-mail, it is more accessible to people with vision impairment than older paper memoranda. So in some ways, e-mail is the glass that is half full.

The main adaptive technologies that allow people with vision impairments to read e-mail are

✔ **Extra large type.** In some cases this requires nothing more than adjusting the font size in your mailer program. Also, screen magnification programs are available for DOS, Mac OS, and Windows. The Macintosh program, CloseView, is included for free with the Mac OS.

✔ **Voice to speech.** All Mac OS and most Windows machines sold today include sound output capability. Older PCs can be upgraded by adding a sound card or multimedia package. A variety of speech-synthesis software is available that enables you to have your e-mail "read" to you.

✔ **Braille printers.** A couple of these devices, also called embossers, are on the market. They tend to cost as much as a computer, however.

✔ **CompuServe** claims to let you pick up your e-mail by phone. We haven't been able to get it installed, but if you're highly motivated, it might be worth a try.

People with other disabilities

Disabilities vary widely in their nature and severity. Many people have multiple disabilities. Finding a way for severely or multiply disabled people to use e-mail often requires developing solutions on a case-by-case basis, drawing on assistive technologies that already exist, and in some cases, developing new ones. E-mail and mailing lists are a great way for those who are trying to help to stay in touch and learn about what's new, what works, and what doesn't work.

Resources for people with disabilities

A large number of mailing lists deal with disability issues. See Chapter 16 for information on how to use mailing lists. Table 22-4 contains a few useful lists.

Table 22-4	Mailing Lists Dealing with Disability Issues
Resource Name	*Description*
L-HCAP	A LISTSERV list about all disabilities (moderated)
BLINDNEWS	A LISTSERV list about blindness (moderated)
DEAF-L	A LISTSERV list for the deaf

For additional information on e-mail and Internet resources for the disabled, see "Internet Access for People with Disabilities" by Jim Allan, K.C. Dignan, and Dave Kinnaman in *Internet Secrets* (IDG Books Worldwide, Inc.).

The Net as college

Saying that many people are learning more on the Internet than they ever did in school is no exaggeration. There are many factors to consider, but the Net requires motivation, and motivated learning is much more fun. The Net provides equal opportunity beyond the imagination of those locked in physical settings. The Net is open to everyone of any color, height, belief, and description. People previously locked out of educational opportunities by physical handicap, economic need, or geography find the Net an empowering, life-altering experience.

Beyond the informal education that's already available, organizations are actively working to establish formal online colleges. Virtual Online University (VOU) just completed its first full semester. It's not yet accredited, but all colleges and universities begin that way. For more information, you can send an e-mail message to billp@showme.missouri.edu.

Part VII
The Part of Tens

The 5th Wave   By Rich Tennant

IT'S FRICASSEE OF PYTHON WITH FRIED ANTS AND CRISPY GRASSHOPPERS.

YOU'RE GETTING RECIPES OFF THE INTERNET AGAIN, AREN'T YOU?

In this part . . .

No ...*For Dummies* book would be complete without our handy lists of helpful hints. By the strangest coincidence, we have exactly *ten* entries in each list. (Note to the literal minded: You may have to cut off and/or glue on some fingers to make your version of ten match up with ours. Perhaps it would be easier and less messy just to take our word for it.)

Chapter 23

The Ten Commandments of E-Mail

Thou shalt include a clear and specific subject line.

Thou shalt edit any quoted text down to the minimum thou needest.

Thou shalt read thine own message thrice before thou sendest it.

Thou shalt ponder how thy recipient might react to thy message.

Thou shalt check thy spelling and thy grammar.

Thou shalt not curse, flame, spam, or USE ALL CAPS.

Thou shalt not forward any chain letter.

Thou shalt not use e-mail for any illegal or unethical purpose.

Thou shalt not rely on the privacy of e-mail, especially from work.

When in doubt, save thy message overnight and reread it in the light of the dawn.

The Golden Rule of E-Mail

That which thou findest hateful to receive, sendest thou not unto others.

Chapter 24

Ten Cats and Dogs: Mailing Lists You Can Chew On

. . . .

*T*o give you, gentle reader, some idea of the vast variety of e-mail mailing lists that are available, we present ten sets of polar opposite e-mail lists.

Cats and Dogs

Humanity is divided by many fault lines. Pet preference is one of the most telling divisions. Some people claim to like both cats and dogs.

Meow

CYBERCAT

This amazing cat fancier's mailing list offers support, love, and feline skullduggery for the serious cat lover.

To subscribe, send the message `join cybercat` *youremailaddress* to `listserv@getaway.net`.

To send mail to the members, write to this address: `cybercat@getaway.net`. (Start the subject line with the word `CHATTERS` if you want to send a message to other cats on behalf of your cat.)

Arf! Arf!

CANINE-L

The dog lover's list. Lots of people like dogs, it seems.

To subscribe, send the message `sub CANINE-L` *yourfirstname yourlastname* to `listserv@psuvm.psu.edu`.

To send mail to the members, write to `CANINE-L@psuvm.psu.edu`.

Macintosh and PC

If pet preference is one of the most telling divisions in humanity, choice of personal computer platform is certainly the most emotional. Some people even claim to like UNIX.

Macs

Mac lovers, always a clannish group, are circling their wagons against the evil Windows empire.

Mac-L

The Macintosh questions and discussion list. This list is not sponsored by Apple Computer and is not dominated by propaganda.

To subscribe, send the message `sub mac-l` *yourfirstname yourlastname* to `listserv@list.nih.gov`.

To send mail to the members, write to `mac-l@list.nih.gov`.

TIDBITS

TidBITS is an excellent newsletter for Macintosh users, edited by our friend Adam Engst.

To subscribe, send *any* message to `tidbits-on@tidbits.com`.

EvangeList

Guy Kawasaki's Macintosh newsletter is essential for the true believers.

To subscribe, send the message `sub macway` *yourfirstname yourlastname* to `listproc@abs.apple.com`.

PCs

PC users aren't as clannish, but they're just as chatty.

WinNews

All Windows 95 stuff, tips and hints, new products, and general propaganda.

To subscribe, send the message `subscribe winnews` to `enews99@microsoft.nwnet.com`. The subject should be blank.

WIN95-L

Windows 95 Give-And-Take List

To subscribe, send the message `sub WIN95-L` *yourfirstname yourlastname* to `listserv@peach.ease.lsoft.com`.

To send mail to the members, write to `win95-l@peach.ease.lsoft.com`.

New and Old

E-mail is new. People talking to each other is old.

New-List

This handy list will let you know about new mailing lists as they appear. (***Note:*** the first part of the domain name is spelled "vee em one.")

To subscribe, send the message `sub NEW-LIST` *yourfirstname yourlastname* to `listserv@vm1.nodak.edu`.

ARCH-L

General archaeology list, covering all aspects of archaeology worldwide.

To subscribe, send the message `SUBSCRIBE ARCH-L` *yourfirstname yourlastname* to `listserv@tamvm1.tamu.edu`.

To send mail to the members, write to `ARCH-L@tamvm1.tamu.edu`.

Single and Married

The grass is always greener . . .

SINGLES

SINGLES is a forum for the discussion of issues related to the single life. This includes, but is not limited to, such topics as living alone, meeting people, the biological clock, and flirting.

To subscribe, send the following message `subscribe SINGLES` to:`majordomo@indiana.edu`.

To send mail to the members, write to `singles@indiana.edu`.

WME-L

Worldwide Marriage Encounter discussion

To subscribe, send the message `sub WME-L` *yourfirstname yourlastname* to `listserv@american.edu`.

To send mail to the members, write to `wme-l@american.edu`.

Rich and Poor

Learn to write *...For Dummies* books and you can go from one to the other. (We're not sure which way, though.)

Business Ethics

People on this list don't think the topic is an oxymoron.

To subscribe, send the message `sub BUSETH` *yourfirstname yourlastname* to `listproc@callutheran.edu`.

To send mail to the members, write to `buseth@callutheran.edu`.

Straw Bale Housing

To subscribe, send the message `subscribe strawbale` *yourfirstname* *yourlastname* to `majordomo@crest.org`.

Republican and Democrat

To people who aren't in or from the United States, let me assure you that the differences between these political parties are profound. (Don't ask us what they are.)

REPUB-L

To subscribe, send the message `sub REPUB-L` *yourfirstname* *yourlastname* to `listserv@vm.marist.edu`.

To send mail to the members, write to `repub-l@vm.marist.edu`.

CDLIST

College Democrats Discussion and Information Group

To subscribe, send the message `sub CDLIST` *yourfirstname* *yourlastname* to `listserv@gwuvm.gwu.edu`.

To send mail to the members, write to `cdlist@gwuvm.gwu.edu`.

CLINTON

Discussion of Bill Clinton's Presidency

To subscribe, send the message `sub CLINTON` *yourfirstname* *yourlastname* to `listserv@vm.marist.edu`.

To send mail to the members, write to `clinton@vm.marist.edu`.

Jocks and Couch Potatoes

Sending e-mail can really build up your wrist muscles.

D-SPORT

Sports for Persons with Disabilities

To subscribe, send the message `sub D-SPORT yourfirstname yourlastname` to `listserv@maelstrom.stjohns.edu`.

To send mail to the members, write to `d-sport@maelstrom.stjohns.edu`.

SPORTSOC

Sociological aspects of sports discussion

To subscribe, send the message `sub SPORTSOC yourfirstname yourlastname` to `listserv@vm.temple.edu`.

To send mail to the members, write to `sportsoc@vm.temple.edu`.

SCREEN-L

Film and TV Studies Discussion List

To subscribe, send the message `sub SCREEN-L yourfirstname yourlastname` to `listserv@ua1vm.ua.edu`. (That's a numeral one between "ua" and "vm.")

To send mail to the members, write to `screen-l@ua1vm.ua.edu`.

FRIENDS

List about the NBC Comedy *Friends*

To subscribe, send the message `sub FRIENDS yourfirstname yourlastname` to `listserv@listserv.dartmouth.edu`.

To send mail to the members, write to `friends@listserv.dartmouth.edu`.

Near and Far

Folks on Mars will stay in touch with their friends on Earth by e-mail.

Roadside mailing list

The discussions on this list concern great cheesy tourist attractions across the U.S. They focus on those that are still in operation but would also enjoy tales of gone-but-not-forgotten ones. If you love old-fashioned roadside attractions, if you'd rather visit an alligator ranch than EPCOT Center, if you'd drive out of your way to dine in a restaurant shaped like a coffeepot, if you'd opt for Route 66 over I-40 in a heartbeat, this list is for you.

To subscribe, send the message subscribe roadside *yourfirstname yourlastname* to listproc@listproc.echonyc.com.

To send mail to the members, write to roadside@listproc.echonyc.com.

Earth and Sky mailing list

Earth and Sky is a radio broadcast on public radio stations. It covers questions on geology, earth science, and astronomy, and many of the questions are sent in by listeners. The transcripts of the radio broadcasts are sent out once a week, along with references and sometimes additional information on a topic.

To subscribe, send the message subscribe to earthandsky- request@earthsky.com.

Serious and Funny

Okay, so some of the poetry isn't serious. Not all the jokes are funny.

POETRY

Electronic Poetry Mailing List

To subscribe, send the message subscribe poetry to majordomo@laplaza.org.

To send poems and comments to the members, write to poetry@laplaza.org.

HUMOR

University of Georgia, Athens, Humor List

To subscribe, send the message `sub HUMOR` *yourfirstname yourlastname* to `listserv@uga.cc.uga.edu`.

To send mail to the members, write to `humor@uga.cc.uga.edu`.

Quick and Dead

Mailing lists cover everything.

ECENET-L

Early childhood education/young children (0–8)

To subscribe, send the message `sub ECENET-L` *yourfirstname yourlastname* to `listserv@vmd.cso.uiuc.edu`.

To send mail to the members, write to `ecenet-l@vmd.cso.uiuc.edu`.

ROOTS-L

General Genealogy List

To subscribe, send the single word `SUBSCRIBE` to `roots-l-request@rootsweb.com`.

To send mail to the members, write to `roots-l@rootsweb.com`.

JEWISHGEN

Jewish Genealogy Discussion Group

To subscribe, send the message `sub JEWISHGEN` *yourfirstname yourlastname* to `listserv@mail.eworld.com`.

To send mail to the members, write to `jewishgen@mail.eworld.com`.

Part VIII
Appendixes

The 5th Wave   By Rich Tennant

"Awww jeez- I was afraid of this. Some poor kid, bored with the usual chat lines, starts looking for bigger kicks, pretty soon they're surfin' the seedy back alleys of cyberspace, and before you know it they're into a file they can't 'undo'. I guess that's why they call it the Web. Somebody open a window!"

In this part . . .

Finally, a part of the book containing nothing but facts. The list of countries help you figure out what country an exotic address hails from. (One of the few disadvantages of e-mail is that you don't get any colorful foreign stamps on the virtual envelopes.) The glossary tells you what the geek-speak terms about e-mail actually mean. And all the way at the back, we give you info about what's on the CD-ROM and tell you how to use it.

Appendix A

Internet Country Codes

• •

*T*his appendix contains a list of the two-letter country codes found at the end of Internet e-mail addresses and in World Wide Web domain names.

New countries join the Net every month. For the latest version of this table, visit `http://net.dummies.net/countries/`.

In this table, *I* means the country is connected to the Internet, and *M* means there is an e-mail-only connection.

Country Code	Connection Type	Country
AF		Afghanistan
AL	I	Albania
DZ	I	Algeria
AS		American Samoa
AD	I	Andorra
AO	M	Angola
AI	M	Anguilla
AQ	I	Antarctica
AG	I	Antigua and Barbuda
AR	I	Argentina
AM	I	Armenia
AW	I	Aruba
AU	I	Australia
AT	I	Austria
AZ	I	Azerbaijan
BS	M	Bahamas
BH	I	Bahrain
BD	M	Bangladesh

(continued)

Country Code	Connection Type	Country
BB	I	Barbados
BY	I	Belarus
BE	I	Belgium
BZ	I	Belize
BJ	I	Benin
BM	I	Bermuda
BT		Bhutan
BO	I	Bolivia
BA	M	Bosnia-Herzegovina
BW	M	Botswana
BV		Bouvet Island
BR	I	Brazil
IO		British Indian Ocean Territory
BN	I	Brunei Darussalam
BG	I	Bulgaria
BF	M	Burkina Faso (formerly Upper Volta)
BI		Burundi
KH	M	Cambodia
CM	M	Cameroon
CA	I	Canada
CV		Cape Verde
KY	I	Cayman Islands
CF	I	Central African Republic
TD	M	Chad
CL	I	Chile
CN	I	China
CX		Christmas Island (Indian Ocean)
CC		Cocos (Keeling) Islands
CO	I	Colombia
KM		Comoros
CG		Congo
CK	M	Cook Islands

CR	I	Costa Rica
CI	M	Cote d'Ivoire
HR	I	Croatia
CU	M	Cuba
CY	I	Cyprus
CZ	I	Czech Republic
DK	I	Denmark
DJ	I	Djibouti
DM		Dominica
DO	I	Dominican Republic
TP		East Timor
EC	I	Ecuador
EG	I	Egypt
SV	I	El Salvador
GQ		Equatorial Guinea
ER	M	Eritrea
EE	I	Estonia
ET	M	Ethiopia
FK		Falkland Islands (Malvinas)
FO	I	Faroe Islands
FJ	I	Fiji
FI	I	Finland
FR	I	France
GF	M	French Guiana
PF	M	French Polynesia
TF		French Southern Territories
GA		Gabon
GM	M	Gambia
GE	I	Georgia
DE	I	Germany
GH	I	Ghana
GI	I	Gibraltar

(continued)

Country Code	Connection Type	Country
GR	I	Greece
GL	I	Greenland
GD	M	Grenada
GP	M	Guadeloupe
GU	I	Guam
GT	I	Guatemala
GN	M	Guinea
GW		Guinea-Bissau
GY	M	Guyana
HT	M	Haiti
HM		Heard and McDonald Islands
HN	I	Honduras
HK	I	Hong Kong
HU	I	Hungary
IS	I	Iceland
IN	I	India
ID	I	Indonesia
IR	I	Iran
IQ		Iraq
IE	I	Ireland
IL	I	Israel
IT	I	Italy
JM	I	Jamaica
JP	I	Japan
JO	I	Jordan
KZ	I	Kazakhstan
KE	I	Kenya
KI	M	Kiribati
KP		Korea (North)
KR	I	Korea (South)
KW	I	Kuwait
KG	I	Kyrgyz Republic

LA	M	Laos
LV	I	Latvia
LB	I	Lebanon
LS	M	Lesotho
LR		Liberia
LY		Libyan Arab Jamahiriya
LI	I	Liechtenstein
LT	I	Lithuania
LU	I	Luxembourg
MO	I	Macau (Ao-me'n)
MK	I	Macedonia
MG	I	Madagascar
MW	M	Malawi
MY	I	Malaysia
MV		Maldives
ML	M	Mali
MT	I	Malta
MH	M	Marshall Islands
MQ		Martinique
MR		Mauritania
MU	I	Mauritius
YT		Mayotte
MX	I	Mexico
FM		Micronesia
MD	I	Moldova
MC	I	Monaco
MN	I	Mongolia
MS		Montserrat
MA	I	Morocco
MZ	I	Mozambique
MM		Myanmar

(continued)

Country Code	Connection Type	Country
NA	I	Namibia
NR	M	Nauru
NP	I	Nepal
NL	I	Netherlands
AN	M	Netherlands Antilles
NC	M	New Caledonia
NZ	I	New Zealand
NI	I	Nicaragua
NE	M	Niger
NG	M	Nigeria
NU	M	Niue
NF	I	Norfolk Island
MP		Northern Mariana Islands
NO	I	Norway
OM		Oman
PK	I	Pakistan
PW		Palau
PA	I	Panama
PG	M	Papua New Guinea
PY	I	Paraguay
PE	I	Peru
PH	I	Philippines
PN		Pitcairn
PL	I	Poland
PT	I	Portugal
PR	I	Puerto Rico
QA		Qatar
RE	I	Réunion
RO	I	Romania
RU	I	Russian Federation
RW		Rwanda
SH		Saint Helena

KN		Saint Kitts and Nevis
LC	I	Saint Lucia
PM		Saint Pierre and Miquelon
VC	M	Saint Vincent and the Grenadines
WS	M	Samoa
SM	I	San Marino
ST		São Tome and Principe
SA	I	Saudi Arabia
SN	I	Senegal
SC	M	Seychelles
SL	M	Sierra Leone
SG	I	Singapore
SK	I	Slovakia
SI	I	Slovenia
SB	M	Solomon Islands
SO		Somalia
ZA	I	South Africa
SU	I	Soviet Union (still in use)
ES	I	Spain
LK	I	Sri Lanka
SD	M	Sudan
SR	I	Suriname
SJ	I	Svalbard and Jan Mayen Islands
SZ	M	Swaziland
SE	I	Sweden
CH	I	Switzerland
SY		Syria
TW	I	Taiwan, Province of China
TJ	M	Tajikistan
TZ	M	Tanzania
TH	I	Thailand
TG	M	Togo

(continued)

Country Code	Connection Type	Country
TK		Tokelau
TO	M	Tonga
TT	I	Trinidad and Tobago
TN	I	Tunisia
TR	I	Turkey
TM	M	Turkmenistan
TC		Turks and Caicos Islands
TV	M	Tuvalu
UG	I	Uganda
UA	I	Ukraine
AE	I	United Arab Emirates
GB	I	United Kingdom
US	I	United States
UM		United States Minor Outlying Islands
UY	I	Uruguay
UZ	I	Uzbekistan
VU	M	Vanuatu (formerly New Hebrides)
VA	I	Vatican City State
VE	I	Venezuela
VN	M	Vietnam
VG		Virgin Islands (British)
VI	I	Virgin Islands (U.S.)
WF		Wallis and Futuna Islands
EH		Western Sahara
YE		Yemen
YU	M	Yugoslavia
ZR		Zaire
ZM	I	Zambia
ZW	I	Zimbabwe

Appendix B
Glossary

● ●

address: The letters and numbers that tell an e-mail message where to go.

anonymous FTP: A method of using the FTP program to log on to another computer to copy files, even though you don't have an account on the other computer. When you log on, you enter `anonymous` as the username and your address as the password, and you get access to publicly available files. See Chapter 19 for information about FTP-ing via e-mail.

anonymous remailer: Internet site that forwards e-mail messages with return addresses removed. Anonymous remailers allow you to send e-mail that can't be traced to you. See Chapter 17.

archive: A file that contains a group of files which have been compressed and glommed together for efficient storage. You have to use a program like pkzip, tar, or StuffIt to get the original files back out. See Chapter 5.

article: A posting to a mailing list. That is, a message someone sends to the mailing list to be readable by everyone who reads the mailing list. See Chapter 16 for information about mailing lists.

attachment or **attached file:** File sent along as part of an e-mail message.

automatic mailing list: A mailing list maintained by a computer program, usually one named LISTSERV or Majordomo.

bcc: Blind carbon copy. That is, someone who receives a copy of message without the rest of the addressees knowing it.

binary file: A file containing information that consists of more than just text. Examples include an archive, a picture, sounds, a video clip, a spreadsheet, or a word-processing document (which includes formatting codes in addition to characters).

BinHex: Method attaching a file to an e-mail message, primarily used by Mac programs. See Chapter 15.

BITFTP: The most widely available FTP-by-mail server.

bitmap: Lots of teeny, tiny, little dots put together to make a picture. Screens (and paper) are divided into thousands of little, tiny bits, each of which can be turned on or off. These little bits are combined to create graphical representations. GIF and JPG files are the most popular kind of bitmap files on the Net.

browser: A super-duper, all-singing, all-dancing program that lets you read information on the World Wide Web.

cc: Carbon copy. That is, copy of a message to be sent to someone else. Used as a verb, as in "I'll cc you on that message," meaning that I'll send you a copy.

communications program: A program you run on your personal computer that enables you to call up and communicate with other computers. It's a rather broad term, but most people use it to mean a program that makes your computer pretend to be a terminal.

compression program: Software used to squeeze files together so that they take up less room and are easier to transfer from one location to another. Favorite compression programs include ZIP and StuffIt. The opposite of compression is expansion or decompression.

country code: The last part of a geographic address, which indicates which country the host computer is in. An address that ends in `ca` is Canadian, for example, and one that ends in `us` is in the United States. For a complete list, see Appendix A.

digest: A compilation of the messages that have been posted to a mailing list over the past few days.

digital signature: A string of bits that is added to a message which could only be created by someone with that message and a particular secret key. See Chapter 18.

directory: A special kind of file used to organize other files. Called folders in the Windows 95 and Macintosh worlds, directories are lists of other files and can contain other directories (known as subdirectories) that contain still more files. The more stuff you have, the more you need directories in which to organize it. Directories enable you to organize files hierarchically.

domain: The official Internet-ese name of a computer or group of computers on the Net. It's the part of an Internet address that comes after the @. Dummies Central is `email2@dummies.net`, for example, and its domain name is `dummies.net`.

domain name server: (Or just *name server* or abbreviated as *DNS*.) A computer on the Internet that translates between Internet domain names, such as `xuxa.iecc.com`, and Internet numerical addresses, such as `140.186.81.2`.

download: To bring software from a remote computer "down" to your computer.

e-mail: Electronic mail (also called *e-mail* or just *mail*) messages sent by way of computers that talk to each other.

emoticons: *See* smileys.

encryption: Converting a message into a form that can only be understood by the desired recipient, usually by means of a code or cipher. See Chapters 17 and 18.

enriched text: Fancy formatting supported by some newer e-mail programs. "Rich text" allows you to use bold, italics, and different fonts. Use this only if you're sure your intended recipient can read it; otherwise, your message comes through as garbage.

expansion program: Software used to expand a file that has been compressed. Favorite expansion programs include UNZIP and UnstuffIt.

FAQ: *F*requently *A*sked *Q*uestions. A collection of answers to questions that come up regularly in an Internet newsgroup or mailing.

file: A collection of information (data or a software program, for example) treated as a unit by computers. Files have names and are organized into directories or folders.

file-transfer protocol: A method of transferring one or more files from one computer to another on a network or phone line.

filter: In the e-mail world, a tool used to sort incoming messages by particular criteria.

finger: A program that displays information about someone on the Internet.

firewall: A system designed to protect other systems from intrusion via the Internet. The firewall allows only certain authorized messages in from and out to the Internet.

flame: Angry or obnoxious message.

FlashSessions: America Online feature that allows you to send and receive your e-mail automatically at a predetermined time. See Chapter 7.

folder: A structure, sort of like a file folder, used to group items of a like nature. DOS, Windows 3.1, and UNIX call them directories. E-mail programs enable you to store your mail in folders for easy retrieval.

forwarding: Sending a message you received along to someone else.

FTP: *F*ile-*T*ransfer *P*rotocol; also the name of a program that uses the protocol to transfer files all over the Internet.

FTP server: An Internet host computer that stores files which can be retrieved by FTP. Some FTP servers also accept uploads of files.

gateway: A computer that connects one network with another when the two networks use different protocols.

GIF: A type of graphics file originally defined by CompuServe and now found all over the Net. GIF stands for *G*raphics *I*nterchange *F*ormat.

GKA: Government key access. A proposed standard that would insure that your government can get your encryption keys.

gov: When these letters appear in the last part of an address (`cu.nih.gov`, for example), it indicates that the host computer is run by some part of a government body, probably the U.S. federal government. Most `gov` sites are in the United States.

header: Line of information at the top of an e-mail message. Headers start with a word followed by a colon (:), like "To:" or "Subject:" indicating what the header line is about.

host name: The name of a computer on the Internet. *See also* domain.

icon: A little picture on your computer screen intended to represent something bigger, such as a program, a choice of action, or object.

Internet: An interconnected bunch of computer networks, including networks in all parts of the world. See *The Internet For Dummies,* 4th Edition, for more information.

Internet service provider (ISP): A service that enables you to use the Internet on a paying (by the month or hour) basis. If you need to find one, check *The Internet For Dummies,* 4th Edition, for a partial listing and helpful hints.

ISP: *See* Internet service provider.

key: A string of bits that tell an encryption program exactly how to do its thing. You need one key to encrypt a message, another to decrypt it.

key escrow: Handing over your secret encryption keys to some organization (a key escrow *agent*) who will hold them so that your government can get them with a court order (or even without, some suspect). *See* GKA and Chapters 17 and 18.

listproc: A program that automatically manages mailing lists, like LISTSERV. See Chapter 16. *See also* LISTSERV.

LISTSERV: A family of programs that automatically manage mailing lists, distributing messages posted to the list, adding and deleting members, and so on without the tedium of someone doing it manually.

list server: A program that automatically manages mailing lists. *See also* LISTSERV. See Chapter 16.

MacTCP: TCP/IP for the Macintosh. Not very interesting except that you can't put your Mac on the Internet without it.

mail server: The computer that provides mail services.

mailbox: Storage place for your messages. Your mail server keeps your mail in your mailbox until your e-mail program retrieves it for you. Some e-mail programs have their own mailboxes; for example, Eudora has In, Out, and Trash mailboxes and lets you create your own mailboxes for storing your messages.

mailing list: A special kind of e-mail address goes to a computer that remails any incoming mail to a list of *subscribers*.

Majordomo: Like LISTSERV, a program that handles mailing lists. See Chapter 16. *See also* LISTSERV.

mil: When these letters appear in the last part of an address (`wsmr-simtel20@ army.mil`, for example), it indicates that the host computer is run by some part of the U.S. military. Note that the computer may or may not be located in the U.S.

MIME: *M*ultipurpose *I*nternet *M*ail *E*xtension used to send pictures, word processor files, and anything else other than straight text through e-mail. Netscape Navigator, Eudora, Pine, and other hip e-mail programs support MIME. See Chapter 15 for details.

mirror: An FTP server that provides copies of the same files as another server. Some FTP servers are so popular that other servers have been set up to mirror them and spread the FTP load on to more than one site.

modem: A gizmo that lets your computer talk on the phone.

multimedia: Information that is not limited to text, and that can contain pictures, sound, and video.

name server: *See* domain name server.

network: For our purposes, a bunch of computers that are connected together.

online service: Service that lets you dial in with your computer and get information. The two most successful online services are America Online and CompuServe.

password or **pass phrase:** A secret code used to keep things private.

password file: The file in which all the passwords for a system are stored. Most systems are smart enough to keep passwords encoded.

PEM: *Privacy Enhanced Mail.* A standard for encrypted e-mail, similar to but not compatible with PGP. See Chapter 17.

PGP: A popular e-mail and file encryption program. PGP stands for *Pretty Good Privacy.*

PKZip: A file-compression program that runs on PCs. PKZip creates a *ZIP file* that contains compressed versions of one or more files.

POP: *Post Office Protocol,* a system by which a mail server on the Internet lets you pick up your mail and download it to your PC or Mac. There have been several versions, but POP-3 is the one nearly everyone uses.

PPP: *Point-to-Point Protocol,* a scheme for connecting two computers over a phone line (or a network link that acts like a phone line). Like *SLIP,* only better.

private keys: Key used with PGP for encrypting your messages.

protocol: Rules for communicating that two computers agree on.

public key cryptography: A really neat encryption system that uses two keys: your *public key,* which you can tell to anyone and is used to encrypt messages sent to you, and your *secret key* that you tell to no one and lets you read those messages.

secret key: The key you never tell to anyone.

security: In the computer world, a means to allow access to only those who should have it. Security includes the use of passwords to protect your account.

server: A computer that provides a service to other computers on a network. An e-mail server, for example, lets people use e-mail.

service provider: An organization that provides access to e-mail and possibly the Internet. Your service provider might be a commercial online service such as America Online or CompuServe, a big national Internet provider like AT&T WorldNet or Concentric, a local Internet provider, or your school or workplace.

shareware: Computer programs that are easily available for you to try with the understanding that if you decide to keep the program you will pay for it and send the requested amount to the shareware provider specified in the program. In this honor system, a great deal of good stuff is available, and voluntary compliance makes it viable.

shell account: An Internet account that requires you to type UNIX commands when you see the UNIX "shell" prompt.

signature: The line or lines at the end of a message that say who sent it. Some mailers let you make up a signature file that is then added to all outgoing e-mail.

SLIP: Short for *Serial Line Internet Protocol,* a software scheme for connecting a computer to the Internet.

smileys: A short group of characters used to express emotions and irony in an e-mail message. Also called *emoticons.*

SMTP: *Simple Mail Transfer Protocol,* the optimistically named method by which Internet mail is delivered from one computer to another.

spam: Originally a meat-related, sandwich-filling product. The word now refers to the act of posting inappropriate commercial messages to a large number of unrelated, uninterested Usenet newsgroups, mailing lists, or individual e-mail accounts.

StuffIt: A compression program for the Mac.

TCP/IP: The system that networks use to communicate with each other on the Internet. It stands for Transmission Control Protocol/Internet Protocol, if you care. See Part VI of *MORE Internet For Dummies,* 3rd Edition, for the gory details.

text file: A file that contains only characters, with no special formatting characters, graphical information, sound clips, video, or what have you.

thread: An article posted to a mailing list or Usenet newsgroup, together with all the follow-up articles, the follow-ups to follow-ups, and so on. Organizing articles into threads makes it easier to choose which articles in a newsgroup you want to read.

upload: To put your stuff on somebody else's computer.

URL: *U*niform *R*esource *L*ocator, a way of naming network resources and originally for linking pages together in the World Wide Web.

Usenet: A system of thousands of distributed bulletin boards called *newsgroups.*

uuencode/uudecode: Programs that encode files to make them suitable for sending as e-mail.

viewer: A program used by MIME and other programs to show you files that contain stuff other than text. For example, you might want viewers to display graphics files, play sound files, or display video files.

virus: Software that infects other software and causes damage to the system on which the infected software is run. You should download software only from reputable servers and use a virus checker regularly. Safe software is everyone's business. Viral infection can be deadly. Don't let it happen to you.

Winsock: Winsock (short for *Win*dows *Sock*ets) is a standard way for Windows programs to work with TCP/IP. You use it if you connect your Windows PC directly to the Internet, either with a permanent connection or with a modem by using SLIP or PPP.

WinZip: A Windows-based program for zipping and unzipping ZIP files in addition to other standard types of archive files. WinZip is shareware, and you can get it from the Net from `http://www.winzip.com`.

ZIP file: A file that has been created by using WinZip, PKZip, or a compatible program. It contains one or more files that have been compressed and glommed together to save space.

zone: The last part of a computer name. Three-letter zones (like `com`, `net`, and `gov`) indicate what type of organization runs the computer, which is probably in the U.S. Two-letter zones are country codes. See Appendixes A for a list of country codes.

Appendix C

About the CD

In this appendix, we tell you how to install the programs on the *E-Mail For Dummies*, 2nd Edition, CD-ROM. We've organized the programs according to operating system — Windows 95, Windows 3.1, and the Mac. The installation program tells more about each program, including the exact version that's on the CD-ROM.

Shareware and freeware: Most of the programs on this CD-ROM are shareware (programs you can use for free for a while, but must then register and pay for) or freeware (programs you can use for free forever). If you decide you like a shareware program enough to use it, do support the shareware concept by registering the program. None of the programs is expensive to register, and you'll have a good feeling all week for Doing the Right Thing.

If you don't know the letter of your CD-ROM drive: Most computers use the letter *D* for the CD-ROM drive, but yours may not. Here's how to find out the drive letter for your CD-ROM drive:

- ✔ **Windows 95:** Double-click the My Computer icon on your desktop. The window that appears lists all your drives. Your CD-ROM drive appears as a shiny, iridescent disk.

- ✔ **Windows 3.1:** Double-click the File Manager icon in Program Manager. At the top of the File Manager window is a row of icons for your disk drives. The CD-ROM drive has a little CD sticking out of it.

- ✔ **Macintosh:** Don't do anything. When you insert the CD-ROM into the Mac's CD-ROM drive, as icon for the CD-ROM appears on your desktop automagically.

Windows 95

Put the CD-ROM from the back of this book into your CD-ROM drive. On most Windows 95 systems, the installation program runs automatically; just follow the instructions on the screen. If the installation program doesn't run within a minute or two, double-click the My Computer or Windows Explorer icon on your desktop, click the icon for your CD-ROM drive, and click the

Install.exe program that appears on the list of files. The installation program sticks a new item on your Start⇨Program menu, called IDG Books Worldwide. To rerun the installation program later, stick the CD-ROM in the drive and choose Start⇨IDG Books Worldwide⇨E-Mail For Dummies 2E.

Connecting

The connecting folder contains software that helps you get onto the Internet.

AT&T WorldNet Service: If you don't yet have an Internet account, you can use this program to set up an account with AT&T WorldNet Service, a nationwide (for the U.S., anyway) Internet provider. The software provided includes a licensed copy of either Netscape Navigator or Microsoft Internet Explorer with which to browse the Web. To install the software and sign up for an account, click the AT&T WorldNet Service option and follow the instructions. You'll need a credit card and a modem that communicates at 14.4 Kbps or faster. When asked for your registration code, type **L5SQIM631** if you use AT&T for your long-distance calls or **L5SQIM632** if you don't.

Trumpet Winsock: This program lets you connect with any Internet account that provides dial-in SLIP or PPP service. On the other hand, Windows 95's own Dial-Up Networking program does too. We recommend that you talk to your Internet service provider to determine if you should install Trumpet Winsock.

Communicating

The Communicating folder contains programs that let you use the Internet once you're connected.

Eudora Light and Pegasus Mail: These are two superb e-mail programs, so choose one to install. Eudora is described in Chapters 9 and 10, Pegasus is described in Chapter 13. After you install Eudora Light, choose Start⇨ Programs⇨Eudora Light to run it. The CD-ROM contains the Eudora Light manual in a PDF file. Install Acrobat Reader (described later), run Windows Explorer or My Computer, look at the files on the CD-ROM, and double-click the Eul3manl.pdf file.

When installing Pegasus, unless you know that your computer is connected to a Novell Netware network, choose No Netware Support when asked. To run Pegasus Mail after you install it, choose Start⇨Programs⇨Pegasus Mail for Win32.

Free Agent: This is our favorite newsreader for reading Usenet newsgroups. When asked whether to add icons for the program to your Start menu, click Yes. To run Free Agent after you've installed it, choose Start⇨Programs⇨ Agent⇨Agent. For information about Usenet newsgroups, see *The Internet For Dummies*, 4th Edition.

mIRC: This program lets you participate in Internet Relay Chat (IRC; see Chapter 20). Once you've installed mIRC, you can run it by choosing Start⇨Programs⇨mIRC v5.0⇨mIRC32.

NetTerm: This *telnet* program lets you log into other computers over the Internet. After installation, you can run NetTerm by choosing Start⇨Programs⇨NetTerm⇨NetTerm. For more information about telnet, see *MORE Internet For Dummies*, 3rd Edition.

WS_FTP LE: This program lets you use FTP to transfer files to or from other computers on the Net. During installation, click the Accept button if you accept the license agreement terms. After installing the program, you can run WS_FTP by choosing Start⇨Programs⇨Ws_ftp⇨WS-FTP LE. For more information about FTP, see *The Internet For Dummies*, 4th Edition.

Working Offline

The Working Offline folder contains invaluable programs that help with files you download.

HotDog: This is an easy-to-use Web page editor. When the installation program asks whether to add shortcuts to your Start menu, choose Yes. When you see the program's readme file, read it and then close the file's window. To run HotDog after installing it, choose Start⇨Programs⇨HotDog Professional v3. For information about the Web, see *The Internet For Dummies*, 4th Edition.

Adobe Acrobat Reader: This program lets you view and print files stored in Acrobat format, including many documentation files on the Internet. In particular, you need it to view the Eudora Light manual included on the CD-ROM. After installing Acrobat Reader, you can run it by choosing Start⇨Programs⇨Adobe Acrobat⇨Acrobat Reader 3.0.

Paint Shop Pro: This is a great little graphics editor that lets you look at, fool with, and print graphics files, as well as create your own. After installation, you can run Paint Shop Pro by choosing Start⇨Programs⇨Paint Shop Pro⇨Paint Shop Pro 4.

ThunderBYTE AntiVirus: This program protects you and your computer from nasty e-mail-borne computer viruses. When installing the program, click Unzip on the first window you see. After the installation files are unzipped (decompressed), the setup program should run. If it doesn't, run My Computer or Windows Explorer, open the C:\Win95\Temp folder, and double-click the Setup.exe program file. The ThunderBYTE AntiVirus scans your whole system for viruses when you are done installing the program.

WinZip: This program is invaluable for unzipping ZIP files you may receive as e-mail attachments. No Windows system should be without WinZip, in our humble opinion. We prefer the WinZip Classic interface, so that's the one we pick when the installation program asks. After you install it, you can run WinZip by choosing Start⇨Programs⇨WinZip⇨WinZip 6.2 32-bit.

Windows 3.1

To install the programs on the CD-ROM, put the CD-ROM into your CD-ROM drive. In Program Manager, choose File->Run, type **d:\install** in the box that appears, and press Enter. If your CD-ROM drive isn't drive D, replace the letter *d* with the letter of your CD-ROM drive. Alternatively, run File Manager, display the contents of your CD-ROM drive, and double-click the Install.exe file. Either way, the installation program runs, and makes a little program group for itself, called E-Mail for Dummies 2E. To run the installation program again later, just double-click the E-Mail for Dummies 2E icon in this program group.

Connecting

The connecting folder contains software that helps you get onto the Internet.

AT&T WorldNet Service: If you don't yet have an Internet account, you can use this program to set up an account with AT&T WorldNet Service, a nationwide (for the U.S., anyway) Internet provider. The software provided includes a licensed copy of Netscape Navigator with which to browse the Web. To install the software and sign up for an account, click the AT&T WorldNet Service option and follow the instructions. You'll need a credit card and a modem that communicates at 14.4 Kbps or faster. When asked for your registration code, type **L5SQIM631** if you use AT&T for your long-distance calls or **L5SQIM632** if you don't.

Trumpet Winsock: This program lets you connect with any Internet account that provides dial-in SLIP or PPP service. If you install the AT&T WorldNet Service, you don't need to install Trumpet Winsock, because AT&T WorldNet has its own communication software. To use Trumpet Winsock, you need information from your Internet provider to configure the program for your Internet account.

Communicating

The Connecting folder contains programs that help you use the Internet once you're connected.

Eudora Light and Pegasus Mail: These are two superb e-mail programs, so choose one to install. Eudora is described in Chapters 9 and 10, Pegasus is described in Chapter 13. After you install Eudora Light, run it by double-clicking the Eudora Light icon in the Eudora Light program group. The CD-ROM contains the Eudora Light manual in a PDF file. Install Acrobat Reader, run File Manager, look at the files on the CD-ROM, and double-click the EUL3MANL.PDF file.

When installing Pegasus, unless you know that your computer is connected to a Novell Netware network, choose No Netware Support when asked. To learn Pegasus Mail after you install it, double-click the Getting Started with Pegasus Mail icon in the Pegasus Mail for Windows program group. To run the program, double-click the Pegasus Mail icon.

Free Agent: This is our favorite newsreader for reading Usenet newsgroups. When it asks whether to add icons for the program to the Program Manager, click Yes. To run Free Agent after you've installed it, double-click the Agent icon in the Agent program group. For information about Usenet newsgroups, see *The Internet For Dummies*, 4th Edition.

mIRC: This program lets you participate in Internet Relay Chat (IRC; see Chapter 20). Once you've installed mIRC, you can run it by double-clicking the mIRC icon, which usually appears in the Control program group (you may have to search for it).

NetTerm: This program lets you log into other computers over the Internet, using a system called *telnet*. After installation, you can run NetTerm by double-clicking the NetTerm icon in the NetTerm program group. For more information about telnet, see *MORE Internet For Dummies*, 3rd Edition.

WS_FTP LE: This program lets you use FTP to transfer files to or from other computers on the Net. During installation, click the Accept button if you accept the license agreement terms. After installing the program, you can run WS_FTP by double-clicking the WS_FTP LE icon in the WS_FTP program group. For more information about FTP, see *The Internet For Dummies*, 4th Edition.

Working Offline

The Working Offline folder contains invaluable programs that help with files you download.

HotDog: This is an easy-to-use Web page editor. When the installation program asks whether to add HotDog icons to the Program Manager, click Yes. When you see the program's readme file, read it and then close the file's window. To run HotDog after installing it, double-click the HotDog16 Web Editor icon in the HotDog program group. For information about the Web, see *The Internet For Dummies*, 4th Edition.

Adobe Acrobat Reader: This program lets you view and print files stored in Acrobat format, including many documentation files on the Internet. In particular, you need it to view the Eudora Light manual included on the CD-ROM. After installing Acrobat Reader, you can run it by double-clicking the Acrobat Reader 3.0 icon in the Adobe Acrobat program group.

Paint Shop Pro: This is a great little graphics editor that lets you look at, fool with, and print graphics files, as well as create your own. When asked whether to add icons to the Program Manager, click Yes. After installation, you can run Paint Shop Pro by double-clicking the Paint Shop Pro 3 icon in the Paint Shop Pro program group.

ThunderBYTE AntiVirus: This program protects you and your computer from nasty e-mail-borne computer viruses. When installing the program, click Unzip on the first window you see. After the installation files are unzipped (decompressed), the setup program should run. If it doesn't, look at the contents of your C:\WIN\TEMP directory using the File Manager program, and double-click the Setup.exe program file. The ThunderBYTE AntiVirus scans your whole system for viruses when you are done installing the program. For more information about the program, double-click the Read Me! icon in the TBAV for Windows program group.

WinZip: This program is invaluable for unzipping ZIP files you may receive as e-mail attachments. No Windows system should be without WinZip, in our humble opinion. We prefer the WinZip Classic interface, so that's the one we pick when the installation program asks. After you install it, you can run WinZip by double-clicking the WinZip icon in the WinZip program group.

Macintosh and Compatible Computers

Carefully remove the CD-ROM in the back of this book and insert it in your Mac's CD-ROM drive. (No, it's not a retractable coffee cup holder.) Double-click the E-Mail for Dummies CD icon when it appears. You see a license agreement (which you should scrutinize carefully), a Read Me First file (which you should review for any last minute changes), and three folders: Connecting, Communicating, and Working Offline.

Connecting

The connecting folder contains software that helps you get onto the Internet, including these programs:

AT&T WorldNet Service: You can use this program to sign up for an Internet account with AT&T WorldNet Service. The AT&T WorldNet kit includes a free, fully registered version of Netscape Navigator, the most popular Internet browser program around. If you want to try with AT&T WorldNet Service, open the folder and double-click the Install AT&T WorldNet icon. You'll need a credit card and a modem that communicates at 14.4 Kbps or faster. When asked for your registration code, type **L5SQIM631** if you use AT&T for your long-distance calls or **L5SQIM632** if you don't.

FreePPP: This is software that lets you communicate with the Internet using a method called PPP. Later versions of the MacOS have an Apple version of PPP build in. Only install FreePPP if your Internet provider says you need it. If so, drag the FreePPP folder to your hard disk and double click on the Install FreePPP2.5v2 icon. We recommend you keep the Install FreePPP2.5v2 program on your hard disk even after the installation is complete. Reinstalling FreePPP is sometimes helpful after system freezes.

Communicating

The Communicating folder contains programs that let you use the Internet once you're connected.

Eudora Light, Pegasus Mail, and Claris Emailer: These three powerful electronic mail programs make it easy to send and receive Internet e-mail. Eudora is described in Chapters 9 and 10, Pegasus is described in Chapter 13. To install Eudora Light or Claris Emailer, open the appropriate folder and double-click on the installer icon. The CD-ROM contains the Eudora Light manual in a PDF file. Install Acrobat Reader and then open the Eul3manl.pdf file on the CD-ROM. To install Pegasus, drag the Pegasus Mail v2.1.2.sea icon to your hard disk and double click on it. *Note:* You should only use one mailer program.

InterNews: This is a flexible Usenet newsreader that allows you to participate in tens of thousands of online discussions. To install it, drag the InterNews folder to your hard disk. For information about Usenet newsgroups, see *The Internet For Dummies*, 4th Edition.

Ircle: This program lets you chat live with thousands of other Net users via Internet Relay Chat. See Chapter 20. To install it, drag the Ircle folder icon to your hard disk.

Anarchie: This an FTP (File Transfer Protocol) client for the Macintosh. It will let you browse FTP sites, upload or download files, or find them using an Archie or Mac search. To install it, drag the Anarchie folder to your hard drive. For information about FTP, see *The Internet For Dummies*, 4th Edition.

Working Offline

The Working Offline folder contains invaluable programs that help with files you download.

BBEdit Lite: This is a handy text editor, which, among other uses, gives you the power to create and publish your own pages on the World Wide Web using the HTML language. There is also a demonstration version of the full BBEdit. To install either version, just drag its folder onto your hard drive.

DropStuff and StuffIt Expander: These decompression tools let you restore to normal most files stored on the Internet in compressed form. To install Drop Stuff and StuffIt Expander, double click on their installer icons. You will want both.

GraphicConverter: This is a tool that can convert images into different file formats, a process which is especially useful for Web page creation. Just drag its folder onto your hard drive.

Disinfectant: This is a well respected software virus detector and remover. To install it, drag the Disinfectant icon to your hard disk. ***Caution:*** Disinfectant only operates when you run it by double clicking on the Disinfectant icon. It does not scan constantly. We recommend you run Disinfectant every time after you download programs from the Internet and once a month in any case.

Adobe Acrobat Reader: This program lets you view and print out files stored in Portable Document Format (PDF). In particular, you need it to view the Eudora Light manual included on the CD-ROM. Double-click the Install Acrobat Reader 3.0 icon to install it. Acrobat Reader also provides a Netscape Navigator plug-in that lets you view with your Web browser PDF files available on the World Wide Web.

Index

AT&T WorldNet℠ Service

A World of Possibilities…

Thank you for selecting AT&T WorldNet Service — it's the Internet as only AT&T can bring it to you. With AT&T WorldNet Service, a world of infinite possibilities is now within your reach. Research virtually any subject. Stay abreast of current events. Participate in online newsgroups. Purchase merchandise from leading retailers. Send and receive electronic mail.

AT&T WorldNet Service is rapidly becoming the preferred way of accessing the Internet. It was recently awarded one of the most highly coveted awards in the computer industry, *PC Computing*'s 1996 MVP Award for Best Internet Service Provider. Now, more than ever, it's the best way to stay in touch with the people, ideas, and information that are important to you.

You need a computer with a mouse, a modem, a phone line, and the enclosed software. That's all. We've taken care of the rest.

If You Can Point and Click, You're There

With AT&T WorldNet Service, finding the information you want on the Internet is easier than you ever imagined it could be. You can surf the Net within minutes. And find almost anything you want to know — from the weather in Paris, Texas — to the cost of a ticket to Paris, France. You're just a point and click away. It's that easy.

AT&T WorldNet Service features specially customized industry-leading browsers integrated with advanced Internet directories and search engines. The result is an Internet service that sets a new standard for ease of use — virtually everywhere you want to go is a point and click away, making it a snap to navigate the Internet.

When you go online with AT&T WorldNet Service, you'll benefit from being connected to the Internet by the world leader in networking. We offer you fast access of up to 28.8 Kbps in more than 215 cities throughout the U.S. that will make going online as easy as picking up your phone.

Online Help and Advice
24 Hours a Day, 7 Days a Week

Before you begin exploring the Internet, you may want to take a moment to check two useful sources of information.

If you're new to the Internet, from the AT&T WorldNet Service home page at www.worldnet.att.net, click on the Net Tutorial hyperlink for a quick explanation of unfamiliar terms and useful advice about exploring the Internet.

Another useful source of information is the HELP icon. The area contains pertinent, time saving information-intensive reference tips, and topics such as Accounts & Billing, Trouble Reporting, Downloads & Upgrades, Security Tips, Network Hot Spots, Newsgroups, Special Announcements, etc.

Whether online or off-line, 24 hours a day, seven days a week, we will provide World Class technical expertise and fast, reliable responses to your questions. To reach AT&T WorldNet Customer Care, call **1-800-400-1447**.

Nothing is more important to us than making sure that your Internet experience is a truly enriching and satisfying one.

Safeguard Your Online Purchases

AT&T WorldNet Service is committed to making the Internet a safe and convenient way to transact business. By registering and continuing to charge your AT&T WorldNet Service to your AT&T Universal Card, you'll enjoy peace of mind whenever you shop the Internet. Should your account number be compromised on the Net, you won't be liable for any online transactions charged to your AT&T Universal Card by a person who is not an authorized user.*

*Today, cardmembers may be liable for the first $50 of charges made by a person who is not an authorized user, which will not be imposed under this program as long as the cardmember notifies AT&T Universal Card of the loss within 24 hours and otherwise complies with the Cardmember Agreement. Refer to Cardmember Agreement for definition of authorized user.

Minimum System Requirements

IBM-Compatible Personal Computer Users:
- IBM-compatible personal computer with 486SX or higher processor
- 8MB of RAM (or more for better performance)
- 15–36MB of available hard disk space to install software, depending on platform
  (14–21MB to use service after installation, depending on platform)
- Graphics system capable of displaying 256 colors
- 14,400 bps modem connected to an outside phone line and not a LAN or ISDN line
- Microsoft Windows 3.1x or Windows 95

Macintosh Users:
- Macintosh 68030 or higher (including 68LC0X0 models and all Power Macintosh models)
- System 7.5.3 Revision 2 or higher for PCI Power Macintosh models: System 7.1 or higher for all 680X0 and non-PCI Power Macintosh models
- Mac TCP 2.0.6 or Open Transport 1.1 or higher

- 8MB of RAM (minimum) with Virtual Memory turned on or RAM Doubler; 16MB recommended for Power Macintosh users
- 12MB of available hard disk space (15MB recommended)
- 14,400 bps modem connected to an outside phone line and not a LAN or ISDN line
- Color or 256 gray-scale monitor
- Apple Guide 1.2 or higher (if you want to view online help)

  If you are uncertain of the configuration of your Macintosh computer, consult your Macintosh User's guide or call Apple at 1-800-767-2775.

Installation Tips and Instructions

- If you have other Web browsers or online software, please consider uninstalling them according to the vendor's instructions.
- If you are installing AT&T WorldNet Service on a computer with Local Area Networking, please contact your LAN administrator for setup instructions.
- At the end of installation, you may be asked to restart your computer. Don't attempt the registration process until you have done so.

IBM-compatible PC users:
- Insert the CD-ROM into the CD-ROM drive on your computer.
- Select *File/Run* (for Windows 3.1x) or *Start/Run* (for Windows 95 if setup did not start automatically).
- Type *D:\setup.exe* (or change the "D" if your CD-ROM is another drive).
- Click *OK*.
- Follow the onscreen instructions to install and register.

Macintosh users:
- Disable all extensions except Apple CD-ROM and Foreign Files Access extensions.
- Restart Computer.
- Insert the CD-ROM into the CD-ROM drive on your computer.
- Double-click the *Install AT&T WorldNet Service* icon.
- Follow the onscreen instructions to install. (Upon restarting your Macintosh, AT&T WorldNet Service Account Setup automatically starts.)
- Follow the onscreen instructions to register.

Registering with AT&T WorldNet Service

After you have connected with AT&T WorldNet online registration service, you will be presented with a series of screens that confirm billing information and prompt you for additional account set-up data.

The following is a list of registration tips and comments that will help you during the registration process.

I. Use one of the following registration codes, which can also be found in Appendix C of *E-Mail For Dummies,* 2nd Edition. Use L5SQIM631 if you are an AT&T long-distance residential customer or L5SQIM632 if you use another long-distance phone company.
II. During registration, you will need to supply your name, address, and valid credit card number, and choose an account information security word, e-mail name, and e-mail password. You will also be requested to select your preferred price plan at this time. (We advise that you use all lowercase letters when assigning an e-mail ID and security code, since they are easier to remember.)
III. If you make a mistake and exit or get disconnected during the registration process prematurely, simply click on "Create New Account." Do not click on "Edit Existing Account."
IV. When choosing your local access telephone number, you will be given several options. Please choose the one nearest to you. Please note that calling a number within your area does not guarantee that the call is free.

Connecting to AT&T WorldNet Service

When you have finished installing and registering with AT&T WorldNet Service, you are ready to access the Internet. Make sure your modem and phone line are available before attempting to connect to the service.

For Windows 95 users:
- Double-click on the *Connect to AT&T WorldNet Service* icon on your desktop.
  OR
- Select *Start, Programs, AT&T WorldNet Software, Connect to AT&T WorldNet Service.*

For Windows 3.x users:
- Double-click on the *Connect to AT&T WorldNet Service* icon located in the AT&T WorldNet Service group.

For Macintosh users:
- Double-click on the *AT&T WorldNet Service* icon in the AT&T WorldNet Service folder.

Choose the Plan That's Right for You

The Internet is for everyone, whether at home or at work. In addition to making the time you spend online productive and fun, we're also committed to making it affordable. Choose one of two price plans: unlimited usage access or hourly usage access. The latest pricing information can be obtained during online registration. No matter which plan you use, we're confident that after you take advantage of everything AT&T WorldNet Service has to offer, you'll wonder how you got along without it.

Explore our AT&T WorldNet Service site at http://www.att.com/worldnet.

IDG Books Worldwide, Inc., End-User License Agreement

READ THIS You should carefully read these terms and conditions before opening the software packet(s) included with this book ("Book"). This is a license agreement ("Agreement") between you and IDG Books Worldwide, Inc. ("IDGB"). By opening the accompanying software packet(s), you acknowledge that you have read and accept the following terms and conditions. If you do not agree and do not want to be bound by such terms and conditions, promptly return the Book and the unopened software packet(s) to the place you obtained them for a full refund.

1. **License Grant** IDGB grants to you (either an individual or entity) a nonexclusive license to use one copy of the enclosed software program(s) (collectively, the "Software") solely for your own personal or business purposes on a single computer (whether a standard computer or a workstation component of a multiuser network). The Software is in use on a computer when it is loaded into temporary memory (RAM) or installed into permanent memory (hard disk, CD-ROM, or other storage device). IDGB reserves all rights not expressly granted herein.

2. **Ownership** IDGB is the owner of all right, title, and interest, including copyright, in and to the compilation of the Software recorded on the disk(s) or CD-ROM ("Software Media"). Copyright to the individual programs recorded on the Software Media is owned by the author or other authorized copyright owner of each program. Ownership of the Software and all proprietary rights relating thereto remain with IDGB and its licensers.

3. **Restrictions on Use and Transfer**

    (a) You may only (i) make one copy of the Software for backup or archival purposes, or (ii) transfer the Software to a single hard disk, provided that you keep the original for backup or archival purposes. You may not (i) rent or lease the Software, (ii) copy or reproduce the Software through a LAN or other network system or through any computer subscriber system or bulletin-board system, or (iii) modify, adapt, or create derivative works based on the Software.

    (b) You may not reverse engineer, decompile, or disassemble the Software. You may transfer the Software and user documentation on a permanent basis, provided that the transferee agrees to accept the terms and conditions of this Agreement and you retain no copies. If the Software is an update or has been updated, any transfer must include the most recent update and all prior versions.

4. **Restrictions on Use of Individual Programs** You must follow the individual requirements and restrictions detailed for each individual program in the "About the CD" Appendix of this Book. These limitations are also contained in the individual license agreements recorded on the Software Media. These limitations may include a requirement that after using the program for a specified period of time, the user must pay a registration fee or discontinue use. By opening the Software packet(s), you will be agreeing to abide by the licenses and restrictions for these individual programs that are detailed in "About the CD" Appendix and on the Software Media. None of the material on this Software Media or listed in this Book may ever be redistributed, in original or modified form, for commercial purposes.

5. Limited Warranty

(a) IDGB warrants that the Software and Software Media are free from defects in materials and workmanship under normal use for a period of sixty (60) days from the date of purchase of this Book. If IDGB receives notification within the warranty period of defects in materials or workmanship, IDGB will replace the defective Software Media.

(b) IDGB AND THE AUTHORS OF THE BOOK DISCLAIM ALL OTHER WARRANTIES, EXPRESS OR IMPLIED, INCLUDING WITHOUT LIMITATION IMPLIED WARRANTIES OF MERCHANTABILITY AND FITNESS FOR A PARTICULAR PURPOSE, WITH RESPECT TO THE SOFTWARE, THE PROGRAMS, THE SOURCE CODE CONTAINED THEREIN, AND/OR THE TECHNIQUES DESCRIBED IN THIS BOOK. IDGB DOES NOT WARRANT THAT THE FUNCTIONS CONTAINED IN THE SOFTWARE WILL MEET YOUR REQUIREMENTS OR THAT THE OPERATION OF THE SOFTWARE WILL BE ERROR FREE.

(c) This limited warranty gives you specific legal rights, and you may have other rights that vary from jurisdiction to jurisdiction.

6. Remedies

(a) IDGB's entire liability and your exclusive remedy for defects in materials and workmanship shall be limited to replacement of the Software Media, which may be returned to IDGB with a copy of your receipt at the following address: Software Media Fulfillment Department, Attn.: *E-Mail For Dummies,* 2nd Edition, IDG Books Worldwide, Inc., 7260 Shadeland Station, Ste. 100, Indianapolis, IN 46256, or call 800-762-2974. Please allow three to four weeks for delivery. This Limited Warranty is void if failure of the Software Media has resulted from accident, abuse, or misapplication. Any replacement Software Media will be warranted for the remainder of the original warranty period or thirty (30) days, whichever is longer.

(b) In no event shall IDGB or the authors be liable for any damages whatsoever (including without limitation damages for loss of business profits, business interruption, loss of business information, or any other pecuniary loss) arising from the use of or inability to use the Book or the Software, even if IDGB has been advised of the possibility of such damages.

(c) Because some jurisdictions do not allow the exclusion or limitation of liability for consequential or incidental damages, the above limitation or exclusion may not apply to you.

7. U.S. Government Restricted Rights Use, duplication, or disclosure of the Software by the U.S. Government is subject to restrictions stated in paragraph (c)(1)(ii) of the Rights in Technical Data and Computer Software clause of DFARS 252.227-7013, and in subparagraphs (a) through (d) of the Commercial Computer–Restricted Rights clause at FAR 52.227-19, and in similar clauses in the NASA FAR supplement, when applicable.

8. General This Agreement constitutes the entire understanding of the parties and revokes and supersedes all prior agreements, oral or written, between them and may not be modified or amended except in a writing signed by both parties hereto that specifically refers to this Agreement. This Agreement shall take precedence over any other documents that may be in conflict herewith. If any one or more provisions contained in this Agreement are held by any court or tribunal to be invalid, illegal, or otherwise unenforceable, each and every other provision shall remain in full force and effect.

Installing the CD-ROM

• •

*T*o get started with the *E-Mail For Dummies,* 2nd Edition, CD-ROM, please refer to the instructions for your computer's operating system.

Macintosh

Carefully remove the CD-ROM in the back of this book and insert it in your Mac's CD-ROM drive. Double click the E-Mail for Dummies CD icon when it appears. You see a license agreement (which you should scrutinize carefully), a Read Me First file (which you should review for any last minute changes), and three folders: Connecting, Communicating, and Working Offline. See Appendix C for details on how to install the programs within these folders.

Windows 3.1

To install the programs on the CD-ROM, put the CD-ROM into your CD-ROM drive. In Program Manager, choose File⇨Run, type **d:\install** in the box that appears, and press Enter. If your CD-ROM drive isn't drive d, replace the letter *d* with the letter of your CD-ROM drive. Alternatively, run File Manager, display the contents of your CD-ROM drive, and double-click the Install.exe file. Either way, the installation program runs and makes a little program group for itself, called E-Mail for Dummies 2E. To run the installation program again later, just double-click the E-Mail for Dummies 2E icon in this program group.

Windows 95

Put the CD-ROM from the back of this book into your CD-ROM drive. On most Windows 95 systems, the installation program runs automatically; just follow the on-screen instructions. If the installation program doesn't run within a minute or two, double-click the My Computer or Windows Explorer icon on your desktop, click the icon for your CD-ROM drive, and click the Install.exe program that appears on the list of files. The installation program places a new item on your Start⇨Program menu called IDG Books Worldwide. To rerun the installation program later, stick the CD-ROM in the drive and choose Start⇨IDG Books Worldwide⇨E-Mail For Dummies 2E.